Israel at Forty

1948–1988

ISRAEL

at forty

H L Willmington & Ray Pritz

Tyndale House Publishers, Inc.
Wheaton, Illinois

First printing, December 1987

Library of Congress Catalog Card Number 87-50980
ISBN 0-8423-1801-1
Copyright 1987 by Harold L. Willmington and Ray Pritz
Printed in the United States of America

Contents

PART ONE: A RELIGIOUS OVERVIEW

PART TWO: A TOPICAL OVERVIEW

PART THREE: A CHRONOLOGICAL OVERVIEW

Introduction

Many important dates have marked history since Jesus ascended back into heaven. In 324 Constantine came into full power and made Christianity a legal religion. In 476 the Roman Empire fell. In 1054 the eastern and western branches of the Christian church split. On August 3, 1492, Columbus set sail. On July 4, 1776, the American Declaration of Independence was signed. On August 6, 1945, the first atomic bomb was dropped on Japan. On July 20, 1969, man first walked on the moon. But the most important date of the past twenty centuries is May 14, 1948. It was on that day, at 4:30 P.M., that Israel officially became a nation again. In his book, *Abraham to the Middle East Crisis*, Dr. G. Frederick Owen writes of this:

> Early that morning Great Britain's flag, the Union Jack, was hauled down. During that sunny day a multitude gathered at a roped-off, guarded section of Rothschild Boulevard in Tel Aviv (the new capital). The chief rabbi leaders along with many representatives of the world press awaited. At exactly 4:00 P.M., David Ben-Gurion called the meeting to order. The Assembly rose and sang the Jewish national anthem, "Hatikvah," while in an adjoining room the Palestinian Symphony Orchestra played. The music had hardly ceased when Ben-Gurion rose and read in Hebrew, in a firm voice, the Declaration of Independence of the new nation of Israel. The entire assemblage rose and applauded, and many of them wept. (Eerdmans, 1957, p. 316)

What a joy that was! But how powerless and pitiful the new state seemed to be. In fact, the almost universal consensus was that this tiny Israeli lamb, surrounded by mighty wolves, would never survive. But survive it did! Today, by any acceptable standard, the little lamb has become a seasoned lion!

This book gives a brief overview of the statistics, events, and citizens connected with the Holy Land during the period from 1948 to 1988, forty fateful years.

ONE

A Religious Overview

1

THE CHURCH

Israel of the 1980s is a land of marked contrasts, and this is as true of the church in Israel as it is of politics and other areas of daily living.

The Book of Daniel provides us with some valuable information about the nature of spiritual warfare and the forces lined up against each other in the heavenly places. Chapter 10 begins with a revelation to Daniel in the third year of Cyrus, king of Persia, a revelation of *tzavah gadol* (in Hebrew). Literally the phrase means "great army" or "great warfare." The word *tsavah* is the same word frequently translated "host," as in Lord of Hosts. God is the God of the armies of heaven.

In the three chapters that follow this introduction, Daniel is involved with angels and, in fact, most of the end of Daniel (10:11-14, 10:19-12:4) details what one unnamed angel tells Daniel prophetically. This angel speaks of battles he has had with "the prince of Persia" and will have with "the prince of Greece" (10:13, 20). Evidently, these princes are not the political rulers of those countries, but rather "principalities, powers, rulers of the darkness of this world, wicked spirits in high (or heavenly) places," which correspond to those political kingdoms.

It is evident from Daniel 12:1 that countries have not only wicked forces over them but also good angelic forces. Michael is called "the great prince" (the same word found in Daniel 10:13, 20, KJV) "which standeth for the children of thy people." The children of Daniel's people, of course, are the people of Israel. The opposition of these different spiritual forces accounts for the "great warfare" of Daniel 10:1.

If we follow Michael through other Scriptures, we find that he often comes up against Satan himself—for example, "When contending with the devil he disputed about the body of Moses" (Jude 9, KJV). (What better symbol for the people of Israel than the body of Moses!) Again in Revelation 12:7-9 (KJV): "There was war in heaven: Michael and his angels fought against the dragon . . . that old serpent, called the Devil, and Satan."

If it is true that every country has its particular "wicked spirit in a heavenly place," then most evangelical Christians living in Israel would agree that the dominant spirit over the Holy Land is a "religious spirit," and Jerusalem is its headquarters. Numerous wars have been fought over the Christian "holy places." Some reached far outside the borders of Palestine and into Europe. The Crimean War of 1853-1856, for example, was fought over the removal of a small silver star in the Church of the Nativity in Bethlehem.

This religious spirit manifests itself in various ways within the Christian community. An initial impression may be gained by looking at a few statistics.

The total number of "Christians" in Israel today is roughly 147,000. This total includes both believing and nominal Christians, Protestants, Catholics, and Orthodox and is less than 4 percent of the overall population. As the only country in the world with a Jewish majority, Israel is, of course, the only country where a Christian minority lives among a Jewish majority—a unique fact in world history since the first century A.D.

The largest religious communities are the oldest, and the largest of these is the Catholic, which is subdivided into Greek Catholic (or Melkite), Latin (Roman) Catholic, and Maronite. There are about 87,000 Catholics within these groups. In the early nineteenth century the Orthodox church accounted for 80 percent of the Christian population of the Holy Land. Today they are less than 25 percent. The Orthodox churches are proud of the fact that through nineteen centuries they carried the name "Christian" and preserved that name in the land during times of hardship and persecution.

The Protestants of Israel make up less than 15 percent of the total Christian population, or less than one-half of 1 percent of the total population of the country. Among those Protestants, probably 70 percent would have to be classified as nominal Christians. To complete the fractured picture, out of the entire Christian community in Israel, there are more than sixty separate denominations, most of these, of course, among the Protestants.

The name "Christian" does not carry all the same connotations in the Middle East that it does in the United States. In the Middle East everyone is born with a religion. The communities are religious communities, and thus every child is born into one of these religious communities. That a person "decides" to become a Christian is a very strange concept for the average Israeli or Arab.

This cultural difference has perhaps been brought to light more in recent years with the news of the factional fighting in Lebanon. Western Christians were undoubtedly shocked to hear that hundreds of Palestinians in two refugee camps in Beirut were systematically murdered by Christian Falange forces. The event itself was, of course, shocking enough, but the whole report took on an added sting in the juxtaposition of the words *Christian* and *massacre*.

Many well-meaning evangelical tourists have been totally misled by the cultural difference in the definitions of the term *Christian*. Walking into a shop in Jerusalem's Old City, a tourist asks the salesman, "Are you a Christian?" Flashing a big smile, the salesman gives an affirmative reply. That salesman may never have made a decision for Christ, but within his cultural context he is being totally honest. In addition, he will surely know that the right answer will be good for business. Many stories could be told about merchants exploiting the spiritual gullibility or naiveté of Christian customers.

Tour guides usually get well acquainted with the people on the tour bus during the course of an intensive week or more. Every tour guide in Israel has encountered countless would-be evangelists, and most have heard the gospel in one form or another many times. (The same can be said to a lesser degree of the bus drivers.) Each guide must learn to accept this as one of the hazards of the job, or refuse to work with evangelical groups. A few guides, however, have learned to turn this religious zeal to their financial profit. If they time it right, they will "have a conversion experience" a couple of days before the end of the tour, just in time to be baptized in the Jordan River or the Sea of Galilee. The announcement of the decision of the guide or driver brings waves of goodwill over the group, which is further reinforced by the baptism. It follows that tips and extra personal gifts are substantially increased. One Muslim guide, at last count, has been baptized twenty times.

When the title "Christian" is used in this chapter, it is used in the Middle Eastern cultural sense, unless it is qualified by some adjective such as "born-again" or "believing" or "evangelical."

RELIGIOUS SPIRIT

The religious spirit as it has invaded Christianity in the Holy Land may be illustrated in another way. The traditional church in Israel has at least two or three of everything. There are three dates for Christmas (December 25 for Catholics and Protestants, January 6 for Greek churches, and January 19 for the Armenians); two dates for Easter (they were more than a month apart in 1983); two sites of Jesus' birth (one in Nazareth, and one in Bethlehem—around which three denominations have built churches); and three churches spread out around the Mount of Olives, each marking the site of Jesus' ascension. The oldest of the Ascension churches is a greatly enlarged and beautified copy of the Muslim Dome of the Rock to commemorate the supposed site of Muhammad's ascension into heaven. Both churches were built by the same architect.

And there are two Calvarys with two nearby tombs. The more traditional of these last two sites is the church of the Holy Sepulchre, or, as some prefer to call it, the Church of the Resurrection. It is shared by four ancient Christian denominations, but through the centuries there has been so much bickering or outright fighting between these groups that the keys to the church were long ago entrusted to Muslim watchmen.

The other candidate for the place of Jesus' crucifixion and resurrection is the Garden Tomb. Aesthetically this is one of the nicest and warmest of the Christian tourist stops in Jerusalem, and the staff are evangelistic in their approach to visitors. Scholars are somewhat divided in their opinions as to the validity of the two sites of Calvary, but one Jerusalem pastor likes to recall how one Jewish immigrant from Russia solved the problem after first hearing of the two rival sites for Jesus' burial. "I think I have it figured out," he told a pastor friend. "When Jesus died, they buried him in the Garden Tomb, and that's where he rose. Then when he died the second time, they buried him in the Holy Sepulchre."

In many ways the church in the Holy Land is a microcosm of the church worldwide. The divisions in Christendom are well represented and are probably more obvious because of their concentration in the land where the church started. However, the resident evangelical with any degree of commitment to Christian work in Israel knows that below the division on the surface is an increasing phenomenon of unity in fellowship. This, too, may well be representative of what is happening on a broader spectrum in the body of Christ.

In Israel this move toward unity began less than a dozen years ago. It is limited primarily to Protestant groupings, although there is a section of the English- and French-speaking Roman Catholic church that is also involved. One finds very little of the partisan backbiting that is so familiar in many Christian countries. Where problems do exist, they are generally personal and not denominational in character. Within the small English-speaking Protestant community of Jerusalem it is not uncommon to find pulpit exchanges and communion across denominational lines. As with the religious spirit and the divisions, there are also several manifestations in the growing fellowship.

For some years, pastors from all over Jerusalem have been meeting every Thursday for prayer. They meet at 6:00 A.M., the only time compatible for so many busy pastoral schedules. In attendance on any given Thursday one may find representatives of Anglican, Baptist, Dutch Reformed, Presbyterian, Pentecostal, Nazarene, Catholic, Lutheran, Messianic Jewish, West Bank Arabs (themselves of various denominations), and several nondenominational groups.

The main activity of the meeting is prayer, but there is time in each sixty-to-ninety-minute session to share burdens, relay information (perhaps to warn of strange winds of doctrine encountered), and to plan common activities. The men and women who attend these meetings are pastors and leaders responsible for the spiritual oversight of a large percentage of Jerusalem's evangelicals. Attendance is by invitation only.

The need for this unusual group can be attributed to the isolation and minority status of the church in Israel. Division is a luxury in which minority cannot afford to indulge and still survive. The things that once seemed so important to fight about fade into insignificance in the light of the basic need to survive.

UNITED CHRISTIAN COUNCIL IN ISRAEL (UCCI)

It was the sense of this need for a common stand that led to the formation in 1957 of the United Christian Council in Israel (UCCI). In the beginning just four or five Protestant evangelical organizations felt the need for some sort of umbrella setup that would also provide a forum for the discussion of larger issues. One of the primary intentions was to have a context in which Jewish and Arab believers could meet and fellowship.

In some ways the UCCI itself is a kind of microcosm of the church in Israel. At present it has twenty-two member bodies. Not all are church or denominational representatives; the membership also includes some parachurch organizations. The breadth of its roster is somewhat indicative of the growing unity; yet at the same time it may be an even stronger indicator of the divisions that have existed for so long. The UCCI, for instance, has never succeeded in including any group outside of the Protestant evangelical circle. At the beginning it was hoped that it might also encompass traditional churches such as the Catholic and Orthodox, but after twenty-six years, the circle is still small.

And as far as the intention of providing a meeting place for Jews and Arabs is concerned, what meetings there are often seem to turn into jousts. Messianic Jews have accused the Council of anti-Semitism because it rarely votes Jews onto its executive committee. This fact is probably attributable to the far greater proportion of Arab believers in the country, as well as to the fact that Jewish attendance at Council functions has traditionally been low and unenthusiastic. On the few occasions when more Messianic Jews have attended, there have been immediate cries from the Arab camp that the organization is going Zionist.

A representative scene occurred at the 1982 annual meeting. A Jewish member presented a talk on the Scriptures as the Word of God and gave special emphasis to the necessity of including the Old Testament in this definition and in teaching about it. In the time of questions and comments that followed, the most influential Arab pastor on the Council strongly objected to the line taken, saying that the emphasis must be on Jesus as the Living Word of God. The undercurrent, of course, was political, and the discussion soon turned very heated and almost proved disastrous to the existence of the UCCI.

ABRAMOWICH LAW (ANTI-MISSION LAW)

Despite mixed results in the areas of reconciliation in the matter of providing an umbrella for Christians in Israel, the UCCI has achieved some positive results. In late 1977, certain religious factions in the Begin government's coalition caught much of the Knesset napping and pushed through a bill that immediately became known as the anti-Mission law. It is more accurately referred to as the Abramowich law, after the name of its sponsor. The law made it a crime, punishable by fine and imprisonment, to offer or accept any material inducement to change religions.

The evangelical community, of course, was not the least bit interested in someone who had become a Christian because he had been offered enough money to do so. The same could be said of the remainder of the Christian community who were, in any case, not interested in people from outside their group becoming Christians. Nevertheless, the law caused angry reactions from all shades of the Christian spectrum. To the outsider the whole matter raises two immediate questions: If no one in the Christian community was interested in buying Jewish souls, then why would such a law be seen as necessary? And if Christians were also opposed to such mercenary converts, then why did they get so upset?

A comprehensive answer to the first question would be too lengthy to present here, but perhaps a brief discussion will suffice. Through the centuries the church, particularly in Europe in the Middle Ages, gained a deserved reputation for being unscrupulous in its attempts to convert Jews. Methods employed included forcing Jews to listen to a conversionist sermon once a month; economic, political, and social pressures to make Judaism unattractive and Christianity attractive (i.e., lucrative); and thousands of sword-point baptisms, where the only other option offered was immediate death. The worst period for such pressures was during the Crusades. In terms of Jewish evangelism, it seems highly unfortunate that in recent years we have chosen to call our largest gospel campaigns "crusades."

As the Middle or Dark Ages gave way to the Renaissance and the Enlightenment, the inducements for a Jew to become a Christian did not lessen. They only took on more subtle forms. In the Jewish mind, the idea already implanted took firm root: The church knows almost no ethical restrictions and will stop at nothing to get a Jew to become a Christian. By "the church," the Jew means Roman Catholicism. The average Jew knows little more of the division of Christendom than the average Christian knows of the divisions in Judaism.

The traditional churches in the Holy Land did little to merit any reputation as being conversion oriented, but when the first Protestant missionaries appeared in the early nineteenth century, their behavior often revived many of the old spectres in the minds of their Jewish neighbors. The missionaries were not violent or even unethical, but their zeal for soul-winning and the charity that accompanied it were easily mistaken for their medieval counterparts' forced sermons and material inducements. The enticements offered by the missionaries took the form of schooling, free medical care, and even food and lodging. Being supported from abroad, the missions could often afford to offer charity above the local standard of living. A promising young student who did "become" a Christian might be sent abroad at mission expense for further schooling.

Over the decades the Jewish mind in the Holy Land developed a sterotype of "the Mission." It was still conceptually bound up with the church as he understood it; the Mission was some great monolithic organ with unlimited funds, using all available means to convert Jews. It is small wonder that today in Israel the names "mission" and "mission-ary" are extremely pejorative in their application to Christians, and no thinking Christian worker will openly accept the name of missionary. When religious zealots want to vent their displeasure on some Christian organization they think is being too evangelistic, they paint swastikas and the word *mission* on the walls of the offending place.

Why did Abramowich and his colleagues feel it necessary to pass the anti-Mission law? Because in their minds the threat of the Mission was a very real one, which must be outlawed.

But why did Christians, particularly the Protestant evangelical mem-bers of the UCCI, become so incensed over a law that stated nothing that Christians would not endorse? The law itself had been put through the Knesset under highly irregular circumstances. It received its second and third readings and final vote without prior notice and at a time when those parties most likely to oppose it were absent from the plenum. Even though there was no explicit mention of Christians in the text of the law, attached to it was a body of explanatory matter that did mention Christians, making it clear that the object of the law was to restrict the Mission. It specifically accused Christians of doing some-thing they felt they were not doing.

That accusation was enough to make the UCCI raise its collective voice, but there was more. The Abramowich party let it be known that this was only the first in a planned series of laws that would eventually make it illegal even to witness publicly. This, many Chris-tians—and Jews—felt would be a direct infringement on the right of freedom of speech. Also implied in the Abramowich law was a restric-tion on the freedom of religion itself. The UCCI set up a kind of watchdog committee and enlisted the willing help of many influential Israelis who were in complete agreement with the Christians as to the principles at issue. To date there has not been a case to test the law, so it is not known how the courts might react. However, the UCCI action probably had a lot to do with the fact that none of the promised follow-up legislation has ever been attempted.

JEWS WHO BELIEVE IN JESUS

The history of the church's treatment of the Jewish people, especially in the Middle Ages, makes very unpleasant reading. The sensitive Christian, striving to emulate the love of Jesus and the attitude of Paul when he said, "I could wish that myself were accursed from Christ for my brethren, my kinsmen according to the flesh, who are Israelites" (Rom. 9:3-4, KJV), finds himself shocked and ashamed by the record of injustices, and even crimes, perpetrated by "Christians" on Jews. It is no wonder that the gospel has made so little headway with Jesus' physical family.

One manifestation of the strong reaction to Christian persecution is the attitude of Jews generally to one of their brethren who makes a profession of faith in Jesus as his Messiah, and particularly one who is baptized. In Israel today it is not difficult to find Jews who practice transcendental meditation or claim to follow the teachings of Buddha. Here and there one may encounter a witch with a small coven, and a sizable percentage of the populace will say that they do not believe in God at all. But all of these are reckoned by the average rabbi as Jews, deluded but still Jews. The basic definition of a Jew is one who was born of a Jewish mother or who was converted. What he believes or practices has no real relationship to his Jewishness. There is one exception to that rule, however: if a Jew has been baptized or (most would agree) has even professed faith in Jesus, the average rabbi would declare that he has ceased to be a Jew.

Despite some rather high estimates, the actual number of Jews in Israel who believe in Jesus is probably not very high. Those high estimates come from two very divergent sources: overly optimistic Christians and overly pessimistic Jews. Christian workers who have lived in Israel for some years testify that until recently, one rarely heard of an Israeli coming to believe in Jesus. Generally speaking, the ones who did were typical of those who might get saved in a street mission in a large American city—the lonely ones, rejected by society. In Israel this did not seem to be the material from which a self-sufficient indigenous church might be expected to grow.

To add to the problem, if a more promising Israeli did accept Jesus, he was whisked abroad by some well-meaning Christian group who wanted to send him to Bible school or give him a chance to become rooted in the faith in a more amenable environment. The problem was that such believers never came back. The United States or Britain or Canada was much more the "Promised Land," where they could have regular fellowship, find a Christian spouse, enjoy a higher standard of living, and live without the constant threat of another war. Consequently, those who could have formed a nucleus of Israeli believers were not in Israel at all but scattered abroad, while the indigenous church limped along. The same pattern was followed with promising young Arab believers.

What Jewish believers there were in the land were generally immigrants, mostly Europeans at first, who were appreciably more European and Christian than they were Israeli or Jewish. Gradually, they became an older generation without much hope of rejuvenation. In more recent years there was an influx of young Americans from the Jesus People phenomenon of the 1970s and, more specifically, from Jews for Jesus. These came with the zeal of youth and got a fair amount of publicity for a time. But most left the country after failing to find a place in the society or after failing to relinquish their love for their home countries. Some of these were refused permission to stay in Israel after they were too outspoken about their faith.

The older immigrant groups of believers formed relatively small fellowships in the larger cities. One was in Tel Aviv, revolving mostly around one large family. In Jerusalem there were two such fellowships, one Protestant and one Catholic. For many years they had little to do with each other. Even in these the membership was not exclusively ethnic Jews. The cohesive factor was the Hebrew language. Some individuals attended the meetings because they could not find satisfactory fellowship in their native tongues, while others chose those meetings as a means of supplementing their Hebrew studies. The Protestant group came to be known as the Messianic Assembly. It was founded in the 1960s by a French immigrant named Ze'ev Kaufmann and three other men, one of whom was not Jewish.

As in many fellowships, both Jewish and non-Jewish, the main weekly meeting is held on Saturday. This day was chosen not for any particular doctrinal reason but pragmatically, because Israel operates on a six-day work week. Saturday is the one day off. To the degree that local Christians are working and identified with the society in which they live, Sunday is the first day of the week and a work day.

The Catholic Jewish fellowship meets in a place called Isaiah House. Many priests and nuns in Israel were sheltered as young Jewish children in monasteries and convents or in private homes while their families were being sent by the Nazis to their deaths. Hundreds of children rescued by both Catholics and Protestants were later returned to what remained of their families. However, some of them chose to adopt the religion of their rescuers, and of these some took religious orders.

Quite a few from this converted remnant from the Holocaust found their way to Israel. Most of these show little desire to maintain any kind of Jewish identity and some seem to go out of their way to repudiate their physical descent. But there are some—and their number is growing—who have made the rediscovery and understanding of their roots their main area of study. One of the recognized leaders of the community at Isaiah House is, in fact, not Jewish. He is Father Marcel Dubois, a French Dominican priest who came to Israel about fifteen years ago. In a land overflowing with anomalies, Dubois is the head of the philosophy department of the Hebrew University in Jerusalem.

Jewish believers in Jesus are not identified as "Christians." They are quick to remind us that Christ means Messiah, which comes from a Hebrew word and a Jewish concept. As a matter of fact, believers call themselves *mesichi'im*, a modern Hebrew word that is the etymological equivalent of *Christians*, but in Hebrew it does not carry the overtones that the word *Christians* does in other languages. In modern Hebrew, the usual word for Christians is *notzrim*, or Nazarenes.

Jewish believers say they are not "converted" to another religion. It is the Gentiles who have converted to the God of Israel through Jesus the Jewish Messiah. For them it is "Jewish" to believe in their Messiah, so why should they call themselves by a Greek translation of their own original name? *Ma'aminim* is another common name for Jewish believers.

In the past five or six years there has been an upswing in the number of Israelis receiving Jesus. These believers are average, well-adjusted Israelis, not those on the fringe of society. This factor, perhaps more than any other, has brought with it a renewed search for identity, both on the communal level and on the individual level.

Israeli society is rife with well-defined, identifiable communities. Most of these find some sort of recognition in the laws of the land, and as such they may also be recipients of special privileges and tax exemptions, as the law provides. Not so with the Messianic Jewish community. At best, it is ignored or barely tolerated; there are certainly no special privileges. When the declaration of the State of Israel was formulated in May of 1948, it included a promise of freedom of religion, each man according to his conscience. In those early days, it was the intention of the State's founders to draw up a basic law or constitution that would include among its provisions a more clearly defined expression of freedom of religion. To date, Israel still has no constitution, and the Messianic community must turn to others for the performance of such important community events as marriages, circumcisions, and funerals.

On the personal level, the Israeli Jewish believer has identity problems no less serious than those on the communal level. Any sincere Christian is concerned about how to be in the world and not of the world. But being a Jew who believes in Jesus has its own particular difficulties, difficulties that center around the Law. To non-Jews the matter seems crystal clear: We are not under the Law but under grace (see Rom. 6:14). However, as one local non-Jewish Christian scholar points out, that verse, and verses like it, were not written by Paul to Jewish believers, but to believers from among the Gentiles. In fact, he insists there is no evidence in the New Testament that Jewish believers in Jesus ever stopped keeping the commandments of the Law. It seems that Paul himself offered animal sacrifices and helped others to do so long after the death and resurrection of Jesus (see Acts 21:23-26). This scholar did his doctoral work at the Hebrew University on the subject of the post-New Testament Jewish Christian sect of the Nazarenes. He points out that the Jerusalem community headed by James and those who came later continued to have a reputation—among both non-Jewish Christians and non-Christian Jews—for adherence to the commandments of the Law of Moses.

While this dilemma is not one that all or perhaps even the majority of Jewish believers worry about, each has to ask himself whether or not he should follow the Law of Moses. The solution is not as easy as it might seem at first. Since the New Testament was written, the interpretations of the Law have undergone nineteen centuries of defining and adaptation. Even Jesus, while he obeyed the law of God, had points of disagreement with the religious authorities over how that law should be interpreted. How much of the covenant made at Sinai (which God calls "everlasting") is still incumbent on the one who becomes a partaker of the New Covenant in Jesus? Is this still part of his national culture and heritage?

In the past few decades missionaries in Africa, India, and other countries have learned that new converts do not have to become westernized. They do not have to change the way they eat or dress or change other ethno-cultural habits in order to be New Testament Christians. To what degree may this also be true of Jews? How much of their Judaism is cultural, and how much of it is religious (and how much of that is incompatible with belief in Jesus)? These are not easy questions, and it is doubtful that any consensus will be reached. But for the Jewish believer, who still feels himself part of his family (and in many cases this identity is even more strongly felt after he becomes a believer), these may be questions over which he will puzzle for a long time.

The increase in the number of Israelis coming to Jesus has manifested itself in several ways and places. For several years two couples who are talented musicians have been composing and writing dozens of Scripture-based choruses in Hebrew, in a musical style that could be called more Jewish. Until recently, places such as the Messianic Assembly were limited in their singing to hymns translated from English. As precious as old hymns may be to those of us raised with them, we can not expect that they will carry the same meaning for Christians from very different backgrounds. As one young Jewish believer put it, "When I open the hymnal and see 'Crusader hymn' under the title or that the song was written by an anti-Semite such as Martin Luther, something inside me chokes."

The flow of new songs led to the establishment of an annual music conference for the explicit purpose of sharing new songs. The conference has encouraged others to compose, and today there is a growing series of chorus booklets. The impetus and enthusiasm for these conferences has come largely from the younger generation of Jewish believers who have carried the songs back to all parts of the country. One can go just about anywhere there are Hebrew-speaking believers and join in the singing without the use of a book.

Another manifestation of this rejuvenation of the Messianic Jewish community has been the appearance in the last several years of youth conferences in Hebrew, which cut across all denominational lines. Apart from spiritual benefits, these conferences are needed for other reasons. In a society where believers are such a pronounced minority, the danger exists that the young people will find marriage partners among nonbelieving classmates in school, or during the universal army service. They may even look outside the country for a spouse.

At first, such conferences were sponsored and organized by the older Messianic fellowships, and the results were encouraging. After a while, however, the young people themselves decided to take the initiative. In

1982, during the week of Passover, they held a Hebrew-speaking youth conference at the Baptist Village near Tel Aviv, the largest to date. More than 100 young people attended for five days of praise, prayer, Bible study, and other activities.

Word of the conference reached a couple of churches in the large West Bank town of Ramallah, and many young Arab believers decided to attend. When they arrived at the conference they learned that most of the young people were Jewish and everyone spoke Hebrew. There were a few moments of tension, but in the spirit of Christian love, the Arabs and Jews worshiped and prayed together, taught each other songs, and saw many barriers and biases broken down. The real test of their Christian love for one another—the evidence of God's perfect timing—came on Friday, Good Friday, as the news was broadcast that a fanatical American-born Jewish reserve soldier had shot his way into the Dome of the Rock, killing one Arab and wounding many others as he shouted out his hatred of Arabs. At the Baptist Village the young people, Jews and Arabs, together prayed for peace.

ARABS WHO BELIEVE IN JESUS

Jews and Arabs are meeting in Jesus' name in several places in Israel, and with greater success than in the forum of the UCCI. In the northern Christian village of Kafr Yusif, the local Arab church meetings are regularly attended by Jewish believers from the coastal town of Nahariya. Small numbers of Arabs and Jews, along with the bulk of expatriates, attend some of Jerusalem's larger evangelical churches.

A Jewish believer set up a factory several years ago in Galilee with the idea of providing employment for Jewish believers in the area. Recently he began hiring believing Arabs as well. Several years ago, a series of biannual conferences were initiated to bring Jewish and Arab believers together for fellowship. They were called "Shalam," a hybrid of the Hebrew and Arabic words for peace. Like the Passover conferences at the Baptist Village, they are attended mostly by young people. Unlike the Passover conferences, however, most of those who attend are Arabs, with a smaller but growing number of Jews participating.

If the Jewish believer has identity problems in Israel, the believing Arab has his own complex dilemmas. As a believer, he is in the minority among Arab Christians; as an Arab Christian, he is greatly in the minority in the wider Arab society, which is mostly Muslim; and, as an Arab, he finds himself in a political situation where Jews are in the majority and many aspects of his life are ruled by an Israeli authority. And, he finds it increasingly difficult to separate his identities as believer, societal Christian, and Arab.

In recent years the world has witnessed an Islamic revival. In its extreme form it is known as "khoumeniism." Because cultural factors dictate that everyone is born with a religion and that religion and nationality are not to be separated, this revival has taken on nationalistic overtones. Little or no distinction is made between the revival of Islam and the concomitant revival of Arab nationalism. The Arab Christian, of course, can only view the Islamic revival with justified alarm; but he must not seem to be less the patriot, less the nationalist. For this reason, some of the most outspoken Arab nationalists are members of the Christian community. Naturally enough, the most fervent expression of this nationalism is heard in pronouncements against Israel.

The believing Arab may also find himself caught up in this spiral. As a member of a closely-knit society, he is distressed by reports of injustices committed on Arabs by the occupying Israeli army. It makes no difference, of course, if the reports are correct or incorrect. All of us have had our political opinions and views of local and world events formed by the source from which we most commonly receive our news, whether it be *Time* magazine, the Voice of Israel, Radio Damascus, or the person next door. Most of us subconsciously believe that our particular news source is objective and correct. As far as the Arab Christian is concerned, one thing is sure: almost all of the reports he hears about what the Israelis are doing are bad reports. Some reports may be true and some may be false, but few, if any, will be favorable to the "forces of occupation."

If the factors that help form political perceptions are so subjective, the same is true about much understanding of Christian doctrine. One may ask: Can't the Arab Christian see from the Scriptures God's place for Israel? The answer is that he sees no such thing in the Bible. It is a fact far too little realized in Christian circles that our doctrine can be a product of our environment. Consider an example from America.

One hundred fifty years ago in the southern United States it was commonly taught that slavery was a divinely sanctioned (if not, in fact, divinely ordained) institution and that the white race was superior to the black race. Books were written by sincere and respected Christian teachers supporting those "facts." Sermons were preached on slavery, and the average churchgoer would have been surprised to find that what they heard wasn't "gospel truth." The idea of the superiority of the white race is supported today by most Bible-believing churches in South Africa.

ENVIRONMENT AND DOCTRINE

Nowhere is this principle of "environmental interpretation" better illustrated than in the Middle East. For many Christians within Israel, the Bible speaks mostly about Israel. Cross any of Israel's borders and one finds that the average Christian does not own and probably has not read the Old Testament. As far as they are taught, God finished with the Jewish people when they rejected Jesus, and there is no theological significance to the existence of the State of Israel. For a number of years, a couple of pro-Israel missionaries in Israel felt their main calling was to get Arabic Old Testaments to Christians in Lebanon so they could see that it was all about Israel.

So the Arab believer is not aided in his dilemma by a strong, positive theology of Israel. In fact, his dilemma actually has little or nothing to do with a theology of Israel. His dilemma is how to love his enemy, how to bless those who persecute him, and pray for those who despitefully use him and his family. He is troubled by the difficulty of forgiving—both the nonbelieving Israelis and the believing foreign Christians who seem to go so far out of their way to support Israel in oppressing him. The objective realities of the situation have little bearing on all of this. Unforgiveness is a problem we all face, but unforgiveness as a personal spiritual problem is quite independent of the facts of the case.

There is also a political aspect to the Arab believer's dilemma. On one hand he would like to feel that he and his people can determine their own fate politically: "No taxation without representation." For that reason he agrees with his Muslim and nominally Christian neighbors that Israeli rule in the West Bank and Gaza must end. On the other hand, he knows that a PLO government could be a disaster for Christians. If the Islamic revival has shown anything, it is that minority groups can find themselves in a very precarious position. Many Arab Christians in the West Bank quietly admit that Israeli rule is better for them than the prospect of a PLO-led Islamic state. One thing is sure: In no other country in the world is there a Christian minority surrounded by a Muslim majority where it is possible to share the gospel without fear of official repression. The committed Arab evangelical knows that the day Israeli control comes to an end, so too will end the freedom to evangelize among Muslims.

THE EVANGELICAL CHURCH IN ISRAEL

A description of the evangelical church in Israel today would not be wholly accurate without some account of the revival which took place on a surprisingly broad scale in the early 1970s. The earliest beginnings of what came to be called "the renewal" are difficult to trace. This is not for lack of witnesses, because most of the people originally involved are still active in the land. The difficulty arises because each one seems to remember the course of events as they appeared to him at the time. In other words, there was a personal level to the changes before there was a corporate or collective level. One thing does seem clear: There was no one individual organization responsible for initiating what happened.

The earliest traceable events occurred in the Tel Aviv area, where five couples began to meet together to pray and discuss common problems. The group ran across denominational lines and included Baptists, Mennonites, and Anglicans. What they all had in common was a dissatisfaction with the reality of their spiritual walk. In one of their meetings they prayed for the stiffening back of a seventy-year-old woman in the group, and much to the surprise of most of them she was immediately healed. This and similar incidents led some of the group to pray for more power in their lives. Before long, they reported that they had had an encounter with the Holy Spirit, which might best be described in the terminology of the Book of Acts as being "filled with the Spirit." These incidents took place in 1970 and 1971.

A short time later, two teachers from the Anglican School in Jerusalem asked Chuck Kopp, the young representative of the United Fundamentalist Church, to direct them in a study of the work of the Holy Spirit. (The name of the church is somewhat misleading, as the church was founded in the 1940s when the name "fundamentalist" carried different connotations than it does today. The name as well as the doctrines of the UFC are akin to what today is called "Full Gospel," or Pentecostal.)

Chuck Kopp and his wife suggested that the teachers come to their home and listen to cassette tapes on the Holy Spirit. Before Lent, a number of Jerusalem's pastors and their wives joined the sessions and, as in Tel Aviv, individuals soon began to have the encounter of being "filled with the Spirit." Strangely enough, most of them did not speak of their experiences outside the group.

Another parallel between what was happening in Tel Aviv and Jerusalem was that both study groups included pastors from a large segment of Protestant evangelical churches. It is significant that this was a revival which began among the leaders, not the laity.

A weekend retreat was organized for members of both groups, which was held at the Anglican retreat center of Stella Carmel, near Haifa. There were several outcomes of this event where participants prayed, studied Scripture, and shared their experiences more openly. There was a greater awareness of dependence upon the Holy Spirit and a growing unity in fellowship. The small tape study sessions in Jerusalem soon grew into a weekly city-wide meeting, which moved from church to church. The 6:00 A.M. pastors' prayer time was a direct outgrowth of this renewal. Many date the start of the upsurge in the number of Israelis coming to Jesus at this time.

Several churches began to grow rapidly soon after their pastors experienced revival in their own lives. In Jaffa, a suburb of Tel Aviv, the congregation at Immanuel House (Anglican) grew from a handful to an excited group of about 120 young people, mostly Israelis (both Jews and Arabs). Leadership of the Passover youth conferences comes chiefly from Immanuel House.

The largest regular Christian gathering in the country is also a result of that revival, according to its pastor. Ten years ago, the congregation in the little wooden chapel of the West Jerusalem Baptist Church rarely numbered more than fifty. Dr. Robert Lindsey, a native of Oklahoma, originally came to Israel in 1939. He studied at the Hebrew University and worked for the Southern Baptist Convention for several years before returning to the States to complete his studies and to get married. In 1946 he returned to Jerusalem with his wife and took over Baptist work until 1957. They served in several areas in the country then returned to the church on Jerusalem's Narkiss Street in 1962.

The Lindseys participated in the Bible studies and in the retreat at Stella Carmel, and soon afterward the little ninety-seat chapel began to overflow. To make room for more seating, the baptistry was filled in. Since then, baptisms are performed in pools formed by natural springs in the Judean wilderness. Soon more seating space was needed. Pastor Lindsey and Chuck Kopp took a sledgehammer to the walls of the two small counseling rooms behind the pulpit to enlarge the chapel. But even that did not provide enough space. They removed a side wall opening onto the garden area between the chapel and the stone Baptist House next to it. The garden area was tiled and the space between the buildings was covered with a flimsy roof.

The final expansion was unplanned. On Thursday night, October 8, 1982, someone poured kerosene under the Plexiglas sidewalls of the old garden area and the entire structure burned down within minutes. One thousand people attended the service on Saturday, many of them Israelis coming to express their sorrow at the destruction. The synagogue next door offered the use of their facilities for meetings, and later donated a beautiful Hebrew Old Testament for pulpit use.

In the fall and winter months that followed, the Narkiss Street congregation never missed a service. Attendance grew to between 300 and 400 people. At first they met outside behind the black shell of the old church building. Eventually they moved into a sturdily constructed wooden "tent" on the parking lot, which actually holds more people than the old church. Plans have been approved for the construction of a new 500-seat building with a cost of about one million dollars. The old chapel had been built for $1,000.

Church members and Israelis believe that the fire was probably set by the fringe anti-Mission groups that were responsible for continued harassment of the church in recent years. Within hours of the fire, dozens of neighbors and passersby came to express their regret and anger. Many contributed money to help rebuild, and the municipality opened a bank account in which Israelis could deposit donations. About one-fourth of the needed money has been given or pledged.

Lindsey likes to call the Baptist congregation "transdenominational." Whatever that means, it is certainly transnational. On any given Saturday, more than a dozen nationalities are represented. The service is best characterized as charismatic, although Lindsey and other pastors attribute the lively atmosphere to the Middle East location and to what they call "going back to our roots in the New Testament." Occasionally they meet a disgruntled visitor who was expecting to find a more familiar Southern Baptist service. Generally speaking, Lindsey and the church have stayed on good terms with their foreign mission board, and their guest preachers have included figures in the highest echelons of Southern Baptist hierarchy. Since its increase in size, the church has become essentially self-supporting and even manages to help support some local Arab Christian churches.

PROPHETS IN JERUSALEM

Jerusalem draws countless would-be prophets, a sorry assortment of deluded religious characters who have been somehow drawn to the Holy City to end their search or to deliver their message. Most of these figures are lonely and harmless, and go their way, leaving behind them nothing worse than a few shaking heads. Some are more threatening, trying to help the Almighty in his eschatological designs, as they interpret them.

One of the earliest of these was Michael Rohan, an Australian Christian who, in 1969, thought he would help the Messiah return by burning the mosques on the Temple Mount, thus expediting the building of the temple. This, he believed, had to happen before Jesus could come back. The latest in this line was the American-born Jew, Alan Harry Goodman. On Good Friday of 1982, Goodman shot his way into the Mosque of Omar on the Temple Mount, killing one man. Like Rohan, Goodman said God had told him to do it.

By far the largest number of these prophets are armed with only their Bibles and a minutely worked out timetable of the last days. Perhaps the most popular identity is that of the "two witnesses" of the eleventh chapter of Revelation. Longtime residents of Jerusalem's Christian community say they have met enough of the "two witnesses" to start a small denomination. Some of the "witnesses" come in pairs, expecting soon to die in the streets of Jerusalem. Some appear by themselves, looking for the other "witness."

THE CHURCH TODAY

The image of the church today is created mostly by the media in Israel. It is referred to as the Mission, a huge monolithic organization with unlimited funds whose primary goal is to use these monies to buy Jewish souls, either by direct offers of money or by any other effective means. This stereotype depicts missionaries walking the streets, offering candy to poor unsuspecting children if they will just be baptized. This and other similar accusations have been circulated for a long time, far longer than there has been a State of Israel. Some of them, unfortunately, may have some root in fact in the days when missions first began operating in Palestine. Today they bear no resemblance to the reality of Christian operations in Israel, but they have been repeated so often and so sincerely by such respectable people that almost everyone believes them.

Many Israelis are paranoid where evangelistic Christians are concerned. In recent years a number of individuals and organizations have emerged whose entire purpose in life seems to be to combat the Mission. Increasingly these anti-Mission groups are using sophisticated equipment, such as computers, to compile dossiers on the thousands of missionaries they believe they see at every turn. This effort entails high expenses and the groups are supported by what they can raise from private donations. Donors, of course, are more numerous and more generous if they believe the threat is great and their investment worthwhile. Ironically, the anti-Mission groups have adopted a method sometimes used by financially frustrated, well-meaning—but less than honest—Christian missionaries. They exaggerate both their difficulties and their success rate.

Increasingly, the anti-Mission groups are exploiting the media in order to push their cause and arouse public awareness to the "danger." The Mission is portrayed as a many-headed monster, totally unscrupulous in its methods, deceitfully claiming to support Israel while actually stopping at nothing to exterminate the Jewish people by converting them all to Christianity.

In all fairness, it must be remembered that throughout history these people have been the victims of persecutions and attempted genocide. A personal illustration may help put the Jewish viewpoint in perspective. A few years ago, not long after I had come to Israel, I was helping to guide a group of young Christians around the country. Our tour guide, a Jew by birth who had come to believe in Jesus, suggested that we go to the Western Wall on Friday evening and sing some Scripture songs. Friday evening is the second holiest day in the Jewish calendar, the time when the religious Jew welcomes the Sabbath. The Western Wall is the spot most revered by Jews, and the area is always crowded on the Sabbath.

We stood at the back of the large plaza, away from the wall itself, and began to sing songs from the Old Testament. As expected, a crowd began to gather to listen quietly and respectfully. We had agreed to sing only songs that would be considered nonoffensive by those in this holy place. We sang the first verse of a song and began the second verse before we remembered that it mentioned the name of Jesus. The song quickly faded into a mumble. Immediately a young man, whose dress showed he was an Orthodox Jew, approached and quietly asked us to stop singing. He was polite and proper, but firm. Our guide, not nearly as politely, replied that we had every right to be where we were, that our intentions were good, that we could keep singing if we wanted to. The young man only replied, "I have to ask you to stop."

"Who are you, anyway?" shot back our guide.

"I am a Jew," was the simple reply.

We assured him that we would sing only songs from the Hebrew Scriptures, but he said he didn't care what we sang, he wanted us to stop.

Why, I wondered, did he not even want to hear songs from his own revered Scriptures? Trying to put myself in his place, I could understand. He didn't want us, believers in Jesus, to sing songs based on his sacred Scriptures.

ANTI-MISSION ACTIVITIES

Under the heading "Sex to the Aid of the Mission: Volunteer Women from Abroad Help the Disseminators of Christianity," a Haifa newspaper in August 1983 published a brief article about the supposed new, sophisticated system initiated by various missionaries in the north. The story, provided by Yad l'Ahim, stated that young men were invited to spend weekend holidays with volunteer girls from abroad and thus encounter the principles of the Christian faith. Another newspaper in the northern town of Kahariya published a similar story, adding that the International Christian Embassy in Jerusalem (ICEJ) had originated these activities.

Yad l'Ahim ("a hand to brethren") is the largest anti-Mission organization in Israel. It has about ten branches, four of them in Jerusalem. Heading Yad l'Ahim's operation in Jerusalem is Moshe (Moses) Porush. In an interview with a leading paper in January 1984, Porush said: "The most dangerous ones [Christians] are precisely those who appear to us as friends of Israel. . . . We are not fighting against Christianity. We recognize the right of members of other religions to live in Israel and to respect their religion. Our struggle is against the attempt to intrude into our lives. . . . Whoever declares that he is a good Christian but is not a missionary either is lying or isn't a good Christian. Whoever is familiar with theology knows that in their eyes mission is an obligation."

While Porush acknowledges that members of other religions have a right to live in Israel and practice their religions and that one tenet of the Christian religion is to evangelize, that is the very thing he is fighting. His belief that Christians must engage in "mission" is the reason his organization regularly advertises to about 4,000 "missionaries" in Israel. The actual number of missionaries, in the Christian definition of the term, is probably fewer than 200, and the total number of born-again believers is fewer than 4,000. Clearly, Porush does not understand the Christian meaning of the word—someone sent forth by a church body to spread the gospel. Or does he? The public statements of Yad l'Ahim include references to a "massive infiltration of Jewish and non-Jewish missionaries from abroad."

Yad l'Ahim, also known as the Pe'ilim (Activists), claims to have been active since the early 1950s, but it has become widely known to the Israeli public only in the last several years. Christian groups knew of the organization earlier. Its activities included breaking into Christian meeting places, burning book shops or mailing lists, harassing and even threatening individual believers whom they considered to be dangerous, smashing windows, and painting slogans and swastikas on the walls of buildings. Recently the group has changed its image by using more sophisticated methods of harassment. They have also gotten publicity from the media.

One example of their new activities occurred when one mission organization was sending boxes of free New Testaments through the mail throughout the country. The Pe'ilim searched postal regulations and proved to harried postal officials that they were not required to deliver such mail. The Ministry of Communications, in one instance, ordered the postal workers in one of Israel's more religious towns to deliver the New Testaments. The workers went on strike against the order. But the Yad l'Ahim's research prevented the delivery of the books and the strike ended.

The organization claims to have computerized files of the 4,000 so-called missionaries and has published booklets with pictures, addresses, and methods of evangelizing used by various individuals. They also publish a bulletin regularly. When a missionary is rumored to be in a given neighborhood, Yad l'Ahim may send an investigator posing as a prospective client to check him out and also to interview neighbors about the suspect's life-style. If he has a regular job, the organization may inform his employer of their suspicions. In some instances, landlords have been influenced to evict the suspected missionaries.

Sometimes handbills, with a picture of a suspected missionary and critical comments about him, are stuffed into every mailbox in the neighborhood and posted on walls and light poles around town. Another method has been to picket the home of a victim, with picketers carrying placards announcing, "This is a missionary."

In the fall of 1984, three Christian establishments were singled out and hit on the same day with both placards and handbills warning local residents and listing the times of the "missionary" meetings. Several days later, the Christian organizations tacked posters in the neighborhood thanking Yad l'Ahim for the free advertising.

On one occasion Yad l'Ahim sent to municipal marriage registrars and burial societies information about 300 Jews who, they said, had been recently baptized. The objectives were to prevent these persons from marrying another Jew who might be unaware of the fiancé's baptism and to prevent their burial in a Jewish cemetery.

Recently, two Israeli men in their mid-twenties, who were baptized in the northern town of Nahariya, were refused permission to marry on the grounds that they had left the Jewish faith. The men decided to return to Judaism and the Nahariya rabbinate appointed a special rabbinical court to oversee their reconversion to Judaism. They were baptized in a ritual immersion pool, called a *mikve*, as part of the normal process of a non-Jew converting to Judaism.

In the spring of 1983, someone informed the Burial Society of Rishon LeZion that the bodies of two Gentiles had been interred in a Jewish plot in the local cemetery. The Society made plans to exhume the bodies of the two women and to reinter them in another area of the graveyard despite objections of the next of kin. Teresa Engelovitz, a Gentile woman wedded to a Jew for fifty years, had lived as a Jewess in Romania and in Israel but had not undergone formal rabbinic conversion to Judaism. A local religious authority denied this, claiming she had continued to visit the church in Israel. In the eyes of traditional Jews, whether or not she identified with the church, she was a Christian, as were her offspring. According to Jewish religious law, Jewishness is transmitted only through the mother.

One of Teresa's daughters formally converted to Judaism. Another daughter, who did not convert, died before her mother and was buried in a Jewish family plot. When Teresa died in 1983, her body was interred in the same plot. A week later, two rabbis informed the family that the two bodies must be removed from the cemetery. The family objected, various government officials intervened, and the exhumation was stopped. Later, when the next of kin applied for permission to erect a tombstone over the mother's grave, the Burial Society threatened to exhume the bodies of the two women. Religious authorities were no help, and the family turned to the Ministry of Religious Affairs, which ordered a delay in the exhumation.

The media, certain Knesset members, an Israeli Humanist Society, and others raised an outcry about what they termed "reversion to the Dark Ages," and disrespect for the dead. An editorial in one of Israel's largest newspapers read:

"It is difficult to describe a more serious combination of inhumanity and disregard of family feelings than this plan [to disinter]. . . . It is certain to be used by anti-Semites and anti-Israelis in order to portray Israel in the darkest of hues."

Defenders of Jewish orthodoxy denied that racism or medievalism were factors in the traditional Jewish view of death and burial. "Jewish believers give the highest priority to traditional Judaism, not only in relation to laws and customs concerning life but also concerning death," wrote one man. "The matter is related to belief in life after death and in the resurrection. None of this means anything to the Jew who regards personal immortality and resurrection as a relic of 'primitive religion' . . . but if there is no life after death and a corpse is nothing more than a home for dust and worms, why is exhumation such a calamity?" he asked.

As the furor continued, the surviving daughter attained an interim injunction from the Israeli Supreme Court of Justice forbidding the disinterment until the Burial Society could show reason why it should not comply with the family's wishes.

The attitude of many Israelis was echoed in a letter by a Haifa lawyer to the editor of a newspaper: "The disinterment . . . is an inhuman act and will alienate every enlightened person. I hope that the government will spare us this shame. But if the deceased is removed from her burial place, I ask the pardon of all Christians and assure them that this is an act of fanatical Jews who enjoy no support among the wider public in Israel. I propose that everyone opposing this shameful act place a wreath on her grave."

While Yad l'Ahim formerly got its information about missionary activity from the occasional infiltrator into Christian groups or articles published abroad by Christian workers in Israel, now its data bank has swelled considerably. It includes names and addresses of organized missionary efforts, as well as identification of some unsuspecting Christian who has shared his testimony with a fellow worker in response to a question. Someone may overhear the conversation and inform the Pe'ilim. Suddenly an unsuspecting Christian finds himself harassed, out of a job, and perhaps out of a place to stay. If he is not Jewish and is in Israel on a visa, he may soon be denied permission to stay in the country.

YAD L'AHIM ACTIVITIES

Yad l'Ahim purportedly discovered a new method being used to convert Jews. They claimed to have made a thoroughgoing investigation of residents of the Christian nursing home Ebenezer on Meir Street in Haifa. Most of the old men and women in the home, they say, are Jews despite the fact that the urban construction committee determined twelve years ago that the building permit would be granted for service to the Christian population only. The group claimed that some of the Jews there were baptized into Christianity in the baptistry in the building. Others who have not been baptized are under pressure to do so. Also they regularly attend worship services in the adjoining churches and celebrate Christian festivals alongside Jewish feasts. Yad l'Ahim in Haifa sent urgent letters to the mayor, members of the Municipal Council, the chief rabbis, members of the Knesset, and others, calling for an investigation of how Jews have come to be sheltered in a Christian nursing home set up by the World Lutheran Society some fifteen years ago. They also proposed that the supervising agency of nursing homes refuse to renew the licenses of Christian nursing homes unless residents are restricted to Christians.

In a press release Yad l'Ahim declared, "It is inconceivable that Jews, sometimes from lack of alternatives, should spend their last days in the shadow of the cross." The group threatened to organize stormy demonstrations against the nursing home, which they claim is engaged in soul hunting, "if there is no immediate action by the proper authorities."

A similar row, stirred up by Yad l'Ahim and encouraged by a female member of the Knesset, has been going on for some time over the fact that in certain parts of the country Jewish children study in Christian schools.

The five books of Moses are divided into weekly synagogue reading portions so that in the course of the year the entire Pentateuch is read through. Early in 1984, during the week in which the portion about Amalek's attack on the children of Israel (Exod. 17:8-16) is read, Yad l'Ahim set up a mobile exhibit containing samples of missionary literature and displayed it at various places around the country. The connection to Amalek? Just as Amalek, against whom the Lord will have war "from generation to generation," tried to wipe out Israel in the wilderness, so today, said Yad l'Ahim, the soul hunters are Amalek and are to be fought and eliminated.

The Mission is not the only target of Yad l'Ahim's activity. They also collect data on and attempt to fight the incursions of the various cults that are active in Israel. Of course, the anti-Mission organization does not always draw the fine theological distinctions that evangelicals do. For example, in their literature on the Mission they are quite likely to include Jehovah's Witnesses, Mormons, and even Scientology.

An interesting dichotomy arises for Yad l'Ahim when it comes to young women who are involved in cults and who come to age for service in the army. Almost all Israelis—men and women—serve in the army, but some orthodox groups Yad l'Ahim among them, oppose army service by women. (One rabbi member of Israel's Knesset caused an uproar by stating publicly that the deaths of so many Israeli soldiers in Lebanon was God's judgment on what he termed the "sluttish behavior" of the women in the Israeli Defense Forces.) However, Yad l'Ahim prefers that female members of cults go into the army to pull them out of contact with the cult. One of Israel's chief rabbis supports this view.

Not all Israelis are especially enamored with the work of Yad l'Ahim. On occasion a newspaper publishes a letter or an article claiming that the organization is creating a tempest in a teapot, that the effectiveness of the Mission (even those who don't agree with the anti-Mission fighters will use the term) is minimal, and that the church has done, and is doing, far more good than harm to Israel. A further criticism (although the two are related) is found in an articles appearing in late 1983 in a weekly magazine in the town of Nahariya:

> The rabbi of Nahariya, Dr. Aharon Keller, has told our correspondent that most of the reports of the Yad l'Ahim organization in Nahariya are half-truths for the sake of publicity. Rabbi Keller stated that the purpose of Yad l'Ahim is to be alert to all problems relating to the Mission and to warn the rabbis of religious functionaries locally, and to come to their aid as it becomes necessary for solving such problems. This work can be successful in most cases when it is done modestly and not in the limelight for the sake of publicity. This was the way the organization worked for many years, but recently an organization spokesman has appeared on the scene, one Aharon Kornfeld, whose lust for glory and

publicity has unbalanced him. A striking proof of this may be seen from the following incident: "An unfortunate woman is married to a man who, according to her, is a 100 percent disabled war veteran, with three children. One child is problematic and could not find his place in a Nahariya school. The woman came to me and threatened to send her child to the Mission for want of an alternative. Immediately, I contacted Yad l'Ahim, seeking their aid. A few days ago the same woman phoned to say that Kornfeld, the organization spokesman, instead of helping her, reprimanded her and made various threats against her. I ask, then, is it for this that Yad l'Ahim exists?"

Another incident deals with exaggeration. Most newspapers ran an item just before Rosh Hashana (Jewish New Year) about two Nahariya people who had been baptized. The newspaper correspondent requested Yad l'Ahim to provide the names of the individuals. They could give only one name. But on the eve of Sukkot (Feast of Tabernacles) the spokesman increased the number to three—all of this in order to publish the name of Aharon Kornfield.

Special damage was done to Beth-El in Shavei Zion (a German Christian hostel for Holocaust survivors). After I learned that this institution had invited a group of believers in the Messiah, Jews who were about to convert to Christianity or had already converted, I contacted the director and demanded that he cancel the meeting. The director complied with my request and cancelled the meeting. I immediately notified Yad l'Ahim of the cancellation; nevertheless, the spokesman again published before Sukkot an item about the holding of a meeting at Beth-El, again for the purpose of publicity, which this time was damaging to me personally and to the Orthodox community in Nahariya. The director of the institution, Beth-El, claims—and this time rightly so—that the confidence he had placed in me did not prove itself, and he is being defamed even though he complied with my request.

In conclusion, I suggest that great caution be exercised with respect to all the notices which are conveyed to the media about the problem of the Mission.

The story of anti-Mission activity in the mid-1980s would not be complete without coverage of one Samuel Golding, who professes to have been a Christian missionary once but who is now a crusader for

Judaism. He was born of Jewish parents perhaps fifty years ago in the Ukraine, his mother from Russia, his father from Turkey. His parents and almost all the rest of his family were killed by the Nazis. After World War II, Golding went to live with more distant relatives in Turkey. There, according to his story, he became assimilated and lost his Jewish identity.

He ended up in England, where he married the daughter of a clergyman and took a Bachelor of Divinity degree. In 1959 he became a minister in a church in Manchester and later became a missionary to France, Vietnam, and India. Before he left England, he was a well-known evangelist and shared the platform on occasion with such personalities as Billy Graham and Oral Roberts. Somewhere along the way, while he was in India, he began to doubt his Christian faith and soon denied it. Then he began a return to his Jewish roots, and in due course he divorced his Christian wife. Returning to Istanbul, he met a devout, old uncle who convinced him to make a full return to Judaism.

In Paris he met his second wife, she too a penitent, and together they returned to Turkey where they began actively to contact Jewish students who were in danger of assimilating. This activity brought on them the wrath of the Turkish authorities, and they were forced to flee to Israel in about 1977. In one of the more orthodox neighborhoods near Tel Aviv, Golding was ordained a rabbi and then moved to the Negev development town of Yeruham, where he made his livelihood as a scribe. After suffering a heart attack, he had to stop his work of copying the Hebrew Scriptures. He then began to see that he was uniquely qualified to work refuting missionaries.

This is Golding's life story as told by Golding. Some of it, at least, should be taken with a grain of salt. After he began his anti-Mission activities, certain concerned Christians with contacts in England and elsewhere began to check out aspects of his story that could be verified. People in Manchester who should be in a position to know had no recollection of anyone answering to Golding's description. Neither was there any such clergyman's daughter to be found, and Graham Crusade people knew nothing of him. In at least partial confirmation of these findings, the World Zionist Press Service sent out the following "Note to Readers" in March 1984:

> Some months ago the WZPS published an article by Dvora Waysman called "The Amazing Life of Rabbi Samuel Golding." It was widely used in the Jewish press. Much of the material

provided by Rabbi Golding himself to our correspondent has turned out to be inaccurate. Dvora Waysman wishes to disassociate herself from the information provided by Rabbi Golding, and the WZPS regrets the publication of the article.

Other investigations have even cast doubt on whether Golding was ever validly ordained as a rabbi. There is no doubt, however, that he is indeed active, and Israeli newspapers regularly publish his ads offering his books, tapes, and counsel on how to refute the missionaries and on subjects such as "the contradictions of the New Testament."

Not only Christians were suspicious of Golding's background. It was reported that local Jewish authorities began to investigate him, and doubt was cast on the authenticity of his ordination as a rabbi. For a time in 1985 his posters and newspaper ads disappeared, and then at the end of the year they reappeared, this time without the title of rabbi.

A sampling of Golding's religious intolerance can be seen by the following statements taken from one of his booklets entitled *A Critical Criticism of the New Testament:*

> Why is it that Jews who study Torah and live Torah never convert to Christianity? Why is it that the only Jews who do convert are the unobservant? Evangelical Christianity takes most of its converts from broken homes, sick and suffering people, lonely hearts, drunkards, prostitutes, and those with guilt feelings. . . . And this brings me to my past point that Jesus and his disciples were all ignoramuses. . . . When Jesus paid a visit to his home community and Bet Knesset, they were offended in him and said, "Is not this the carpenter's son?" (Matt. 13:57). In John 7:20 the people thought he was devil-possessed. John 7:15 says he never did any learning.
>
> The apostles were also ignorant men. "They saw the boldness of Peter and John, and perceived that they were unlearned and ignorant men" (Acts 4:13). Little wonder then that their followers were also ignorant. "For ye see your calling, brethren, how that not many wise men after the flesh, not many mighty, not many noble are called" (1 Cor. 1:26). They were immoral. "It is reported commonly that there is fornication among you, and such fornication is not so as named among the Gentiles, that one should have his father's wife" (1 Cor. 5:1). In fact, it is against Christian teaching to be wise. "Let no man deceive himself. If any

man among you seemeth to be wise in this world, let him become a fool that he may be wise" (1 Cor. 3:18). Paul says of himself, "I speak as a fool" (2 Cor. 11:23) and "We are fools for Christ's sake" (1 Cor. 4:10).

So whilst the fools for Christ read their foolish New Testament, let us Jews become wise in Torah.

Many and varied have been the accusations against the Mission and, generally speaking, they have been made so often and so long that they have been practically canonized as self-evident truths in the minds of the average Israeli. This psychological phenomenon is not unknown. It was the motto of Hitler's Propaganda Minister Joseph Goebbels that if you repeat a lie long and loud enough, it will become the truth. Goebbels employed this principle in slandering Germany's Jews until the Nazis were able to carry out their anti-Semitic program with at least the tacit approval of most of the population. The Jews had suffered many persecutions at the hands of Christians throughout the Middle Ages because of the success of this metamorphosis of lie and truth.

The average Christian peasant in fifteenth-century Europe "knew for a fact" that Jews regularly killed Christians and drank their blood; that Jews were masters in the use of poisons and often poisoned the wells of Christians; that Jews were in the habit of stealing the bread consecrated for the communion so they could continue to persecute Christ's body by stabbing it, boiling it, etc.; that Jews were not actually even human beings but rather demons in human form (which they maintained by drinking blood).

This same phenomenon of misinformation has created in Israel a body of what might be called "standard missionary methods" to win Jews, and it is aided by the commonly expressed idea that Christians *must* be resorting to unethical means to steal Jewish souls, because "no Jew would convert to Christianity unless he was paid or tricked." Some of these supposed methods have already been mentioned, such as offering candy to children to get them to listen to the gospel. One newspaper reported recently that a beleaguered fellowship in the town of Rehovot was accused of offering not only candy but pictures of Wonder Woman to children.

One of the most popular notions is that if an Israeli converts, the missionaries will solve all his financial difficulties or provide him and his family with a free ticket out of the country. This idea, unfortunately, has its roots in certain incidents that took place a number of years ago.

When a bright, promising Israeli would get saved, there was no place for him to deepen his knowledge of his new faith, a common problem in Christian mission work around the world. Some mission groups solve the problem by sending such students to a Bible school or seminary abroad. In other places the solution has been to start local training institutions, but in places where this is not feasible, sending students abroad—with the hope that they will return to their homeland—has been the only alternative. Of those few who left Israel to study abroad, both Jews and Arabs, most seem to have found mates, jobs, and homes in the new land, where it was easier to live as professing Christians.

The "financial aid" idea also seems to have its roots in efforts that also have been misinterpreted. At a time when conditions were worse, when people were unable to feed themselves and their children, and disease was more prevalent, a number of charitable institutions, hospitals and orphanages, came into being. Many of these institutions have remained, although the needs that brought them there originally have largely been met in other ways. But, like the institutions, the idea that the Mission has unlimited funds and knows no scruples in "buying" as many Jewish souls as possible has stayed around.

Any of the personnel in several Christian bookstores around Jerusalem will tell you that in any given week they can expect several Israelis to walk in and announce that they want to become Christians. The workers in these shops, who have grown wise and wary from experience, begin to question the inquirers' motives. In almost every case, they have personal problems ranging from fights at home to debts to a desire to avoid military service. These inquirers honestly believe that the Mission is their way out. Since most are not religious people anyway, they think becoming a Christian simply means getting baptized and having the information about religious affiliation changed on their personal documents. Obviously, this is not the life-changing personal encounter with Jesus that is the basis of true conversion, and most of these inquirers leave disappointed when they are told, "Silver and gold have I none. . . ."

Because so many believe the stories they have heard about the Mission and, even more important, because they know the Israeli religious authorities believe them, many try to use "going to the Mission" as a lever to get their demands satisfied by the Jewish institutions they feel should be championing their cause.

Edith Harpaz, for example, faced eviction from her home on Nordau Street in Tel Aviv after she lost an appeal to the High Court, which ordered her to return the flat to its owner. She threatened to set the flat afire with herself and her children in it. An attempt to implement the eviction order was frustrated by the woman, who locked herself in. Then she claimed that two days later, people who identified themselves as missionaries offered to send her to Canada and care for her there on condition that she and her three daughters convert to Christianity.

Harpaz claimed that the two people who spoke to her were Ruth and Hans, a couple from Scotland, who asked her to keep the matter a secret. "I felt that this was the solution for me," Harpaz said. "I'm not religious and am not an observant of Judaism, and just by chance I was born Jewish. The main thing is that someone cares for me and my daughters."

Harpaz said that the woman gave her a picture of the Virgin Mary and four medallions for herself and her children. When she told the story to friends, they advised her to contact Jewish religious institutions who might help her. "It doesn't matter who helps me, so long as I find shelter for me and my daughters," Harpaz said.

Another story was about a man, the head of his family, with no place to live. He and his family were being forced to leave their apartment and find temporary shelter in a storeroom where the man worked. He told the ultra-orthodox newspaper *HaMahane HaHaredi* that a mysterious person came from Jerusalem and offered him a ticket overseas and a flat on condition that he convert to Christianity. The newspaper reported that the man was afraid his situation would deteriorate if no help was found. "Perhaps some righteous person will read your paper about my problem and will take an interest," he told the newspaper reporter.

In the first example, it is inconceivable that a Christian worker who has been in Israel for any time at all would just walk in and identify himself as a missionary. None of the real missionaries from recognized mission boards use the term in Israel because of its negative connotations. These "missionaries" mentioned in the story supposedly gave Mrs. Harpaz items that are distinctly Catholic. There are many Roman Catholic workers in Israel, but since the early 1960s, they do not call themselves "missionaries." It is interesting to note that the threat to "accept the Mission's offer" came only after she had lost her court appeal, threatened suicide, and resisted eviction, all unsuccessfully.

Of the second story, it seems the man took a somewhat different approach. Unlike Mrs. Harpaz, he was a "religious" man, so in his story he immediately refused the offer of Mission help. But the object of his story was the same as hers—to use leverage on those who before had not been willing to help.

Others have threatened to "go to the Mission" if aid was not forthcoming from school authorities. Four children, residing in the mostly religious town of Safed in Galilee, were refused admittance to a religious school because their father was not a Sabbath observer and kept his shop open on the Sabbath. He claimed to be in dire financial straits, and if help was not forthcoming, he would emigrate to France and convert to Christianity. In Tel Aviv, fifteen parents threatened to enroll their children in a Christian school in Jaffa if the school authorities insisted on transferring the children under the terms of an educational reform plan. The local director of education expressed dismay and doubt over the threats. He claims he gets about 800 threats of this kind each year.

In July 1982 two prisoners at the Kfar Yona jail—one serving time for fraud, the second for unlawful entry—threatened to convert to Christianity. In a letter to a newspaper they wrote: "Inasmuch as the Jewish people have been gifted with a nature of contempt for lawbreakers, we have succeeded in finding our place among another people. We have appealed to a missionary church to undergo conversion to Christianity, and a number of prisoners want to follow in our footsteps." Later in the letter they suggested that if someone in the government took an interest in their plight and saw to an improvement in their conditions, or if the governor of the prison system was ready to invite them to his office, they would agree to revoke their decision to convert.

WHY THE ANTI-MISSION LAW?

Are these myths about Mission work mostly old wives' tales believed by the more credulous, less educated people of Israeli society? Take a look at the the Abramowich "Anti-Mission Law" passed by the Knesset in December 1977, which reads in part:

> He who gives or promises to give money, an equivalent of money, or another material benefit in order to entice a person to bring about the change of another's religion, his sentence will be five years imprisonment, or a fine of IL 50,000. . . . He who receives, or agrees to receive money, an equivalent of money, or a material benefit in exchange for a promise to change his religion, or to

bring about the change of another's religion, the sentence due to him is three years imprisonment, or a fine of IL 30,000.

Needless to say, this law caused no little uproar in the Christian community, since its obvious purpose was to silence the message and ministry of born-again believers. A number of protests from both Christian and Jewish organizations followed passage of the bill. The Christian protests, led by the United Christian Council in Israel, were not against the wording of the law itself but against the reasons given for its enactment. But one wonders if this distinction was made by the average Israeli newspaper reader. The newspapers usually quoted only the words of the law itself, not the explanatory matter. If one lays down the rule that children are not to play with matches and then the children begin to fuss and protest loudly, one is sure to get the impression that they want to play with matches. It may be that the Christian protests, and surely some sort of protest had to be registered, only served to reinforce in the Israeli mind the myths stated in the explanatory matter.

One statement in the explanatory notes of the law claims that the Mission is at work among the soldiers of the Israel Defence Forces, trying to influence them to desert from their units. If such is true, it probably reflects activities of members of the Jehovah's Witnesses, opposing army service as they do everywere else. It is one of the frustrations of evangelical Christians to be confused with the activities of such cults and made responsible for their actions.

In the seven years since its passage, the law has never been brought to a test case in court. In fact, it has never been invoked by the authorities. But every once in a while, some member of one of the religious parties in the Knesset will question a government minister as to why it is not being applied, since everyone knows that it is being broken regularly by "the missionaries."

All of this shows that, while there is freedom of religion in Israel, evangelical Christianity is accepted there with something considerably less than open arms.

2

ORTHODOX JUDAISM

Some evangelical Christians might believe, as I once did, that they share much theological ground with Orthodox Jews. Clearly, we disagree on the Trinity and the identification of Jesus Christ as the true Messiah and of his atoning sacrifice on the cross. But apart from these, one might assume that there was a lot of ground for common agreement.

A closer study shows that there are more things dividing the two groups than those that unite them.

Others may be surprised to learn that within Judaism are a number of sects or denominations. The three most prominent, at least in the United States and perhaps throughout the world, are Orthodox Judaism, Reform Judaism, and Conservative Judaism, the latter being mostly an American distinction. Therefore, any comment about the religion of Judaism should take into consideration that not everyone worshiping through the faith of Judaism will hold to the same body of truth or system of beliefs.

Jewishness for many has became a nationalist rather than a religious distinction. For this reason a student of the people and religion of Israel should also be careful to note the distinction between the people and politics of Israel and the religious beliefs of its people. To be a Jew ethnically doesn't necessarily mean that the person participates in any system of worship.

The distinction between Judaism and Zionism should also be noted. While both lay great importance to the idea of *Erets Yisrael*, the land promised to the fathers (the Holy Land), and emphasize the importance of a spiritual revival as conditional to a return to the Land, modern Zionism sees it more as a political realization than spiritual. While Orthodox Judaism is the only form of religion sanctioned by the religious establishment in Israel, polls taken in recent years show that no more than 15 percent of people there are in favor of Orthodox Judaism.

When one speaks of Orthodox Judaism today, he is using a modern designation for what was once considered the traditional sect of the Jewish faith, which was passed down from the first century. A quick overview of Judaism, then, necessitates a careful look at its foundations, best defined as tenets of Orthodox Judaism as we see it today.

THE SCRIPTURES OF JUDAISM

Five words need to be defined and understood in order to know what Jews believe.

1. *Torah*. The word is used a number of ways. The term literally means "the teachings." In another sense, it is the entire body of Law, both oral and written. To the Jew it is the fullest revelation of God given to man. Sometimes it is used to refer to all Hebrew Scriptures. In its narrowest use, however, it refers to the Books of Moses, the Pentateuch. Historically, the Torah is written on parchment and kept in scroll form, and revered ritually as the holiest object in their worship. Numerous laws have been written to preserve its purity and accuracy. Old copies or copies that become torn or dropped must be disposed of through special ceremony.

Orthodox Jews have a high view of inspiration of the Torah, believing that every word was inspired by God. It is considered the most sacred and divine of all the Scriptures. Their view of hermeneutics, however, enables them to hold to a view of literal inspiration, while they legitimately interpret such passages as Adam and Eve and the creation story as allegorical.

While Moses was their spokesman and the man to whom God spoke face to face, God's revelation was to all of his people. All saw God's glory on the mountain. One portion in the Midrash suggests that even the animals and birds heard God giving the Ten Commandments. Orthodox Jews, then, do not think of the revelation of God apart from the revelation of himself to all men through Torah, since the souls of all Jews were present there at Sinai. In Judaism, there is a diminution of religious authority with each successive generation, as we get farther and farther away from Sinai. Further revelations from God, the Prophets, and the Writings—basically all the books that make up the present Old Testament—were compiled by a group known as "the Great Synod" or "Men of the Great Synagogue." This collection, variously called the Hebrew Bible or the *Tanakh*, is generally referred to today as the Torah.

Although all of the Hebrew Bible (the *Tanakh)* is said to be inspired, the Torah section (the Pentateuch) is said to be the most inspired, next the Prophets, and then the Writings. It is in this order that the books appear in the Hebrew Bible.

2. *The Oral Law.* Sometime after the Jewish exile, the religious authorities set about to solve some of the new problems of interpretation of the Torah. During the years an oral tradition had come into existence, the use of the *midrash,* homiletical stories, to interpret and apply the teachings of Torah. They believed that at Sinai God gave Moses the written Law and at the same time instituted the oral Law. This oral Law was passed on from Moses to Joshua and to succeeding religious leaders of Israel, and the tradition continued through all the history of Israel. For example, the written Law says, "Remember the Sabbath Day to keep it holy" (Exod. 20:8). But how does one keep it holy? The answer is shown in detail in the oral Law, given by the priests who followed Moses. This oral Law, which was also considered divine revelation, sometimes differed from the written Law because of the way interpretations were made. Most of this compilation of oral Law was later put in written form and called the *Mishnah.*

3. *The Mishnah.* The Mishnah appeared around 200 B.C. in Babylon and Palestine. As interpretations grew, the collection grew. The collection was arranged in six main sections:

    a. laws dealing with agricultural produce, the portions of the harvest that fell to the priests, Levites, and to the poor

    b. the set feasts

    c. laws affecting womanhood

    d. property rights and legal proceedings

    e. the holy things of the temple

    f. laws concerning uncleanness

It was to these interpretations contained in the Mishnah that Christ spoke in his harsh response to the "righteousness of the scribes and Pharisees."

4. *The Gemara.* In the years that followed, the body of interpretations, illustrations, and commentary material continued to grow until in the fifth century a compilation was made in Babylonia, written in Aramaic. It was called the Gemara. Later a separate form of it, a commentary on the Mishnah, appeared in Jerusalem and elsewhere in Palestine, very similar to the one that appeared in Babylonia.

5. *The Talmud.* The Talmud was a later compilation that included both the Mishnah and the Gemara plus other portions of the oral

tradition that had developed. An English edition of the Talmud has been published. The Talmud in English runs to twenty-two volumes and is more than 2.5 million words long—more than three times the length of the Old and New Testaments combined.

6. *The Thirteen Articles of Moses Maimonides.* Judaism has never had a clear statement of faith such as the *Kalima* of Islam or the Apostles' Creed of Christendom. The closest they ever came to a clear organization or statement of their beliefs was the product of a rabbi, Moses Maimonides, during the twelfth century. His statement of belief, the Thirteen Articles, are:

    a. the existence of God
    b. his absolute unity
    c. his incorporeality
    d. his eternity
    e. the obligation to serve and worship him alone
    f. the existence of prophecy
    g. the superiority of Moses to all other prophets
    h. the Torah as God's revelation to Moses
    i. the Torah's immutability
    j. God's omniscience and foreknowledge
    k. reward and punishment according to one's deeds
    l. the coming of the Messiah
    m. the resurrection of the dead

THE LAW APPLIED

As one reads the Gospels, it appears that Jesus was in conflict with the Law on many occasions. A closer look at the Scriptures will show that it was to the interpretations of the Law that Christ objected. For example, the disciples plucked some grain as they passed through a field one Sabbath day. The rabbinical view was that they had violated a Sabbath prohibition against reaping and threshing because they had rubbed it between their hands to husk it.

Rabbis took prohibitions concerning the Sabbath to incredible extremes. For example, a tailor must not take even his needle into his hand before nightfall lest he forget he has it and go out somewhere. To carry it on his body would be "working on the Sabbath." A person could not read by lamplight on the Sabbath because the reader might tilt the lamp in doing so and that would be work.

Mosaic laws concerning diet (for example, the prohibition: "Thou shalt not seethe a kid in his mother's milk") were probably written to keep the Israelites from some idolatrous Canaanite practices. The rabbinical law took it to the extreme so that today some Jewish homes will have four sets of dishes—one for milk products, one for meat products, and two more sets to be used during Passover meal, one for milk and the other for meat.

Of all the contributions that Judaism has made to the world, Sabbath worship has probably had the most profound and far-reaching effects. One day of rest out of seven has been established as a pattern almost worldwide, among Christians, Muslims, and other groups as well. Sabbath worship was such an important consideration to the Jews that it was the only day of the week given a name. All the other days were referred to by the number of days remaining until the Sabbath.

Even today the Sabbath is central to Jewish doctrine and practice. A Jewish astronaut couldn't celebrate the Sabbath in space because time is calculated on earth according to the sun and moon. A person traveling in space, unaffected by earthly days and nights, simply could not experience a Sabbath or feast day.

DENOMINATIONAL JUDAISM

While there is much ground for agreement among all Jewish worshipers today, there are vast differences to be found among the beliefs and practices of the various denominations today.

1. Orthodox Judaism. As mentioned earlier, the only sanctioned Judaism in Israel today is Orthodox Judaism. Its beliefs are briefly described above. Until the eighteenth century, the term *Orthodox Jew* did not exist. The term is used today as a designation for traditional Judaism, which tends to be most concerned with holding to the historical events of revelation, the Torah, and the immutability of divine law in written and oral form, as binding for all time.

2. Reform Judaism (sometimes called Liberal or Progressive Judaism). During the period of enlightenment, European Jews felt the influence of the mode of grammatical and historical exegesis being put upon the Bible. Rather than the Bible being considered the yardstick to measure the progress of science and philosophy, science itself became the measuring stick of biblical interpretation. As this influence was exerted on Judaism, such matters as dietary laws were considered obsolete.

What remained of Jewish faith was the moral and ethical injunctions of Torah. Reform Judaism was an attempt to modify and enlarge the doctrines of the past to make them consistent with each other and with the highest truth attainable. The result was a view of universalism, but in a way that emphasized the prophetic message of Judaism without the priestly aspects. In later years Reform Judaism seemed to downplay the aspects of *Ahavat Erets Yisrael* (Love of the Holy Land)—Zionism, the concept of Israel as people of the land of Israel. Recent years, however, have shown a revival of Zionism, especially since the reestablishment of the State of Israel. Such a resurgence of interest, however, may reflect more of a social and political or ethnic interest among Reform Jews than religious concern.

3. Conservative Judaism. During the early nineteenth century, Jews in America sought some compromise of the ritualism of Judaism as it was practiced in Europe and elsewhere. Placing itself somewhere between Orthodox Judaism and Reform Judaism, the Conservative movement, while it sought to hold onto the entire structure of the rabbinical system, strives to interpret the Law in accordance with existing cultural needs and convictions. In summary, Conservative Judaism seeks to preserve and foster the unity of universal Israel and perpetuate Jewish tradition, while cultivating the best in Jewish scholarship. Conservative Judaism probably shows more tolerance for divergent views and practices among their constituent synagogues than any other denomination of Judaism.

BASIC DOCTRINES OF JUDAISM

While there are wide variances and great difficulties experienced in looking for authoritative statements, certain common doctrines exist among all the major denominations of Judaism:

1. God. To all Jews, God is a full personality, though free from all limitations and imperfections of personhood as we know it. God is indefinable, his divine character, his will, and his purposes seen directly and personally only through religion. Judaism emphasizes the oneness of God, and ideas of trinitarianism are repulsive to the Jew. In one sense Judaism can be defined by one verse of Scripture: "Hear, O Israel: the Lord our God is one Lord" (Deut. 6:4). Man's knowledge of God's righteousness and his way of life for his creation was made known to man through his revelation to Moses, which was the Torah, though full

revelation of God was not complete in the written Law. Further revelation of him comes gradually through the oral law, given first to Moses and later to the prophets and further to the rabbis. God is to be seen as man's heavenly Father and friend, who is concerned for his welfare.

2. Man and sin. As God is considered a perfect unity, man is seen as a unity of body and soul with no separation of spirit and matter. In contrast to the Christian view of man having a sinful nature, Judaism thinks of man with a divine nature. There is no such thing as original sin in Jewish theology. Rather, Judaism places great emphasis on original virtue and righteousness, which are the common heritage of the people of Israel.

While Judaism has no doctrine of sin, it does accept the possibility of *sins*, offenses or transgressions that are in need of atonement.

3. Atonement. In Jewish theology, human initiative takes great prominence in atonement. Man is seen cleansing himself on the Day of Atonement by self-examination and confession and by resolving not to continue in the offense. While Judaism understands that forgiveness comes from God, man is eminently capable of initiating the return to God. As expressed in a well-known Hassidic saying: "Where is God? Wherever we let him in."

4. The Messiah. There was a time when the term meant a person whom God would send to deliver Israel and restore them to world prominence. In the Authorized Prayer Book there is a phrase going back several centuries that reads: "[Lord our God] Who rememberest the pious deeds of the patriarchs, and in love wilt bring a redeemer to their children's children for thy name's sake." In Judaism today this idea seems more and more to be abandoned, replaced by the concept of a messianic era of flourishing Jewish statehood. Any idea of a messiah invokes only thoughts of a political leader who will unify the nation and bring peace. Reform Judaism now tends to reject any concept of a personal messiah, substituting rather the coming of a messianic era, the coming of a kingdom of justice and peace.

5. The future. One might be surprised, in studying the Bible closely, to discover that very little is said about the future state until certain prophetic references appear in the Psalms and Prophets.

Belief in a bodily resurrection began to develop in Judaism during the time that the Old Testament Scriptures were being completed. It is referred to more clearly in the Book of Daniel than any other. Reform Judaism does not accept the idea of a literal bodily resurrection. Conservative Judaism talks of resurrection as a way of describing the immortality of the soul.

In Orthodox Judaism, however, bodily resurrection is still fundamental dogma, expressed clearly in the liturgy in the form of the daily prayer: "Blessed art thou, O Lord, who makest alive the dead." Since the rabbinical period, resurrection of the body is looked forward to as being a part of the Messianic Era that is to come.

6. Good and evil. One particular tenet of Jewish theology suggests a problem over which both Jews and Gentiles have struggled through the years. Judaism, above all else, is monotheism. With polytheism or pluralism, one could attribute good and evil to different deities. With monotheism, there remains no one else to attribute both good and evil but to one deity. With monotheism, as Judaism is, one would have to say that a good God, who created all things and pronounced them "good" (Gen. 1:31), also allows for evil in the world, and allows for man to have a heart that is inclined to evil, as man was described to be in the time of Noah. A good God who allows for the existence of evil is either not all-powerful or he is not perfectly good, one could argue.

For Judaism the answer is given in the free will God has given man, the freedom and ability to choose to do good and God's willingness to help him to make good choices. While man's deeds are not always good, it is his motives, his desires to do good, that determine the good or evil of any act. To the Jew as for the Christian, the world does not provide the full and final reward of good works but is the proving ground and the preparatory state for the time of eternal retribution and reward.

JUDAISM TODAY

For centuries the people of Israel have suffered repression—sometimes subtle economic pressure, sometimes open pogroms as in World War II when as many as 6 million were exterminated in Europe. Through the centuries, however, it was both an ethnic and a religious bond that kept them as an identifiable people and religion. Despite the pressures that may unify them, Judaism has not been a static system of beliefs, and some of the changes have taken place as a result of the relative freedom they have known.

It was perhaps in America that Jewish people first felt really free. Later the French Declaration of Human rights in 1789 and further movements in Europe allowed for various sections of Jewry to establish themselves. Despite their differences there remains some clear distinct characteristics and beliefs that unify them as a people. As Rabbi Maimonides' articles did in previous centuries, it may be said that the tenets of Judaism as set forth by Dr. E. L. Ehrlich of *B'nai B'rith*, the "Sons of the Covenant," an organization that includes representatives of all the major branches of Jewish faith and practice, has given what may be termed a clear statement of what all Jews believe today:

a. *Ahavat Yisrael*, i.e., love for the Jewish people as a corporate unit of religion and peoplehood.
b. *Ahavat Torah*, i.e., love for the Torah in its written and oral forms, though varying in the degree of acknowledgment.
c. *Ahavat Erets Yisrael*, i.e., love for the Holy Land, promised to the Fathers and regained in our time.
d. *Ahavat Briyot*, i.e., love for mankind as all men were created in the image and likeness of God.
e. *Ahavat Adonai*, i.e., love for God in fulfillment of Deuteronomy 6:5.
Cited in "Judaism," by H. D. Leuner, in *The World's Religions*, edited by Sir Norman Anderson, fourth ed. (Grand Rapids: Eerdmans, 1976).

TWO

A Topical Overview

3

ALCOHOLISM

Through most of Jewish history, persecutions and pogroms have often started when non-Jews, the "Christians," had too much to drink and went looking for someone on whom to vent their aggressions. Traditionally, drinking and alcoholism have not been Jewish problems. With rare individual exceptions, Jews may engage in overdrinking on the festival of Purim. During that celebration of God's deliverance of his people as recorded in the Book of Esther, the rabbis have said, "One should drink enough so as not to know the difference between 'Blessed be Haman' and 'Cursed be Mordecai.' Or is it the other way around?"

The absence of an alcoholism problem among Jews generally was reflected also in the State of Israel in its early years. In the 1950s, the director of a Jerusalem psychiatric hospital searched for Israeli alcoholics and found only a handful. However, in recent years alcoholism has become increasingly a problem in Israel, probably reflecting a trend worldwide among Jews suffering from the symptoms of assimilation. It is estimated that there are presently about 12,000 alcoholics in Israel. While this is proportionately far below the percentage in the United States, it represents a marked increase. Especially alarming is the estimate that between 20 to 25 percent of Israelis of high school age have regular drinking habits and that within the next fifteen years the number of alcoholics will have risen to 50,000.

The minimum age for buying alcohol in Israel is eighteen, but the law is very loosely enforced.

Patterns of alcoholism are somewhat different from those in the U.S. In Israel, 80 percent of alcoholics are married men, 10 percent women, and 10 percent single men. In America, the number of alcoholics is about evenly divided between men and women.

Experts suggest that the severe economic problems and high rate of inflation contribute significantly to the number of alcoholics. Drinking, of course, brings with it increases in road injuries and deaths, wife beating, child abuse, and other violent crimes.

Several years ago the *Jerusalem Post* carried the following ad in very large type: "HALLELUJAH. The liqueur to drink after . . . you needn't ask after what . . . there are so many occasions."

4

ARCHAEOLOGY

Archaeology is often considered Israel's pastime. Thousands of Israelis on a regular basis probe and dig at the almost uncounted hills, caves, and valleys that dot the land, each one a possible hiding place for some priceless historical treasure. There are 3,500 registered archaeological sites in this little country and 22 archaeological museums.

Since the founding of the State of Israel in 1948, a number of exciting Holy Land archaeological discoveries have been reported in newspapers around the world. Only a sampling of these discoveries can be discussed here.

SYNAGOGUE IN CAPERNAUM

In Capernaum, a synagogue has been discovered where, it is believed, Jesus probably preached. Jesus ministered in the synagogue often and worked at least one miracle there, the healing of a demon-possessed man (Mark 1:21-25). Virgilio Corbo, the archaeologist who headed up the excavations in 1981, suggested that this may have been the synagogue built by the centurion whose servant Jesus healed (Luke 7:1-10). The synagogue walls were nearly four feet thick, and the building was 60 feet wide and 80 feet long.

LACHISH TELL

In 701 B.C. Sennacherib, the Assyrian king, laid siege to Lachish, Judah's second most important city next to Jerusalem itself (2 Chron. 32:9).

David Ussishkim, sponsored by Tel Aviv University and the Israel

Exploration Society, began additional excavation at the Lachish Tell in 1973. The workers unearthed a counter wall ramp, dumped against the inner wall of the ancient city to support it from the expected Assyrian attack. This counter wall extends some 360 feet. Ussiskim also excavated the siege ramp built by the attacking Assyrians. It measures 215 feet wide at the bottom and extends to 170 feet. Several dozen arrowheads, apparently fired by the enemy toward the defenders on the wall, were found, along with some scales of Assyrian armor.

MT. EBAL

Just prior to his death, Moses commanded that after crossing the River Jordan and entering the Promised Land, the Law of God should be read upon two mountains for the congregation of Israel. The promised blessings for keeping the Law were to be proclaimed upon Mt. Gerizim, just west of Mt. Ebal, and the judgments for disobeying God's commandments, upon Mt. Ebal (Deut. 27-28).

The actual ceremony on Mt. Ebal in obedience to Moses' command is described in Joshua:

> Then Joshua built an altar unto the Lord God of Israel in mount Ebal, . . . an altar of whole stones, over which no man hath lift up any iron: and they offered thereon burnt offerings unto the Lord, and sacrificed peace offerings. (8:30-31, KJV)

In 1980 Adam Zertel began excavating on Mt. Ebal. This 3,000-foot-high mountain, the highest in northern Samaria, is located some thirty miles due north of Jerusalem. Before the initial project ended some three years later, strong evidence suggested to Zertel that his team may have uncovered the altar built by Joshua some 14,000 years before Christ. He discovered a rectangular altar once filled with alternating layers of earth, ash, and field stones. It was approximately 9 feet high, 25 feet wide, and 30 feet long, with walls 5 feet thick. It was constructed of large, unhewn field stones. Around the altar were the burned bones of young bulls, sheep, and goats. The altar had a ramp leading up to it, instead of steps like most pagan altars. This would correspond to Exodus 20:26, which requires a ramp rather than steps. Pottery shards found near the altar suggest a date agreeable to the time of Joshua.

FORTRESSES BUILT BY SOLOMON

One of Solomon's first projects after securing Israel's throne was to build fortified cities in the central Negev to protect the southern flank of his Judean kingdom (1 Kings 9:15). After his death his son Rehoboam became king. It was during this time that Shishak, ruler of Egypt, attacked Jerusalem and destroyed those southern strongholds (1 Kings 14:25-26; 2 Chron. 12:1-12). In the mid-sixties and seventies, archaeologists Rudolph Cohen, Z'ev Meshel, and others discovered eleven of those oval fortresses built by Solomon. Some were 6 feet high and 406 feet in circumference. The architecture of the houses found in the settlements near the fortresses were of standard Israelite origin. Pottery discovered in the area suggests a tenth-century period, the time of Solomon and Rehoboam.

TEMPLE MOUNT

Since 1968, Benjamin Mazar has been directing excavation of a section of the Temple Mount near its southwestern corner on behalf of the Hebrew University of Jerusalem. Excavators found a huge stone on the southwest corner of the Herodian temple mount retaining wall. Inscribed on the stone were the Hebrew words translated: "The place of the trumpeting." Doubtless this was the actual location where the priest stood when he blew the shofar to announce to all Jerusalem the arrival and departure of the Sabbath. Mazar may also have uncovered the building where King Joash, a Judean monarch (835-795 B.C.), was murdered by his own palace guard (2 Kings 12:20-21).

SODOM AND GOMORRAH

Have Sodom and Gomorrah been found? Walter E. Rast, of Valparaiso University, Valparaiso, Indiana, and R. Thomas Schaub, of Indiana University of Pennsylvania, excavated two sites near the eastern shore of the Dead Sea in Jordan that they strongly believe are the biblical cities destroyed by fire because of their citizens' wickedness, as reported in *Biblical Archaeological Review* (Sept./Oct. 1980).

The principal site, Bab edh-Dhra, lies less than one mile east of the Lissan, a tongue-like peninsula that protrudes into the Dead Sea on the eastern shore. It was occupied during the Early Bronze Age (third millennium B.C.). Overlooking the Dead Sea from a height of 550 feet, Bab edh-Dhra was no doubt built on a bluff for defense purposes. The site consists of a town and a large cemetery. One scholar estimated that the cemetery is composed of more than 20,000 tombs in which more than 500,000 people were buried along with over 3 million pottery vessels. A large rectangular structure found inside the town is thought to be a temple. The archaeologists also uncovered the remains of what they believe was the altar associated with the temple.

Rast and Schaub discovered the second site, Numeira, in 1973 while surveying the area around Bab edh-Dhra. Even before excavation, the archaeologists could see that the site had been burned. Spongy charcoal covered the ground and could be scooped up by hand. Pottery shards found on the site's surface easily dated Numeira to the Early Bronze Age, the same period that Bab edh-Dhra was inhabited.

The two archaeologists spent two seasons digging at Numeira, the second in 1979 with Harvard professor Michael D. Coogan acting as supervisor. Based on these excavations, the archaeological team can pinpoint the occupation of Numeira to a brief 100-year period between 2450-2350 B.C. The town was then consumed by a fiery destruction, the remains of which can still be seen.

Rast and Schaub systematically surveyed the area and found three other sites strung along a line south of Bab edh-Dhra and Numeira, all showing signs of habitation during the Early Bronze Age. These three sites, Safi, Feifa, and Khanazir, like Bab edh-Dhra and Numeira, overlook the Southern Ghor, the circular plain or flatland along the southeast shore of the Dead Sea.

It is significant that there are only five sites located in the Dead Sea area, each located near a flowing spring; that all five date to the same archaeological period, the Early Bronze Age; and that there is no other evidence of occupation in the area until the Roman period more than 2,000 years later.

Sodom and Gomorrah had been part of a coalition of five cities which had rebelled against their overlord. The rebellion was suppressed and Lot, who lived in Sodom, was taken captive. When Abram heard this, he took an army of 318 men, rescued Lot, and defeated the armies that previously had fought against the coalition of five cities (Gen. 14).

These five biblical cities are generally referred to as the Cities of the Plain. In addition to Sodom and Gomorrah, they are Admah, Zeboiim and "Bella," that is, Zoar (Gen. 14:2). Geographical references in Genesis 14 seem to suggest that the five cities were located in the Dead Sea area. One reference is to "the valley of Siddim (that is, the Salt Sea)" (Gen. 14:3, NASB).

The town of Bab edh-Dhra and the four other sites may well be the remains of the five Cities of the Plain, inhabited in the Early Bronze III period (about 2300 B.C.). The foundations of some of the buildings were buried under tons of rubble. Beneath the rubble, there is clear evidence of a fiery conflagration.

RABBINICAL TUNNEL

Since 1967 the Ministry of Religious Affairs, in cooperation with the Department of Antiquities, has cleared out an ancient passage in Jerusalem which they named the Rabbinical Tunnel. Undoubtedly it dates back to the time of Christ.

The tunnel runs north along the Western Wall and is more than 600 feet long. Meir Kusnetz, an American-born civil engineer, has been in charge of the project. Since 1967, more than 17,000 cubic meters of fill have been excavated. The tunnel stops just short of the northwest corner of the Temple Mount. Its starting point is in the hall under Wilson's Arch, which is directly left of the present-day men's prayer section of the Western Wall. The finished stones inside the tunnel are still beautifully preserved, and some are of unbelievable size. For example, near the beginning of the tunnel is a gigantic chiseled limestone rock 46 feet long, 10 feet wide, and 10 feet high, weighing more than 415 tons! By comparison, the largest megalith at Stonehenge, England, is a mere 40 tons, and the rocks used by the Egyptians to build the pyramids were only 15 tons. Other similar stones weighing more than 300 tons have been uncovered in the tunnel. The amazing thing is that all those massive rocks are so well cut that although there is no mortar holding them together, even a thin knifeblade cannot fit between their joints.

TEL EL-QUDEIRAT

Between 1976 and 1979, Rudolph Cohen began excavating at Tel el-Qudeirat, searching for the ancient Kadesh-barnea of Numbers 13-14.

The springs there are the most abundant in Sinai. They water the largest oasis in northern Sinai. Cohen feels there is a strong possibility that Tel el-Qudeirat is indeed ancient Kadesh, the very spot where Moses sent the twelve Israelite men to scout out the Promised Land. In fact, the place is now officially known as Tel Kadesh-barnea.

MT. ARARAT

A unique coin, now on display at the Israel Museum, presents new evidence for the antiquity of the tradition associating Mt. Ararat in Turkey with the landing place of Noah's ark, according to Yaakov Meshorer (*Biblical Archaeology Review,* Nov./Dec. 1981). This large bronze medallion was struck 1,700 years ago at Apameia Kibotos in Asia Minor (modern Turkey) near the mountains of Ararat.

The coin depicts events of the story of Noah's Ark (Gen. 6-8) and is the only coin-type known to bear biblical scenes. The Greek word *kibotos,* which means "ark," is inscribed on the coin.

Three events in the flood story are depicted on one side of the coin. In the center, the ark, depicted as a box with an open lid, floats on water. The heads and shoulders of Noah and his wife protrude from the ark while the lid shelters them from the rain. The side of the ark is inscribed with the three Greek letters NOE *(nu omega epsilon).*

Above the ark's lid, a dove with an olive spray in its beak lands on the cover of the ark, symbolizing the subsidence of the Flood.

The third event is shown to the right of the ark. Noah and his wife are standing with arms upraised in an attitude of grateful prayer for their salvation.

TEL NABRATEIN

Eric and Carol Meyers began excavating in upper Galilee at Tel Nabratein in 1981. This ancient Jewish village dates back to the first few centuries after the destruction of the second temple in A.D. 70.

As reported in *Biblical Archaeology Review* (Nov./Dec. 1981), the Meyers uncovered a magnificent stone fragment weighing more than a thousand pounds, with two lifelike lions carved upon it. This stone apparently rested on top of two pillars, forming a shelter for a wooden

Torah Shrine or Holy Ark in a synagogue. The wooden box would have contained the synagogue's copies of the Mosaic Law. The structure and carvings of this stone aid our understanding of the appearance of the real Ark of the Covenant in the days of Moses and Solomon. Eric Meyers suggests: "It is a kind of missing link. It dates from the third century A.D., a millennium and a half after the Ark of the Covenant (the original prototype) and a millennium before any extant medieval example."

ST. PETER'S HOME IN CAPERNAUM

Italian archaeologists believe they have uncovered St. Peter's home in Capernaum, according to an article in *Biblical Archaeological Review* (Nov./Dec. 1982). When Jesus left Nazareth and settled in Capernaum (Matt. 4:13), it is speculated that he moved in with Simon Peter, who owned a home there (Mark 1:29). It is theorized that Peter's original house was later turned into a Christian house-church during the fourth century A.D. and an octagonal church was built over both during the fifth century. According to the excavators, the original house was located 84 feet south of the ancient synagogue in Capernaum.

James Strange and Hershel Shanks, authors of the article, summarized the evidence for the belief that Peter's house has been found:

> The house in question was originally built in the late Hellenistic or early Roman period (about 160 B.C.). It was constructed of abundantly available, rough, black basalt boulders. It had a number of small rooms, two courtyards and one large room. When it was built, it was indistinguishable from all the other houses in the ancient seaside town.

The authors reported that evidence suggests that sometime about the middle of the first century A.D. the function of the building changed. It was no longer used as a house. The center room, including the floor, was plastered and replastered, and walls were covered with pictures. Christian inscriptions, including the name of Jesus and crosses, were scratched on the walls. Some inscriptions may refer to Peter. Remnants of oil lamps and storage jars were found, but domestic pottery had disappeared. Fishing hooks were found between layers of the floor.

The center room and the building were gradually transformed. The lower parts of two pilasters were found in excavations. The pilasters had been erected on the north and south walls of the room and supported a stone arch which, in turn, supported a new roof. This was no longer a light roof of branches, mud, and straw, but a high masonry roof. In the fourth century an atrium about 27 feet long and 10 feet wide was constructed on the eastern side of what had now become a house-church. Finally, a wall was built around the compound.

In the mid-fifth century, precisely over the now plastered central room, an octagonal church was built, covering the same area and with the same dimensions. This was the kind of structure used to commemorate a special place in Christian history.

As early as the fourth century, Christian pilgrims visited the site and saw what they believed to be St. Peter's house.

"Is this then the house of St. Peter?" the authors ask. While it cannot be confirmed, the authors believe there is a considerable body of evidence indicating this is the house once owned by Peter.

JERUSALEM GATE

In April 1969 archaeologist James Fleming was standing in front of the Jerusalem Golden Gate. Suddenly the rain-soaked earth gave way and he fell into a hole 8 feet deep. Disoriented but uninjured, Fleming surveyed his surroundings in the dim light that came through the hole above his head.

As reported in *Biblical Archaeology Review* (Jan./Feb. 1983), he saw an ancient wall below the Golden Gate. "The gate itself," he said, "is built into a turret that protrudes about 6 feet from the wall. The underground stones of the wall south of the turret were large and imposing. . . . On the eastern face of the turret wall, directly beneath the Golden Gate itself, were five wedge-shaped stones neatly set in a massive arch spanning the turret wall. Here were the remains of an earlier gate to Jerusalem, below the Golden Gate, one that apparently had never been fully documented."

Could the Lower Gate have been the gate through which Jesus entered the Holy City? Unfortunately, it is difficult to date this underground gate precisely. According to the *Biblical Archaeology Review*, the best archaeological evidence for dating the Lower Gate seems to be the masonry to the right of the straight joint. Most scholars date this masonry to sometime before the Herodian period, based on archaeological and historical grounds. The Lower Gate would, therefore, also date to a period earlier than the Herodian, and a date as early as the reign of King Solomon is possible. It is possible that such a gate continued to be used for a thousand years or more and thus was the gate through which Jesus entered the Holy City.

Perhaps the most important implication of the presence of the Lower Gate below the threshold of the Golden Gate is that this area has long been identified as a location for the eastern entrance into the Temple Mount. Many Jerusalem maps show a Temple gate due east of the Dome of the Rock in the Haram esh-Sharif. The Golden Gate, however, is located about 350 feet north of this point. We now know that the location of the present Golden Gate was determined by an earlier gate.

SITE OF FIRST AND SECOND TEMPLES

Dr. Asher Kaufman, faculty member in physics at Hebrew University, disputes the traditional view that both first and second temples once stood on the present Temple Mount area now occupied by the Dome of the Rock, a Muslim shrine. Although not an archaeologist, Kaufman claims to have explored the Temple Mount platform more than 100 times.

It is his conclusion that both ancient Jewish temples were located some 30 feet northwest of the Muslim shrine at a place now marked by a small cupola that for centuries was known by the Arabs as the Dome of the Spirits and the Dome of the Tablets. In part, Kaufman's reasons for advocating this new location are as follows:

1. Because of the ancient names for this small cupola. He suggests the title "Dome of the Spirits" may be associated with Numbers 16:22 and 27:16 where the Creator is described as the God of human spirits. To carry the assumption a step further, the Shekinah (the Glory of God) once resided in the Jewish Holy of Holies. Kaufman concludes that the second name for the cupola, Dome of the Tablets, may be even more

significant, serving as as reminder that the Ark of the Covenant once contained two tablets upon which were written the Ten Commandments.

2. Because of the cupola's location in regard to the Eastern Gate. A straight line connects these two objects, from East to West. As the Eastern Gate served as the main entrance from the Kidron Valley and the Mount of Olives to the temple area itself, logic suggests the gate would probably have been built to provide the easiest and shortest route to the temple itself.

3. Because the cupola area alone stands upon a flat bedrock that protrudes from the platform surrounding the Dome of the Rock. The remaining platform area in the vicinity is paved with rough, somewhat uneven flagstones. The Mishnah, an ancient Jewish historical and theological source, states the Ark of the Covenant rested on a foundation stone just inside the Holy of Holies. The Mishnah also describes a nearby pit in which the libation (liquid) offerings were gathered. In 1896 Sir Charles Wilson, a British archaeologist, discovered a cistern just southeast of the cupola.

EBLA

In the early 1960s a farmer in northern Syria ran his plow against a large stone object. When it was eventually dug out, it proved to be a bin for storing cereal, dating back to about 1800 B.C. A short time later Professor Paolo Matthial, of the Near Eastern Studies from Rome University, began excavating the area. His team soon uncovered the remains of a fabulous and forgotten city that dated to between 2000-1600 B.C. In 1968 a male statue was discovered with a twenty-six-line inscription dedicated to the king of Ebla. The city was thus identified.

Giovanni Pettinato, also of Rome University, served as the original epigrapher of the Italian mission to Ebla. He suggests the possible link of some places and names found on the Ebla tablets to those found in the plain, such as Sodom and Gomorrah. The name Birsha, found on one of the tablets, may refer to the Birsha of Genesis 14:2, said to be the king of Gomorrah. Previous to this, these cities never have been mentioned in nonbiblical ancient sources. The city of Ur is also found in the tablets, but it is uncertain whether this can be identified with Abraham's home mentioned in Genesis 11:31. Apart from the Bible, names such as Adam (Gen. 2:19), Eve (Gen. 3:20), Lamech (Gen. 4:19), Jabal

(Gen. 4:20), Noah (Gen. 5:29), Hagar (Gen. 16:1), Keturah (Gen. 25:1), and Bilhah (Gen. 29:29) were rarely, if ever, found upon ancient documents. But, all these names are mentioned in the Ebla tablets, indicating that they were somewhat common names during that era.

CITY OF DAVID

Some of the most fascinating archaeological finds in recent years were discovered in the summer of 1983 at the "City of David" dig just a few hundred yards from the southern wall of the Old City of Jerusalem.

Twenty-six clay seals were unearthed bearing the names of dozens of persons who lived in Jerusalem in the time of the First Temple—the Holy Temple built by King Solomon that stood on the Temple Mount for nearly 400 years before its destruction by the Babylonians in 587 B.C.

The dig director, Dr. Yigael Shilo of Hebrew University, says the find was made on the floor of a building that dates back to the seventh or eighth century B.C. "This is the biggest First Temple find of bulla [seals] ever," said Shilo, who is rated as one of Israel's leading archaeologists. "It's a sensational find . . . and very well preserved."

Some of the names of Jewish merchants and citizens mentioned in the bulla had been previously unknown, such as Efroah Ben-Ahiyahu and Resa'yahu.

Shilo and his team of diggers—Israelis and volunteers from abroad—also came across the debris of the ancient city caused by the Babylonians' destruction of Jerusalem in the sixth century B.C. Some of the piles of rubble were reportedly nearly 10 feet (3 meters) high.

Probing beneath the ruins, Shilo found remnants of the original Canaanite wall that surrounded the city when young King David took Jerusalem and moved his capital there from Hebron. He also found tools and pottery used by the denizens of Jerusalem in the time of King David and his son Solomon.

SHILOH

According to the scriptural account, after invading and subjecting the land of Canaan, Joshua set up the tabernacle of Moses at a place called Shiloh, north of Jerusalem in the tribal allotment of Ephraim (Josh. 18:1). Here it would remain until destroyed by the Philistines (Judg. 4).

Centuries later, the prophet Jeremiah used its utter destruction as an example of God's judgment upon Israel's sin (Jer. 7:12).

Archaeologists working in Shiloh believe they have discovered the site of the Holy Sanctuary, where the Ark of the Covenant was kept for 369 years until the Philistines stole it and destroyed the sanctuary in 1050 B.C. This discovery came at the end of a five-week dig led by Dr. Israel Finkelstein of Bar-Ilan University, involving more than 400 volunteers, including university students.

According to Finkelstein, there is compelling evidence that the team uncovered the exact site of the Holy Sanctuary mentioned in the Bible. Dug up on the western portion of the site were various bones, which may be the remains of animals sacrificed there, and many clay vessels probably used to carry the sacrifices to the area. In addition, thirty large pitchers, virtually intact, were also discovered. It is doubtful that these large pitchers were for private use, indicating the presence of a public area at the site. Thus, Finkelstein believes that the presence of the bones, the clay vessels, and the large pitchers point to the strong possibility that this site was indeed the actual location of the Holy Sanctuary.

Finkelstein also points out that Shiloh was a Canaanite settlement long before the Israelites arrived. With the help of aerial photographs, the walls of the original settlement, which date back to the time of the patriarchs, have been located. Three stone rings with Egyptian markings, about 3,600 years old, were found also.

THE RIDGE SOUTH OF THE TEMPLE MOUNT

In 1978 Yigael Shilo, professor of archaeology at Hebrew University, began excavating the eastern portion of the ridge south of the Temple Mount in Jerusalem. Shilo's dig has produced the most extensive information thus far available on the last years of the Judaean monarchy. Several houses of the late preexilic period were found. Built on terraces, these structures become progressively poorer the closer in time they come to the Babylonian destruction.

A typical range of small objects of daily life was uncovered. Seals discovered in 1983 bear the biblical names of Eliakim and Micah. But the most sensational find was a hoard of fifty clay seals. Among them was one belonging to "Gemariah, the son of Shaphan"—certainly the same individual mentioned in Jeremiah 36:9-12 as scribe to King Jehoiakim. Shilo believes the building where this seal was found may have been part of the royal chancellery.

OLDEST BIBLICAL TEXT

In June 1986 archaeologists in Jerusalem announced the discovery of the oldest biblical text ever found. On two small silver amulets was part of the text of Numbers 6:24-26. The find was actually made about three years earlier in a dig conducted by Dr. Gabriel Barkay of Tel Aviv University, on the grounds of the Scottish Presbyterian Church across the Hinnom Valley from Mount Zion and the Old City of Jerusalem. The announcement of the find was delayed at first because the dig itself was being kept somewhat of a secret. This was because it was on the site of ancient graves, and any digging around Jewish graves is sure to bring a hostile reaction from some elements in the society. Another reason for the delayed announcement was that it had taken a long time and much tedious work to open up the fragile, rolled-up amulets.

Even when the silver scrolls were opened, the text was so faint that it took some time to decipher the minuscule texts. It was clear early on that it was in the most ancient Hebrew script, not at all like the script in use today, nor like that used in the time of Jesus. The script was, in fact, in keeping with the dating already assigned to the site: First Temple period. In other words, it was written between the time Solomon built the Temple and the time when that Temple was destroyed in 586 B.C. Barkay placed it in the century preceding that destruction, making it about 400 years older than the Dead Sea Scrolls, which provide our oldest biblical text to date. The part which can be read is almost identical to the Hebrew text of the same passage in use today.

The age of the text may prove to be a nail in the coffin of those scholars who have tried to claim that the Pentateuch was not written by Moses nor even in Moses' time. That same school generally tries to place large portions of the first five books of the Bible in the period of Ezra, in the fifth century B.C. In this debate, some of the argument revolves around the use of YHVH, the divine name of God (sometimes mistakenly transliterated "Jehovah"). The texts that have just been found do contain that four letter name of the God of Israel. In fact, this was the first time that the name had been found in any dig in Jerusalem.

These silver amulets were evidently worn around the neck and buried with their owner. An amulet is a kind of protective device worn by the superstitious to ward off evil spirits and bad luck. The text which was found, "The Lord bless thee and keep thee [literally, protect thee] . . . ," would have been considered particularly appropriate for such a purpose. Among other words that have been deciphered on the preserved part, but that are not part of the biblical text, is the word *hara*, the "evil," or the "evil one." Here perhaps was an early device intended to protect its wearer against Satan or against the "evil eye."

Dr. Barkay, who discovered the amulets, began reexcavating burial caves at the site, most of which had been robbed. The squarish burial chambers included benches on three sides where the deceased and their burial goods could be laid out. Eventually space was needed for new burials and the remains and burial goods were placed in a smaller chamber beneath one of the benches. This practice in the First Temple period probably gave rise to the biblical phrase about "being gathered unto one's fathers" (cf. Judg. 2:10; 2 Chron. 34:28).

Barkay found that Cave 25 had not been robbed, and it contained over 700 objects, the richest find in the vicinity of Jerusalem. Among the contents were the largest cache of jewelry and the oldest coin ever found in the country, according to a report by Lawrence T. Geraty in *Ministry Magazine* (Mar. 1984). A crab design from the Aegean island of Kos was found on the sixth century B.C. coin.

5

ARK OF THE COVENANT

There have been numerous attempts to find the lost Ark of the Covenant, but perhaps the most bizarre attempt was led by Tom Crotser, owner of a construction company in Winfield, Kansas. He is also the director of an organization called the Institute for Restoring History International. Crotser claimed to have made several earlier discoveries: the Tower of Babel, the actual stone Cain used to kill Abel, the City of Adam, and Noah's ark.

In October 1981 Crotser and his associates set out for the Middle East, confident that he would find the Ark. He based his search on Mt. Nebo in Jordan for two reasons. First, the apocryphal Book of Second Maccabees states that the prophet Jeremiah hid the Ark in a cave on Mt. Nebo shortly before the Babylonian destruction of the temple (in 587 B.C.). Second, he had studied a sketch made by Antonia Futterer who had made a similar search in the 1920s. On a wall blocking a cave passage on Mt. Nebo, Futterer claimed to have found this inscription: "Herein lies the Golden Ark of the Covenant."

Shortly after arriving in Jordan, Crotser and his associates located the cave they believed Futterer described. Immediately they began illegal excavations inside. Crotser claims to have entered a secret chamber where he saw a gold-covered, rectangular box. Without opening the box, he and his associates measured it. They reported the measurements to be 62 inches long, by 37 inches wide, by 37 inches high. Gauze-covered packages tied with leather thongs were lying in a corner of the cave, Crotser claimed. He assumed they contained the golden cherubim that once sat on the Ark.

Tom Crotser took color slides of what he saw, but has refused to reveal them publicly. In a vision, he reported, God instructed him to release the pictures only to David Rothschild, a London banker. Rothschild, according to Crotser's vision, is a direct descendant of Jesus Christ!

Larry Blasser, of Englewood, Colorado, was also determined to locate the Ark of the Covenant. He and Tom Crotser share several things in common. Both are untrained in matters of theology and archaeology and each heads up his own construction business. Both men felt their divine calling was to discover the Ark of the Covenant. Both created much publicity in their sensational attempts and both failed!

Blasser was influenced by the writings of Ellen G. White, a nineteenth-century prophetess of the Seventh-day Adventist Church. According to White, the Ark was buried in a cave before the Babylonian destruction of the temple, hinting the hiding place was near Jerusalem. Blasser was also intrigued with the description of the cave David used while fleeing Saul. According to 1 Samuel 24, the cave was situated near the Rocks of the Wild Goats. After reading both White and the biblical passage, Blasser concluded that this very cave doubtless would be a perfect hiding place for the Ark at a later date.

While Crotser relied chiefly on divine revelation, Blasser turned to technology. He enlisted the aid of two employees of the United States Bureau of Mines, Frank Ruskey and Richard Burdick. Soon the team felt they had found this place in the En-gedi area down by the Dead Sea. Using sophisticated electrical and seismic geophysical methods, they quickly "discovered" a large, underground, Y-shaped cave. There seemed to be a man-made wall at the entrance of the cave, indicating it had been sealed for some purpose. They concluded that the cap rock on the cliff edge had been removed to channel spring water over the presumed opening to the cave, probably to stimulate the growth of vegetation that would effectively hide all traces of the cave entrance. There seemed little doubt: the cave had been located. All that needed to be done was break through and obtain the Ark.

Blasser's zeal was so great that he persuaded the Department of Antiquities in Israel to grant him an excavation permit. He then enlisted a highly respected scholar, James Strange, dean of the College of Arts and Letters at the University of South Florida, to serve as field director.

It took the trained eyes of Dr. Strange and other archaeologists who had joined him just one day to totally dismiss the evidence gathered by Blasser. Erosion, they pointed out, had worn down the cap rock. The man-made wall was merely a natural limestone feature of the hill. Finally, the mysterious underground cave itself consisted of large fissures, created by weathering of salt from the Dead Sea that had settled in the rock pores. After breakfast on the second day of the project, all involved packed up and went home.

Once again the elusive Ark had outsmarted its would-be finders. Perhaps the failures of both Crotser and Blasser will discourage future spiritual raiders of the lost Ark.

Perhaps, but not likely.

In 1981 an archaeological dig adjoining the Temple Mount, Jerusalem's holiest site, caused a clash between Muslims and Jews.

A mysterious tunnel under the Temple Mount in an area north of the Western Wall, near the foundations of the ancient Temple, had been opened up in late summer by Religious Affairs Ministry workmen. The discovery of the secret subterranean tunnel, which was first uncovered 100 years earlier, then sealed up again, was kept secret for a month. Secrecy was maintained so as not to exacerbate relations with the Muslim authorities, who are in control of the Temple Mount.

The tunnel adjoined an enormous Crusader-built cistern that extended 75 feet under the mount. Archaeologists say it is one of perhaps dozens of such tunnels or cavities that honeycomb the depths of "God's House"—Mount Moriah of the Bible—where Adam was created, Abraham was called to sacrifice Isaac, the First Temple that was destroyed by the Babylonians, and the Second Temple destroyed by the Romans. For the Muslims it is the site of the Mosque of Omar, from where Muhammad ascended to heaven.

At the height of the furor over the archaeological dig, Ashkenazi Chief Rabbi Shlomo Green was interviewed on Israeli television and dropped a bombshell. He announced dramatically that the rediscovered tunnel might lead to the Holy of Holies, the Ark of the Covenant, and other Temple treasures.

Archaeologist Yigail Yadin said no one could know this, but Goren told *Newsview* (Nov. 10, 1981) that he had good reason to believe that the tunnel led to the Holy of Holies, and that he had found some way to find the Ark but didn't know how long it would take. He also said he wouldn't reveal anything more because of "secret and mystical reasons and also archaeological, historic and religious reasons." When asked if there were political reasons, he replied no.

It is against Jewish belief to reveal the real story of where the Ark is hidden. "The secret will be revealed just prior to building the Third Temple," Goren said. "The Ark will reveal the truth of accepting the Ten Commandments from heaven. This is the evidence of what Moses brought to the Jews. It will be the greatest testimony of what we have followed because it contains both the broken tablets and the complete second tablets." (Moses broke the first set when he saw the Israelites worshiping the "golden calf." He went back up Mount Sinai for the replacement.)

Rabbi Adin Steinzalz, Israel's great Talmudic scholar, tried to interpret "what Goren meant to say," *Newsview* reported. "The Holy of Holies was part of the temple and no longer exists. There may be a tunnel that leads to the area. We know the Temple Mount was tunneled and cross-tunneled. Even in the Second Temple times, in the first century C.E. we have information that the Ark was buried in one of the tunnels."

Steinzalz cited traditions about a loose stone and an entrance to the key tunnel. In the rediscovered tunnel, which is regarded as the most sacred spot in the holy area by the rabbi of the Western Wall, a workman accidentally loosened a stone, causing water from the cistern to flow into the tunnel.

Rabbi Moshe Hirsch, spokesman for the ultra-orthodox Neturei Karta sect, believes he can predict when the Ark will be discovered: "The world was created to last 6,000 years. Now it is 5,742, so we're not far. The Messianic era starts prior to the end of 6,000 years." He believes that the Ark will appear "when the Messiah rules and the Temple is rebuilt."

The rabbi of the Western Wall, Neir Yehuda Getz, who often prays in the tunnel, told *Newsview:* "The tunnel is a hint that the Ark may be hidden near there. Who can know? But at present, we don't want to make problems [with the Muslims]. There's no need. We'll know when the time comes. Then there won't be any problems."

6

ARMED FORCES

Zahal, the Israeli Defense Forces (IDF), is perhaps the world's most amazing citizen army. It permeates all aspects of national life. At the age of eighteen, both males and females (with few exceptions) are conscripted—the men for three years, the women for two years.

The 1950 Defense Law requires able-bodied men (and women up to age twenty-four) to serve in the reserves from thirty-two to fifty-four days a year in peace time, depending on unit and rank. However, in times of war, reserve duty is extended. In the 1973 Yom Kippur War, for example, a six-month duty period was common.

Unlike most nations, Israel's military survival depends not so much on the regular army as it does on the number of trained reservists the country can muster during periods of national emergency. The total standing army in Israel consists of 172,000 enlisted men, noncommissioned officers, and officers, according to the International Institute for Strategic Studies in London. With a ratio estimated by experts at six service and backup troops per fighting man, it becomes obvious that the regular army cannot wage a war by itself. Indeed, IDF military doctrine invests the standing army with the task of merely holding off an attack until the reserves can be mobilized.

The Institute estimates the total number of reservists in Israel at 504,000 men. Of them, 400,000 can be called up within forty-eight hours. The IDF has expended a great deal of energy in perfecting call-up procedures in order to achieve a maximum of efficiency. There are two methods of mobilization, one public, and the other secret. The former includes announcement of code words on the radio and in public media, calling on specific units to mobilize, and notices sent out in the mail. The second method relies on telephone calls, couriers, and unit members charged with contacting other members of the unit.

Reserve duty is called *Miluim*, and its influence on Israeli life is all-pervasive. The university student must serve during the summer months instead of working or enjoying a vacation. His professor must serve also, perhaps in the same unit and maybe at a lower rank.

Miluim has a devastating effect on business. All businesses must cope with annual long-term absences of workers. Factories, for example, must fill orders despite long absences of employees, often key personnel. It is not hard to understand how small businessmen could face bankruptcy under such conditions.

The burden of Miluim is so heavy that some Israelis prefer to move abroad rather than suffer the inconvenience of service. Brigadier General Hanoch Milo, deputy of the IDF's manpower, commented: "We send a kid through three years of compulsory service in order to prepare him for thirty years of Miluim."

After age fifty-five, males serve in the Civil Guard, or *Haga* units, providing security for urban and rural centers and institutions.

Relationships between personnel in Israel's army are casual. While higher ranks are saluted by subordinates, they are usually addressed by their first names. Discipline is relaxed. Soldiers don't "look very smart," and, some say, they even look sloppy, yet they are a potent force.

William Frankel, in his book *Israel Observed* (New York: Thames and Hudson, 1980), commented that members of the IDF are like members of an extended family, "offering each other the same mixtures of friction and basic understanding of needs as most families do." In fact, most soldiers are permitted to go home for the Sabbath unless there is a military emergency. "If their homecoming is delayed," Frankel wrote, "a telephone call from HQ will generally reassure parents." After a military battle, first priority is for fighters to communicate with their families.

Pay for conscripts is nominal, but for the regulars it compares favorably with civilian occupations. A full colonel and the director-general of a Ministry in Israel are paid at the same rate and are subject to the same conditions. A major earns about $850 a month, about the same rate a top-rate journalist is paid. However, the comparison is misleading because a major sometimes must work long hours—perhaps twenty hours a day, may be away from his family for weeks, and at times his life may be in danger.

There are few fringe benefits for the military. A car and driver are provided for lieutenant-colonels and those with higher ranks. If a field officer is married and needs a car to get home, one is generally provided, but HQ officers on the staff share a car pool. A subsidized commissary store and subsidized housing, subject to specified conditions, are also offered.

On the national scale, the IDF serves two important purposes beyond its essential function: educational and social. William Frankel made this observation:

> The national education system does not always ensure that the young recruit has mastered the basic elements of education. Some either started school too late, or were hampered by the negative aspects of their environment. An educational program in the army rectifies the omissions. The basic three-month course is an intensive immersion in study for 600 hours, in classes which generally number no more than ten pupils each.

"The army was, and still is, the most powerful instrument of unity for young adults, particularly Oriental citizens who arrived [in Israel] illiterate," wrote Israel T. Naamani in his book, *State of Israel.* He noted that while "defense is the primary aim, not far behind is the goal of galvanizing the antagonistic tribes of Israel into a national entity." To accomplish this, recruits are "put through accelerated courses in Hebrew and are imbued with a sense of historic values, beliefs, self-esteem, and will to self-sacrifice for the security and survival of others. They are made equal partners in a national experience. The psychological impact is obvious."

William Frankel concurs:

> The army has been a unique school, teaching not merely literacy but the basis of ordinary life in a modern society to many whose home background has remained that of the fairly primitive countries from which they came. Not only has the IDF been—as it continues to be—Israel's most successful educational organization, it is also the single most important instrument in creating a unified society from the variegated elements which have gone into its making.

7

ASHES OF THE RED HEIFER

Perhaps the most sensational (if not downright bizarre) happening in Israel today is the much publicized attempt to discover the Ashes of the Red Heifer, led by Vendyl Jones, one-time Baptist preacher from Texas. In reality his efforts along this line served as a backdrop and inspiration for the movie, *Raiders of the Lost Ark*, a "fairy tale" that depicted the heroics of archaeologist Indiana Jones as he rescues the Jewish Ark of the Covenant from some Nazi villains. Needless to say, any resemblance between the film and biblical history is purely accidental. But the original Vendyl Jones story is even more amazing than its Hollywood counterpart. This is the gospel according to Jones.

Through a secret code, supposedly known by only a select few Jewish mystics, Jones has deciphered some utterly fantastic prophecies from an ancient manuscript known as the Copper Scroll. Among the prophecies are:

1. Prior to Messiah's return, the Ashes of the Red Heifer, described in Numbers 19, must be discovered.

2. This will permit the purification and restoration of both the Sanhedrin Court and the Levitical priesthood.

3. After this, the lost Ark of the Covenant will be found, with Aaron's Rod, the pot of manna, and the tablets containing the Ten Commandments all safely inside.

4. Then, the original tabernacle of Moses will be discovered and will function as the Tribulational temple.

5. Finally, based on Amos 9:11, the one effecting these amazing discoveries will be a Gentile, possibly Vendyl Jones himself.

Other mind-boggling claims from Jones include:

1. The man who will officiate over the sacrifices in the Tribulational temple is Shlomo Goren, one of Israel's former chief rabbi leaders. This startling revelation is based on Luke 17:37.

2. The pot containing the Ashes of the Red Heifer is approximately three gallons in size.

3. This pot is hidden in a cave on the road between Jericho and Succakah by the Wadi Hakipa.

4. The coming Antichrist will be a Jew from the tribe of Dan. According to Jones, he is presently living in New York City and he (Jones) has met him.

Needless to say, there exists not the smallest shred of scriptural evidence to support any of Jones' fanciful speculations. No evangelical scholar would be able to even seriously consider his exotic theology.

The real tragedy, however, of pronouncements by such movements is that they are all too often accepted by the unsaved community and immature Christians as actual Bible truths, which is definitely not the case. Like date-setting for Christ's return, such statements excite, but in no way edify. They promise great things, but deliver nothing.

8

BOOKS AND READING

Every spring, soon after the Feast of Weeks, the 100-member Book Publishers Association sponsors National Book Week in Israel. All over the country open-air book stalls are set up, selling nothing but books of every description. Because of the daytime heat and work schedules, the markets open in late afternoon and close an hour or two before midnight. Thousands of Israelis turn out for the sale of new books, and it is usually difficult to get near some of the stalls. Piped-in music, soft-drink and cotton candy salesmen, and the throngs of people give the event a carnival atmosphere as "the people of the Book" engage in a favorite pastime. Avid readers search out new titles as well as better known favorites for their personal libraries.

A 1984 UNESCO survey showed that Israelis read and publish more books per capita than any other people in the world. More than a million Israelis from age fourteen and up read at least one book a month, and 90 percent of the nine- to thirteen-year-olds read a book a month. Even with the economic crisis, the sale of children's books, in particular, has not slackened. It is estimated that Israelis buy $30 million worth of children's books annually. The average home library contains about 300 books.

An average of fourteen new books are published every day in Israel, making it one of the two top nations in publishing, according to the number of different book titles printed annually compared with population figures.

In addition to Annual Book Week, an International Book Fair is held in Jerusalem every two years, which not only attracts local people but a large number of international publishers.

One book that probably won't be found at an open market during Book Week is the New Testament. This does not mean, however, that it is unknown or unread in Israel. One 1983 survey showed that 12 percent of Israeli homes have a New Testament, usually in Hebrew and bound together with the Old Testament. The same survey revealed that 94 percent have the Old Testament. Just under half of these are read with any kind of frequency, a figure considerably down from the 63 percent in a similar survey in 1970. About 23 percent of those polled had read at least a little bit of the New Testament, but more that 75 percent said they never had read it.

Forty-three percent of those questioned felt that it was desirable that the New Testament be used to supplement the teaching of history and religion in schools, while about the same number (including both those who had read some of the New Testament and those who had never read it) felt that its distribution and sale in Israel was harmful to Israeli society.

The average Israeli is quite ignorant of matters of the New Testament and Christian doctrine. Even an average university student will probably say that the Trinity consists of the Father, the Son, and the Mother. One Christian pastor, who taught a semester at a Beersheba university, was asked by one of the comparative religions students if Jesus went to church on Saturday or on Sunday. Most Israelis rarely see or come into contact with even nominal Christians, and those who live in areas such as Jerusalem, where there is some sort of Christian presence, will know only strangely garbed priests and nuns of the ancient churches.

9

CHARISMATICS

The Christian tourist who visits Israel today will probably see lots of church buildings. Most likely, however, he will not see any churches, that is, the people who meet inside those buildings. If he were to stay long enough to visit different fellowships, he would almost certainly notice that services are not quite like they are back home. That, of course, is primarily due to cultural difference.

But if that tourist had visited those fellowships in 1970 and then again in the mid-1980s, would he have noticed any particular changes? Probably.

What kinds of changes would he note? He would recognize the differences in worship as attributable to what is generally known as the charismatic movement. Granted, not a few of those differences he had seen on his first visit might have looked charismatic, too, even though their source was actually cultural. But a surprising number of evangelical fellowships throughout Israel are now worshiping in that style peculiar to the charismatic churches.

How and when did this come about? What follows is an attempt to trace objectively the progress of this phenomenon in Israel from the early 1970s to the present day.

One thing that becomes immediately evident is that the "renewal," as local people like to call it, began in several places around the country—unconnected to each other either geographically or denominationally—at about the same time. In 1970 several couples, including Anglicans and Mennonites, as well as Baptists, began to meet together regularly for Bible study and sharing at the Baptist Village near Petah Tikva. A number of the individuals had been going through personal dry times, and they felt the need to be built up by fellowship.

One Saturday afternoon, while they were discussing the implications of Agnes Sanford's *The Healing Gifts of the Spirit*, someone suggested that they pray for a seventy-year-old woman in the group whose back had been badly stiffened ever since a fall some six years before. It was reported that as they gathered around her to pray, she was immediately healed and began to touch the floor with the palms of her hands. That small group began to delve into the ramifications of the whole thing for themselves. In the following months they saw a number of people healed as a result of their prayers.

At about the same time, two Anglican school teachers in Jerusalem asked a young Assemblies of God pastor and his wife if they had any material on the baptism of the Holy Spirit. Before long they began meeting with the pastor weekly to listen to tapes made by some American teachers. Within a short time a number of pastors from various Protestant denominations joined them. By February 1971 the Jerusalem and Tel Aviv groups had become aware of each other and their common questions, so it was decided to arrange a weekend conference at a retreat center near Haifa.

Thirty-five people attended the retreat, most of them in positions of leadership in a wide range of Protestant denominations. By all accounts the high point of the weekend was the sharing of the Lord's Supper. Several of those attending testify to having had a charismatic experience during that retreat. Most of those involved up to this point were expatriates, that is, neither Jews nor Arabs.

However, an event took place at about the same time in a different area of the country which involved the Arabic-speaking churches. A newsletter written shortly after the retreat reported:

> A family of Muslim Arabs in a village near Genin on the West Bank had been tormented by a "demon" which was cutting their clothing and destroying their household furnishings. They placed a notice in the newspapers calling on spiritual leaders to exorcise the demon. As a result of the newspaper article the pastor of East Jerusalem (Baptist Church), Rev. Fahid Karmout, was led to pray for these people. Through a series of dreams he was assured of God's power in overcoming the power of the demon in the name of Christ. In the process of visiting the tormented family, a local Muslim leader and a Christian Arab teacher were brought under deep conviction and a series of meetings were started in the village of Zebabdi, on the West Bank of Jordan. As a result of the ministry of visitation and prayer the Muslim family has reportedly been freed from the demon and Pastor Karmout is having a continuing ministry in dealing with people in the area who are

disturbed by the occult. We visited among these people and saw evidences of these events, along with doctors from the Nazareth Hospital. It has proved to us anew the power of Christ to cast out demons, just as he did in the same area almost 2,000 years ago.

The newsletter, written by a noncharismatic Baptist missionary, described a series of meetings in Nazareth that featured a leading member of the Foreign Mission Board of the Southern Baptists. The meetings were described as a "revival in the Nazareth Baptist Church that resulted in more than 100 decisions for Christ. We saw a moving of God's Spirit for which we have been praying for years."

By the end of that spring it was evident that something was happening around the country. Father Michael Harper, a charismatic Anglican priest, was invited to conduct a one-day conference that June, and ninety people attended.

A Nazareth newsletter reported:

> The miracle acts of God in the past few months here in Nazareth have made the Christmas story take on a strange new relevance. They have convinced us anew that God's Spirit is still the comforter for a lost world, as he was when he visited a young devout Jewish maiden at a spring which still flows near here, and she brought forth a son, Jesus, the Savior of the world. These acts have been the literal re-creation of the New Testament stories in all their realness.
>
> First and foremost was the healing of our sister missionary, A.T. She was stricken by a severe case of peritonitis. When the efforts of local doctors and modern medicine appeared to be failing, we all gathered in prayer for her. Each of us was directed by the Spirit to go immediately to the hospital to pray for her and anoint her with oil as related in James 5:14. She related later that this was the turning point in her illness. She is referred to as "Lazarus" by the hospital staff who marveled at her sudden reversal and quick recovery.
>
> The fires of revival were fanned by this obvious act of the Lord. Church attendance has increased. The local population has been more open to the gospel than ever before. Bible study attendance at the Nazareth Baptist Church increased fivefold. There have been professions of faith even among young men from prominent Muslim families. Deacons, pastors, and mission-

aries have been meeting almost daily for prayer, and God keeps bringing answers. Even the local mission has been revived and held a conference to study the work of the Holy Spirit.

Pastor Fahid Karmout was one of three men who had come to the Lord years before in the town of Ramle. One of the others was Costa Deir, who had gone to live in the States and had become a recognized leader in the charismatic movement. He was one of the speakers on those cassettes that had helped get the meetings started in Jerusalem. It was learned that he would visit Israel in the spring of 1972, so he was invited to conduct a conference. One report describes it as being "attended by nearly 100 people—ministers, workers, doctors, nurses, and teachers—from such diverse fellowships as Anglican, Catholic, Lutheran, Mennonite, Pentecostal, Scottish Presbyterian, Southern Baptist, including Jewish and Arab believers, from such places as Jerusalem, Tel Aviv, Haifa, Tiberias, and the missionary hospitals of Nazareth and Gaza." Deir conducted another conference for leaders of the Arab churches around the country.

The charismatic movement is now well entrenched among Protestant congregations in Israel. It soon spread also to Roman Catholic prayer groups.

10
CITIZENSHIP

The Law of Return confers citizenship with its rights and obligations to all Jews as soon as they enter the country. Israeli Jews can maintain dual citizenship for they are not required to renounce their previous nationality. It was hoped that Jews from lands of "prosperity and freedom" would be more likely to emigrate to Israel if they were assured that they could leave if they wished.

Only those who are considered to be acting against the Jewish people or who may endanger the health, welfare, and safety of the land are denied citizenship.

Naturalization of non-Jews is similar to the naturalization process in other nations. Each applicant must be currently living in Israel; must have lived in Israel at least three years before applying; must be eighteen or older; must be entitled to reside permanently in Israel; must have some knowledge of Hebrew; must renounce his former nationality; and must make Israel his legal domicile. Some exceptions to these rules have been made.

11

CLIMATE

Israel's climate ranges from temperate to tropical. In the north it rains in winter but rarely in summer. The Mediterranean influences climate in the north central part of the country. The rainy season extends from October to March. Along the shoreline of Tel Aviv, the climate is warm and humid. Average daily summer temperatures range from 79 to 103 degrees Fahrenheit, and in winter temperatures range from 47 to 65 degrees.

The Galilean mountains and Jerusalem are favored by fresh, invigorating breezes, and temperatures range from 67 to 84 degrees in summer, and 40 to 50 degrees in winter.

Southern Israel is dry the year round, except for sudden, unexpected downpours in the Negev.

12

COMMUNICATIONS

RADIO AND TELEVISION

Five radio stations broadcast daily. Three of them are local, while the other two broadcast overseas in twelve languages.

There is only one television channel in Israel.

THE PRESS

There are eighteen dailies, two evenings, and fifty weekly newspapers. Most are printed in Hebrew, but some appear in Yiddish, English, Arabic, German, French, Polish, Hungarian, and other major languages.

Israel's largest newspaper is the *Haaretz* (The Land), which attracts about 15 percent of all newspaper readers in the country. The stated circulation is 50,000 daily with a weekend rise to over 70,000. The paper employs approximately 400 people.

However, the best-known newspaper on a worldwide basis is the *Jerusalem Post.* For most non-Israelis, this is the only source of news and views read concerning Israel. Printed in English, it has subscribers in all major countries. Created in 1932, the Post served as a voice of Zionism against the hated British.

There are some 650 periodicals and magazines published on a regular basis in Israel.

13

CRITICISM OF ISRAEL

UNESCO

The "Old City of Jerusalem and its walls" has been included in UNES-CO's list of 136 sites on a World Heritage list. In view of Israel's expulsion from the United Nation's Educational, Social, and Cultural Organization, it may seem strange that Israel's capital should have found its way onto the list.

But according to UNESCO's information bulletin, the site was nominated for the list of properties "of outstanding value" by Jordan. The bulletin failed to point out that the Old City and its walls have been under Israeli control for the past seventeen years. The report notes that the Old City contains "four synagogues dating from the sixteenth, seventeenth, and eighteenth centuries." It does not state, however, that these were vandalized and wrecked during Jordan's nineteen-year occupation of the Old City and restored to their pristine dignity and to daily use by Israel.

INTERNATIONAL RED CROSS

When a new country becomes independent, two things have high priority. One is for it to join the United Nations and the second is to join the International Red Cross. "The first is simple; the second is not," said Panayotis Stanissis, head of the North African and Middle East Department in the International League of Red Cross Societies, during a recent visit to Israel.

Stanissis had been asked why Israel's Magen David Adom (Red Star of David, the Israeli equivalent of the Red Cross) has never been accepted as a member of the league. The problem, he said, is the Israeli Society's refusal to accept the Red Cross emblem. "Our cross is not shaped like the Christian cross and has nothing to do with Christianity," he said. "Non-Christian countries like Japan and Bangladesh use the red cross."

The Red Crescent used by Muslim countries was presented to the League as a *fait accompli* after czarist Russia and the Turkish Ottoman Empire agreed to its use by the Ottomans during the truce in a war between them. Stanissis writes that accepting the crescent was a mistake and says the same for the red lion and sun—the symbol used in Iran under the shah. "If an African had founded the movement, the symbol would probably have been a red elephant and nobody's feelings would be hurt," he said.

Dr. Uri Hassis, head of Magen David Adom's International Relations Department, feels the symbol is only an excuse and the real problem is political. "Those who wanted to introduce the red crescent and to keep it in use all these years simply have more votes than we do," he said.

ISRAEL-CHINA ARMS RELATIONSHIP

The *London Sunday Times* reported that Israel has developed a top-secret arms relationship with Communist China. Quoting unnamed "intelligence experts," the newspaper reported that during the Chinese military parade through the streets of Peking on October 1, 1984, to celebrate the country's thirty-fifth anniversary, some of the tanks on display were updated with new guns believed to have been supplied by Israel. Instead of the clean lines of the Soviet-designed 100mm gun, there was a telltale fume extractor sleeve halfway along the barrel—typical of the British 105mm tank gun. But Britain did not supply the gun. A major part of the alleged arms relationship between Israel and China, the report adds, is "tank collaboration."

The *Times* reported that China is thought to have approached Israel several years ago because of its experience in improving Soviet tanks captured from Arab armies during the 1967 and 1973 Middle East wars. Israel saw the deal as a way of subsidizing its own military production. It has license to make parts of the British L7 tank gun and has successfully developed its own version. Britain has also modernized the L7 gun, adapting it for use in either Soviet T54 and T55 tanks or a slightly different version for the Chinese model, the type 69. Though the British are trying hard, they have yet to sell any of this equipment abroad. By using the latest ammunition supplied by Israel, China's reequipped tanks could be a match for the latest Soviet models.

In the 1982 war in Lebanon, the Israelis knocked out many Soviet-supplied Syrian T72 tanks, using a new tank shell developed by Israel. It is this type of ammunition that was made available to China. China has more than 9,000 battle tanks, all of a basic 1950s design. The deal to reequip them is, therefore, worth hundreds of millions of dollars. According to the *Sunday Times,* Israel has beaten Britain in this commercial battle, even though there are no diplomatic relations between Israel and China. One possible adverse consequence for Israel could be that its links with Taiwan may suffer. Ironically the Nationalist Chinese navy already uses the Israeli-made Gabriel missile.

Israel later denied this report, as did China.

AUSTRIAN ANTI-SEMITISM

A survey published by a scientist in Vienna says that 25 percent of Austrians are firmly anti-Semitic, and very few others are free of negative attitudes toward Jews. The survey was sponsored by the Austrian National Bank and covered a cross section of 1,000 Austrians between 1976 and 1980. Every fourth person had "markedly anti-Semitic attitudes" and another 25 percent showed "midway" anti-Semitic views by agreeing with the negative historical images of the Jewish people. Only 15 percent of those interviewed showed no prejudice against Jews.

The fact that Kurt Waldheim was accused of taking part in Nazi war crimes in Yugoslavia during World War II (allegedly he took part in the extermination of Jews) seemed to have little or no effect on his election to president of Austria on June 8, 1986.

Austrian anti-Semitism is expressed chiefly in the view that Jews wield too much economic and political power. About 56 percent of those canvassed said the Jews have too much influence on international finance.

Most of Austria's Jews were driven out of the country or sent to Nazi death camps during World War II.

UNITED NATIONS

The United Nations as a body generally disfavors Israel. Time and again that world body has shown itself to be controlled by a majority of states that are opposed to Israel as a matter of national policy. For the last several years, Iran has attempted to have Israel put out of the United Nations organization by having Israel's credentials rejected. In 1982 the vote was 74-9 with 31 abstentions (mostly by Arab countries) to kill the Iranian motion. In 1983 the Norwegians moved to table the Iranian motion indefinitely, and that time it was tabled by a vote of 79-43, with 19 abstentions. This year the tabling motion was made by Denmark, and the vote was 80-41, with 21 abstentions. In previous years Iraq (which is at war with Iran) had voted for the Iranian proposal; in 1986, Iraq abstained. All other Arab states voted with the Iranians, with the exception of Jordan and Lebanon, which abstained, and Egypt, which voted to kill the motion.

The People's Mujahedeen Organization, the main Iranian opposition group, claimed that while Iran continues to push for Israel's expulsion from the UN, the Teheran government is buying military equipment from Israel. "The people's Mujahedeen Organization of Iran has published today documents and information showing that on request of the authorities in Teheran, the Khomeini regime's purchase of arms and ammunition from Israel has been continuing during the current Christian year," the Paris-based organization stated. The Mujahedeen reported that while the government of the Ayatollah Ruhollah Khomeini "is making noisy propaganda regarding the proposal to expel Israel from the UN," Iran was taking shipment of military supplies from Israel via Frankfurt. (This accusation was made earlier, and it was denied by Israel and Iran.) Events of the last few months of 1986 and early 1987 concerning American involvement in alleged arms-for-hostages negotiations, using Israel as a middleman, add more credence to these claims. Despite the allegations, charges like this should be considered carefully, because it is a well-known trick in the Arab world to slander opponents by claiming they have links with Israel.

POISON OR HYSTERIA IN JENIN?

In early March 1983, fifty Arab school girls near Jenin on the West Bank were rushed to the hospital after complaining of nausea, dizziness, and headaches. The school was immediately closed. An Israeli medical team was sent to check out the air, food, water, and earth samples. They found nothing.

Another outbreak occurred on March 24 when 280 girls were hospitalized. Again a check found nothing.

On March 28, a car with Israeli license plates drove down a street in Jenin belching fumes from its exhaust pipe, followed by Arab school girls shouting, "Poison gas!" Immediately seventy-five people rushed to the hospital and were later released when local doctors found no evidence of gas poisoning.

Due to continuing skepticism, Israel invited the International Red Cross, the World Health Organization, and the highly respected Center for Disease Control in Atlanta, Georgia, to conduct independent inquiries. Some Arab girls confessed to feigning illness. Others were doubtless victims of mass hysteria.

POLITICAL CARTOONING

One of the most popular cartoon series in the world is "Dry Bones," which appears regularly in the *Jerusalem Post*. The following appeared after a visit to Israel by Jimmy Carter at which time he chastened the Israeli government for some of its policies.

First Speaker: Jimmy Carter . . . southern gentleman! Hah! We wine him, dine him, show him around, and before he leaves, he denounces our government!

Second Speaker: Aw . . . he'll do the same thing in Jordan.

First Speaker: You think so?

Second Speaker: Sure. They'll wine him, dine him, show him around, and before he leaves, he'll denounce our government!

FALSE REPORTS

As an example of false reports that are accepted as truth, *Newsview* published the following account in its issue of November 30, 1982:

Moshe Yegar, Assistant Director General of the Ministry of Foreign Affairs, recalls the wire service photo of a bandaged "armless baby," which President Ronald Reagan showed in protest to Israeli Foreign Minister Yitzhak Shamir. It turned out that the baby in question not only possessed both arms, but was in a hospital under Israeli auspices and was expected to make a full recovery.

Yegar said he met the photographer who took the picture in Beirut. When asked why he didn't verify the caption before sending the picture to his editor, the photographer shrugged and said, "In this business we have to work against time."

14

CULTS

It is not easy to cull extensive reliable information on the activities of the various cults in Israel. The Mission law has caused non-Jewish groups to show extreme caution as to how they expose themselves to mainstream information sources. Information gleaned from the press has mostly been supplied by Yad l'Ahim and the accuracy of such information is open to question.

Even so, it appears that cult activity is quite limited in Israel today. The number of these cults is quite small and overt proselytizing seems almost nonexistent. Information in this report has been gleaned from news reports over the past several years.

In February 1982 Dr. Seymour Lachman, a Jewish activitist, noted that there were 2,500 identified cults and missionary groups in the United States. The New York Jewish community set up a task force headed by Martin Dean, a sociologist, to warn Jewish communal leaders about missionary and cult activities that might affect Jews.

The New York Task Force on Missionaries and Cults reported that several of the cults were establishing centers in Israel to attract young Israelis and American tourists, and that several young Israelis visiting the United States had been ensnared by the Unification church. "A significant number of Israelis have become involved in such groups as the Church of Scientology, the Unification church, and the Divine Light Mission. Israelis visiting the United States are recruited and indoctrinated here and then sent on proselytizing missions to Israel," a Jewish anticult leader was quoted as saying.

In July 1984 a Task Force report was given that "dangerous influences" of missionaries and cults have made serious inroads in cities, kibbutzim, and college campuses in Israel. The Task Force, comprised of government officials and private organizations, was formed to combat the proliferation of Hare Krishna, Scientology, and other sects throughout Israel that had been seen trying to proselytize citizens.

The Mormons believe their future is "embodied in their unification with the Jewish community," the report said. The newly-formed Task Force attempts to serve as a monitoring force on all missionary activity as well as provide education programs for the community that will publicize the problem and propose solutions.

MORMONS

Israel and Jerusalem have a very deep significance in Mormon religion. According to remarks attributed to Dan Rona, president of the Mormon community in Jerusalem, "We are the sons of the tribe of Joseph, and the Jews are the tribe of Judah," This is said to explain the origins of Mormonism in Judaism. It also explains the Mormons' longstanding attachment to the belief in the return of the Jews to Zion and of their need to "convert" the Jews to the true faith.

A few years ago it was said that Mormon leaders in Utah proclaimed, "Joseph must pour water over the hands of Judah." Professor David Flusser of Hebrew University in Jerusalem, a specialist in religions, explained that this meant that the Mormons are to work for the conversion of Jews in Israel. Because they see their destiny as so intertwined, they go about their mission with great zeal. Flusser explained, "They work in a delicate manner, but are careful not to sell their goods with a loud voice. They begged me to lecture about them before a Jewish audience, but they met with a polite refusal."

David Galbraith, another Mormon community leader in Israel, does not deny the top-level decision in Salt Lake City, but he tried to explain it by saying, "If we engage in missionary activities here, they will reject us, oppose us, and misunderstand us. In recent years there have been instructions to us from the Utah leaders to explain and detail the essence of the Mormon religion in Israel. If someone should be convinced and desires to be a Mormon, we will accept him in love, but without ceremony or sacrament, because this is forbidden to us here, unlike every other area in the world where we engage in intensive mission activity."

Dr. Jonathan Shunari, also of Hebrew University, is in the last stages of his translation of the Book of Mormon in Hebrew, which he also worked on when he was at Brigham Young University. Shunari was impressed by the warm and hearty attitude of the Mormons, though he says, with a smile, that he never became a "Jewish Mormon," as they desired of him.

Israeli officials abroad are very well treated by the Mormons. Dr. Moshe Yegar, former Israeli consular in Los Angeles, was allowed to enter their genealogical center in Salt Lake City. The Mormons tried to work with *Yad VaShem*, the Holocaust memorial center in Jerusalem, in compiling genealogies of the Holocaust victims, but they were refused. The Mormons in Israel are well integrated into Israeli life with some 140 members in Jerusalem, about 100 of them students taking study courses, and about 40 in Tel Aviv and 20 in Tiberias.

Some 2,000 Mormons visit Israel anually on some sort of church-sponsored program. Many of them are students who have studied at Mormon headquarters at Kibbutz Ramat Rahel, just south of Jerusalem. However, in 1983, after having gone through normal channels, Mormons received permission to build an educational center on Mount Scopus near the Hebrew University, overlooking the Temple Mount. Work began on what will be the largest Mormon facility outside the United States.

After the permits were obtained and work began, the Orthodox Jewish community began to object to the project. In 1985 it became a burning issue, frequently in the headlines. Demonstrations were held at the building site and several times a week outside the office of Jerusalem's mayor Teddy Kollek. Frequent assurances came from Mormon officials in Israel and in Utah that there would be no proselytizing. The demonstrators were unconvinced and continued to look for ways to stop the construction, but to no avail. The center is far along toward completion and will soon become just another part of the multifaceted Jerusalem skyline.

SCIENTOLOGY

Two articles appeared in an Israeli newspaper in January 1983 about the Scientology church. One article gave a negative appraisal of the Scientology courses, which were said to provide "spirituality at the rate of 15,000 shekels per course." The second article reported on the pronouncement of the international headquarters of the sect on the ban of two Israeli Scientology leaders, Professor Yehoshafat Givon, math lecturer at Beersheba University, and Yovel Dor, a professional entertainer, as "subversive persons." They were charged with insubordination toward their superiors and setting up an independent branch of Scientology with a selective application of the sect's teachings. Contacted by the newspaper, the two leaders affirmed their desire for an autonomous Israeli Scientology, but Dor claimed that the ban was based on misunderstanding. Yoav Shefi, chairman of the Tel Aviv authorized Scientology branch, admitted that the ban on the two leaders had demoralized various members of the sect.

HARE KRISHNA

Some fifteen young people, ten of them Israelis, quartered themselves in Kiryat Tivon, a town some eleven miles from Haifa, where they lived according to the principles of the Hare Krishna sect. Five are former members of kibbutzim. A "resistance" movement of concerned citizens and parents has been developing in opposition to the Hare Krisha and other sects. At the sect's headquarters in Kiryat Viton, there is no excitement over the opposition, and they seem to have no intention of moving out. "We are not threatening Judaism," they say. "All we want is to do good to people—Jews, Christians, and Muslims."

In a report from Italy, the correspondent of an Israeli daily newspaper noted that an Israeli girl of Italian extraction is the voice of the Hare Krishna sect in Italy through the medium of radio. In an interview, she claimed that the sect was growing in numbers, even in Israel where a new center in Tel Aviv was to be opened. Israel is very close to the heart of the present Hare Krishna leader, she claimed, not only because it is the Holy Land for millions of believers in the monotheistic religions, but mainly because "Jewish blood flows in his veins," and he has visited Israel several times. During the Krishna festivals, many foreign guests come to the sect's centers in Italy, and recently a dozen Israelis were among them. Another Israeli in Italy is connected with the sect, it is also reported.

In Haifa, the Hare Krishna sect opened a branch in the form of a restaurant called "Maharajah" near the Beit Rothschild. Yad l'Ahim brought out a circular, calling for a campaign to close the restaurant and to oppose the promulgation of their poisonous spiritual food.

JEHOVAH'S WITNESSES

In June 1981 Yad l'Ahim reported that in Lod and Netanya, new nests of missionaries of the Jehovah's Witnesses sect were uncovered, although precise details were not yet known. Appeals were made to organize a demonstration, and Yad l'Ahim reported that they had begun to prepare such a demonstration.

TM

There has been enough activity involving Transcendental Meditation to make it a concern in Israel. A local newspaper in Israel carried a letter recently concerning the dispute. The letter denied the claim that TM was not a religion and cited anticult literature and first-person accounts of its underlying Hinduism. The writer of the letter was supporting a "long overdue" investigation of this and other cults in Israel.

YOGA

Another ultra-orthodox newspaper reported that a notice had recently appeared in another local paper for those seeking "good company" by taking lessons in yoga. "And where are these lessons given?" the paper asked. "At the Anglican Church in Israel. In this school Arab children and the children of diplomats living in Israel study together with a not insignificant number of children from the intellectual strata of Jewish society." The writer reminded the readers that one of Israel's Chief Rabbis had ruled that yoga and other pagan cults are in the nature of idolatry.

EMIN

The Emin sect had an estimated 600 members in Israel in February 1983. Based in England, this group is headed by a man named "Leo." The sect allegedly disdains Judaism to the extent that members use mainly English in their meetings, considering Hebrew "primitive." It also regards the Bible as passé, although the sect is said to incorporate elements of Christianity, magic, and the teachings of Leo and his agent in Israel, one Matthew. Testimonies of former members of the sect in Israel claim that huge sums of money were raised from participants in sect meetings. A one-paragraph statement by the sect representative says that Emin is "not a missionary sect but a nonprofit society, and that the Israel branch has no tie to the English center."

An exhibition of paintings of the Emin sect at a municipal gallery was closed in January 1983 following a protest of the city councilman who charged that it was sponsored by a "missionary body." The councilman claimed that he had been investigating reports that there was "missionary activity" behind the exhibition. According to reports, the sect has about 1,000 followers in Israel, and it is based on "ancient Egyptian beliefs with traces of mysticism, parapsychology, astrology, and more." Reports like that one must be treated skeptically regarding both numbers and doctrines, realizing the strong local prejudices against any outside groups who attempt any kind of proselytism.

BAHA'I

The world headquarters of the Baha'i sect are in Haifa. The temple and extensive surrounding gardens are magnificent, overlooking the Mediterranean, and are a favorite tourist attraction for Israelis.

INDIGENOUS CULTS

When speaking about cults in Israel, it is not enough to mention those groups known to have been imported from abroad. Israel has produced several of its own groups. One such group, known as the Black Hebrews, will be discussed in chapter 22, "Ethiopian Jews." Another group, the so-called "Lifta group," will be discussed in chapter 47, "Temple Mount." A third group was started by Simha Perlmutter in a place called Ir Ovot.

An article appeared in November 1982 under the heading: "Ir Ovot: The Messiah who will come from the Edom Mountains will find Simha Perlmutter with one wife and five children only!" What followed was a feature story relating the escapades of a group of eccentrics.

The group, some of them so-called Christians who had immigrated to Israel sixteen years before and settled in the Arabah, was said to have "risen on the staircase of Judaism," under the guidance of its prophet, Simha Perlmutter. The article stated that the group was entangled in indebtedness, but that they had discovered a fountain whose holy waters had healing powers. The article said that one of the wives of the leader fled in the darkness of night, snatching away four of his children.

According to the story, most of the group had abandoned their leaders several months before when they had run out of money and were having to live on little more than bread and water.

Perlmutter was at first thought to be a member of the group Jews for Jesus. The group had settled in the Arabah because of Perlmutter's belief that the Messiah would come from the Edom mountains to a great plain. Water was drilled, and the sulfurous waters were said by Perlmutter to be healing "holy" waters. At one time there were more than eighty followers but the group dwindled.

In June 1983 the Jerusalem ultra-orthodox "judiciary" ruled that Perlmutter was nothing but a missionary disguised as an ultra-orthodox Jew. Members of the group were said to be American "penitents" (secular Jews who returned to orthodoxy), who did not recognize the State of Israel, took no part in Knesset elections, boycotted the census, and did not serve in the army or celebrate national holidays.

Through the efforts of Yad l'Ahim, it was discovered that Perlmutter's book, entitled *The Tents of Shem*, was filled with propaganda for Christianity and Jesus. As a result, a grave warning was issued by the ultra-orthodox judiciary: "In the wake of reliable testimonies, we declare that this place [Ir Ovot] is a frightful menace to every Jew, that he [Perlmutter] is an extremely dangerous person who, under cover of an ultra-orthodox mantle, seeks to persuade Jews to believe in that man [meaning Jesus]. Heaven forbid! We therefore warn each and every Israeli not to set foot in that place nor to be in the presence of that man at all."

This episode shows the energy with which non-Jewish groups are sought out, examined, and discouraged in Israel.

15

DAILY LIVING

Life in Israel is an ever-changing panorama, a strange blend of the old and the new. Sometimes staying alive can depend on how agile and resourceful one can be. The nation exists despite the volatile political environment, a territory surrounded by tense Arab nations and with sometimes hostile Palestinians in their midst. An angry look or misunderstood gesture or a shouted slogan could turn a peaceful street scene into a war zone. Someone described an Israeli citizen as a soldier who happens to be on a lengthy furlough. Almost all citizens—men and single women—serve their time in conscription and remain in military reserve units for most of their lifetime.

The description of this land, given by the ten fearful spies sent out by Moses, with Joshua and Caleb, was, "This is a land that devours its inhabitants." At certain times in the recent past, this description could be considered as still being true of Israel. It is a land where no one takes peace for granted.

In a nation of ever-rising tax and import duties, an automobile might be taxed as much as 350 percent of its original value. Inflation makes price tags meaningless from day to day. Compared with other nations, salaries often seem to have no relation to one's occupation. An automobile mechanic may earn more than a white collar worker or a government official, and a plumber may earn twice what a doctor or university professor receives.

The language itself is a measure of the country and the people. No other nation in the world has been known to choose to put back into common use such a difficult language that was for centuries all but extinct. No other people would pursue its revival with such persistence and patriotic zeal. Bringing the language back into existence was quite an accomplishment. Some even question whether or not the pronunciation today bears any real resemblance to the language as it was spoken years ago. Someone has said, however, that "Israel without Hebrew would not really be Israel."

Israel is a land of struggle and of a struggling and persistent people, yet thousands attempt to immigrate yearly and take up the challenge of settling there. One can compare it in many ways to eighteenth- and nineteenth-century America, where people from all nations and tongues came to a free land to enter into the struggle of establishing themselves. The commonality of those who seek Israeli soil today is, as much as anything else, the ethnic attraction, the realization of what it means to be a Jew and living on Jewish soil.

Some might find it incongruous to see a young American Jew with several academic degrees side by side with a young European Jew in their new land of freedom, both struggling with the nuances of an ancient Semitic language during a weekend military exercise as they learn to field strip their M16 rifles. Others would wonder at a "peace-loving" people who spend so many hours in military training and in clambering over miles of desert terrain in armored vehicles..

The boatloads and planeloads of people who crowded toward Israeli soil in the past decades came looking for role models, someone to teach them a new way of life in a new land. They found their role models in the Sabras, the native-born Israelis. The Sabras were mostly veterans of the early kibbutzim, which were so successful in making, through their spectacular agricultural feats, the "desert . . . rejoice and bloom as a rose" (Isa. 35:1). The hardness of their lives and their diligence set the pace for all those who came to join them. Their quiet ridicule of the softness of the newcomers, and their wincing at the accents of people trying to speak their newly acquired Hebrew, spurred the newcomers on to learn it better. Someone with several academic degrees would be considered illiterate if he didn't speak Hebrew well. Their casual dress made the man's tie obsolete, even on the floor of the Knesset.

Education is relevant only as it applies to Jewishness and temporal relevance. While they might teach their young people every nook and cranny of Israeli soil, the student might never learn to find the Virgin Islands on a map. With a population approaching 4 million, of which nearly one-third are students, it is clearly a nation of youth with all the accompanying energy and potential.

Israel is a land of unusual settlements. One might picture it as a nation made up entirely of kibbutzim, planned agricultural and industrial settlements. Actually there are less than 250 such settlements with little more than 100,000 members. Yet kibbutzim members furnish a disproportionate number of representatives as cabinet ministers, members of Knesset, and are among the highest ranking military men. This is largely true because these kibbutzim members are considered the veterans of the land, the true Israelis, with all others thought of as the latecomers who have not yet paid their dues.

Most of the citizens live in cities and suburbs along the coastline, from Haifa in the north to Ashkelon in the south. City streets are generally crime-free and safe, and supermarkets, movie houses, and restaurants abound. Nightlife might compare favorably with any city on the Mediterranean. The densest inland settlement is around Jerusalem. Tel Aviv and its suburbs account for about 500,000 of the nation's 4 million people.

After the cities and suburbs and the kibbutzim, the rest of the people live in small villages and farm communities.

The nation of Israel has a life all its own, one that has developed from the struggles and opposition its people have faced from their neighbors. Israelis see themselves as different, but no better or worse than other people of the world. Perhaps, however, they have fewer hangups about themselves and are more eager to live with the differences than most others.

Their often-quoted slogan, "Never Again," could apply to more than just the Holocaust of Europe. It could mean also that never again will they be a nation without a land, a people without a place to be.

16

DEATH PENALTY

The five Books of Moses, the basic canon of Jewish law, contain what seems a very harsh code, with its frequent references to offenses meriting capital punishment, some of which we would consider as minor infractions today. In practice, however, the laws concerning capital punishment were rarely applied and always surrounded by numerous qualifications and conditions.

A rabbi's quotation, recorded in the Mishna, compiled around A.D. 200, said that any Sanhedrin ordering even one execution in seven years would be considered a murderous one. Another rabbi extended the seven years to seventy years, statements that suggest to us that capital punishment has always been considered a rarity among the Jewish people.

Israel abolished capital punishment in 1954 except for convicted Nazi war criminals, and specifically those who took part in the Holocaust. In 1961, Adolf Eichmann, one of the Nazi executioners, was tried and hanged, after his controversial abduction from his hiding place in South America.

Israel, however, did not repeal the Defense Regulations of the British Mandatory Government, which imposed the death penalty for the illegal use of firearms and for membership in groups that illegally used firearms. After the Six-Day War, a Security Regulation, valid under the Geneva Conventions, was passed, making the possession or use of illegal weapons a capital offense. But the regulation has never been imposed because of the people's deeply rooted objections to the death penalty.

17

DIVORCE

Divorce is another matter demonstrating the negative effects Western society has had upon Israeli life and culture. The degree of the problem has not yet approached the level in America, but the problem grows. The divorce rate in America is still four times that of the State of Israel.

The reason divorce is so difficult for Israelis is that divorce in that country, like marriage, is in the hands of the religious authorities, who do their best to keep couples together by not granting divorce so readily as the American courts.

According to Jewish law, a writ of divorce will be granted only if both parties are in full agreement. Though this does prevent some divorces from taking place, it has the effect of giving the unwilling partner the advantage of stating conditions for the divorce that seem almost like blackmail. One wife, for example, granted her husband a divorce on the conditions that he pay her $10,000, give her full ownership of the apartment, sole custody of the children, and "the return of her virginity"! (This latter condition, strange as it may sound, since she already had children, had some religious significance, something that would aid her in marrying again.)

In some ways, the divorce laws are somewhat one-sided. If the husband refuses to grant the divorce, even if he has no desire to see the marriage saved, it is impossible for the wife to ever remarry. Any children she might have from another relationship would legally be *mamzerim* (bastards), unable to marry anyone except other *mamzerim* for seven generations. If, on the other hand, a wife should refuse to agree to a divorce, any children the husband might father in a later relationship would be considered legitimate.

The rulings concerning a *mamzer* only put limitations on the person's rights to be married. In everything else, inheritance and even social standing, he is considered a brother, an equal. Ironically, one way of avoiding the seven-generation taboo is to marry a Gentile woman. Since religion goes according to the mother, the children will be considered Gentiles and can undergo conversion to Judaism with no reference to the fact that their father was a *mamzer.*

18

DUAL COVENANT

One of the most controversial, and to many, disturbing concepts emerging from within the Israeli Christian community today is known as the dual or double covenant philosophy. The idea is suggested that God has made two covenants—one with Jews and one with Gentiles—to open the way to the one true God. According to this contention the two religions have one center, that both Jews and Christians are worshiping the same God, but that Christianity has the mission of reaching the Gentiles to bring them to the Father, a position with the Father the Jews already attain.

Throughout history there has always been some mutual respect by Jews for the moral standards of Christianity and by Christians for the moral standards of Judaism. Moses Maimonides, the twelfth-century rabbi who codified the distinctives of Judaism, expressed a high view of Christianity's ethical standard, seeing in it God's preparation of the world for the coming Messianic Era.

In their respect for Judaism and its morality, some Christians through the centuries have gone farther. In rejecting the thought that Judaism is inferior to Christianity, they have concluded that Judaism was not replaced by Christianity nor the covenant to Abraham superseded by his covenant with the Gentiles. Such an idea would naturally appeal to some Jews. But in the end, few Jews will accept the full ramifications of such a view. Martin Buber, the Austrian-born Jewish philosopher, said, "Whoever regards Jesus as an historical personality, be he ever so high, may belong to us; but he who acknowledges Jesus to be the Messiah already come, cannot belong to us."

The reestablishment of a Jewish nation, returning to the biblical name of Israel, raised hopes in the hearts of many evangelical Christians because of the eschatological implications. The feelings gave rise to what has been called "Christian Zionism," a movement that has given vocal support to Jewish rights. The movement influenced the so-called

"Blackstone Petition" of 1981, which was signed by more than 400 Christian and Jewish leaders in America and was distributed by the State Department to most of the nations of the world, urging the return of the land of Palestine to the Jewish people.

The religious sentiments of Christian Zionism coincided well with the political aims of Jewish Zionism, though the latter was never as precise in its definition of what the new "Zion" would be like except that it was to be established on the moral principles of "the Prophets."

Other Christians in the twentieth century have taken up the view that, despite the territorial claims of Arabs (and even Palestinian Christians living in the land), Israel has an inherent right to the land. Even Billy Graham, speaking to the National Executive Council meeting of the American Jewish committee, called for the rededication of the United States to the existence and safety of Israel.

Some of the controversy concerning Christian Zionism has arisen over the establishment of the International Christian Embassy in September 1980. Some of the goals of the embassy were stated in an information pamphlet as follows:

- To show concern for the Jewish people, and especially for the reborn State of Israel, by being a focus of comfort according to Isaiah 40:1: "Comfort, O my people, says your God."
- To remind and encourage Christians to pray for Jerusalem and the land of Israel.
- To be a center where Christians from all over the world can learn what is taking place in this land and be rightly related to the nation.
- To stimulate Christian leaders, churches, and organizations to become an effective influence in their countries on behalf of the Jewish people.
- To begin or assist projects in Israel, including economic ventures, for the well-being of all who live here, irrespective of race, background, or religion.
- To be a reconciling influence between Arabs and Jews.

Another organization reportedly advocating the Dual Covenant position is Nes Ammin, an international Christian settlement in Galilee, established in 1961 to promote Christian-Jewish understanding and cooperation through dialogue. It is a movement to offset centuries of prejudice against Jews for their "rejection of God." The movement contends that God has not rejected Israel and that Christianity has the task of cooperating with God's people, Israel.

To achieve their goals, Nes Ammin members seek to live with the Jewish people and promote dialogue between them, refraining from any attempts to proselytize them. The message of the church, they say, is to make clear the real identity of Jewish people and their purpose in the land God promised them, and their importance for the life, thought, and actions of the church.

Such ideas have not gone without serious challenges by other evangelical Christians, who fault the so-called "Christian Zionists" for their love of the Jewish people that stops short of evangelizing them or seeing a need to evangelize "God's chosen people."

19
ECONOMICS

Imagine living in a country where everything goes up in price each week, where even basic items become so expensive they are considered luxuries! One might think of the Old Testament reference to such a time of economic disaster when "a donkey's head sold for eighty shekels of silver, and a fourth of a cab of seed pods for five shekels" (2 Kings 6:25).

Israel in the 1980s has had one of the highest inflation rates in the world. It reached higher than 1,000 percent near the end of 1984 and continued to go higher by the day. As it worked out, it took forty-five times as many shekels to buy a given product in 1984 as it did four years before. The cost of living in Israel was rising at a rate of about 25 percent per month! At that rate, anything in America costing a dollar would go up in price a penny a day, and because the rate accumulates, it would cost ten dollars after one year.

It is not difficult to imagine that such conditions created a different attitude toward personal economics. No one wanted to keep much unused cash lying around the house or in a bank. Israeli banks offered what appeared to be fantastic terms. Someone who invested 100,000 shekels one day would receive 100 million shekels in three years—but only if he invested shekels. Dollars, whose currency base is more stable, invested in Israeli banks would receive less than in an American bank.

In the years before the election of Menachem Begin's Likud Party, the annual inflation rate had reached about 30 percent. In the late 1960s the exchange rate was about 3.5 Israeli pounds to the dollar. Then in the early 1970s the government devalued the pound so that there were 4.2 pounds to the dollar. In the years leading to the Likud's victory in 1977 there were several sudden, unannounced devaluations. Each one was usually preceeded by rumors of its approach, and the public rushed to the stores to buy up many price-fixed items at the old prices.

As the economy deteriorated more rapidly after 1977, the new government adopted a policy of more frequent "mini-devaluations" of only 2 or 3 percent in order to avoid the panic hoarding psychology. This policy, in turn, gave way to a system whereby the exchange rates for the Israeli currency was adjusted daily to try to keep up with the inflation. In the meantime, in one of many efforts to stabilize the economy, the government's economists replaced the pound (or "lira," a name left over from Turkish days) with the biblical name "shekel," which was valued at ten of the old pounds. Unfortunately, inflation got worse, and in 1984 the exchange rate was 525 shekels to the dollar.

In some of the markets of the Old City of Jerusalem, piles of old lira coins were being sold as scrap metal, as their value as scrap actually exceeded their face value.

This rapid and accelerating decline in the currency values created new attitudes toward what to do with the paycheck each week. The savings plans offered could be used by the public, especially for short-term investments of just a few weeks. But many people feared that a desperate government might decide the next day to levy taxes on bank accounts, as had been known to happen in the past. (Savings accounts, then, don't have the same respect they enjoy in the United States and other places in the world.) But no one would think of hiding his savings under the mattress, as inflation would make the buying power of the shekels decrease daily. So other methods had to be found as a hedge against inflation.

One solution was to buy needed items as soon as possible. A family's savings then might be put into an apartment, a car, or a video player. Buying an extra apartment was a common method, and even though the property taxes were high, the rise in real estate prices more than compensated for the investment. Most families, however, couldn't afford even their own apartment—much less a rental investment property. Prices for a four-room apartment in Jerusalem started at $100,000. Property investments were normally in the smaller items such as color TVs and furniture or automobiles. While these items were all heavily taxed—the TV at about $1,000 and a small car as much as $10,000—the taxes were the same for almost everyone, so resale value, compared to investment value, stayed relatively high also.

This tendency to invest in material things might give a Western visitor a false impression of opulence. In America a man whose home and clothes are of the best quality probably has a bank account to match. In Israel, as often as not, what you see is all there is—and the person's bank account probably carries a regular end-of-the-month overdraft.

Another solution to solving the inflation problem is to engage in illegal currency exchanges, buying American dollars, Swiss francs, Jordanian dinars, or other relatively stable currency on the black market instead of keeping shekels. (Holding foreign currency in Israel is illegal.) The black market exchange rate is much higher than the banks, but at least the "investor" has a stable currency and escapes the 20 to 25 percent erosion in the value of his paycheck each month.

For generations the Middle East has been known for its black market currency exchanging, and since its founding in 1948, Israel has been no exception. At certain times, under certain governmental policies, the market is more likely to flourish. In Tel Aviv during the early 1950s in the area around Lilienblum Street where the Bank of Israel is located, there also developed a lively trade in Israeli currency. At that time the Israeli government bought and sold its own currency in Switzerland, where such trade was legal, in an effort to slow down the drop in the Israeli pound. A similar situation developed in the 1960s in Tel Aviv, with the government itself secretly buying and selling on the outlawed black market in an attempt to regulate the exchange rate. It is rumored persistently that the same thing has happened even more recently.

Only on rare occasions in the past has there been anything resembling a serious crackdown on illegal moneychanging. When it does happen, it takes the form of a one-time arrest and the payment by the offender of a fine amounting to about one day's profit. Then the offender is back to his street trading. On several occasions the police have raided moneychangers because the crowds in front of their shops have been hindering the movement of traffic in the streets. Blocking the streets is a more serious offense than moneychanging, it seems, leading citizens—even born-again Christians—to conclude that there is nothing wrong with the illegal practice.

There are two centers of moneychanging activity: one in the Lilienblum district in Tel Aviv and, since 1967, a larger one in East Jerusalem. In Tel Aviv, business is generally conducted right on the sidewalks, often with the participants raising their voices in haggling over rates. No one seems concerned that they might be overheard by the police. Such street dealings are for amounts as large as $5,000. Larger deals might be transacted in a local café over a cup of coffee or in a nearby office.

The atmosphere in Arab East Jerusalem is quite different, with moneychangers sitting in street-front offices with large "Money-changer" signs over the entrance. On one major street alone there are more than twenty such shops within a four-block area. One can see a customer enter a shop with a bag of shekels and, in less time than it would take to stand in line at a bank, the customer comes out without the bag but with several large dollar notes in his pocket. Fifty 1,000 shekel notes exchanged for one $100 bill. Later in the day the customers are shop owners, coming to exchange all their money into dollars before putting it into the safe for the night.

There is always a big demand for dollars, some of which are brought in by tourists. There was a time when tourism brought in enough to meet demands, but today the supply comes, ironically, from the Bank of Israel. This official agency tried to step in to stabilize the market and at the same time make 15 to 20 percent profit over the official rate at which it bought the dollars from the country's banks after their dealings with the tourists. However, with the increased demand and the rapid turnover, the main source of black market dollars is a sophisticated operation of couriers from the United States and Switzerland, some of whom are caught in spot checks at air terminals. Most, however, make it undetected to their center of operations in Jerusalem's ultra-orthodox Mea Shearim district.

Counterfeiting is also another attempted means of supplying dollars. In early September 1984, through raids by the U.S. Secret Service in the United States and the police in Israel, an operation that had $12 million in $100 bills ready to circulate was broken up. Ten Israelis were arrested, seven in Israel and three in the United States. The bills found in a print shop in Jaffa were of such high quality that only laboratory tests, and not the standard detection machines, were able to determine they were counterfeit.

The cooperation of U.S. and Israeli currency law enforcement agencies, for the protection of the dollar, may have had symbolic significance for another development, which the high inflation rate of the shekel brought about. More and more in the past years, Israelis had begun to consider the dollar as their unofficial currency. Prices of large items, such as a car or an apartment, even vacation packages or sometimes salaries, were quoted in dollar terms rather than in shekels, but perhaps several weeks after the quotation, when payment was actually made, it was given in shekels at the rate of exchange at that time.

Every morning the exchange rate was quoted, just like a weather report. The weather report was of less interest, however, since it changed less than the exchange rate.

In 1983, the finance minister actually proposed quietly to his fellow cabinet members that Israel begin using the dollar as the official currency. This "dollarization" program would have had several beneficial effects, among them the immediate end to both inflation and the black market. According to the proposal, all goods and services would be reckoned and paid in dollars, which would also have been made legal tender throughout the country. When news of it reached the public there was an outcry over what appeared to be the loss of national sovereignty such a move would have brought about. "After all," they argued, "Israel is not the fifty-first state of the U.S. Adopting U.S. currency as legal tender would take away from the Israeli government control of their own finances."

Unofficial "dollarization" continued under the table, however. One major supermarket chain introduced a system of "dollar chits," vouchers marked with five, ten, and twenty dollars. The customer would buy them at the current exchange rate and use them at the rate of exchange when he bought his groceries. The supermarket was, in effect, creating its own dollars. The problem was so severe in large stores that several full-time employees did nothing but go around the store changing price tags to keep up with the exchange rate. (Computer price coding tags placed on merchandise has helped, but customers never know the exact price until they reach the cash register unless the store posts some way for customers to interpret the price coding system.)

Israelis pay the highest personal income tax in the world, and almost everything is taxed beyond that. A self-employed Israeli will pay 40 to 45 percent tax on his earnings under $1,000 monthly. On income above $1,000 he will pay perhaps 60 percent tax. When he takes his earnings and rushes out to spend it before the inflation rate cuts its value, he may pay as much as 15 percent sales tax on any item he buys, which means the government received at least half of what he earned.

How then can families survive? Most families have at least two wage earners or they wouldn't survive. With a population of nearly 4 million, it is estimated that about 500,000 women work, many of them mothers of young children. Children stay in daycare centers, or an older woman, someone who would be otherwise unemployable, will be hired as a regular baby-sitter.

The government and the Bank of Israel had to consider dropping one or two zeroes from the shekel, a 100-shekel note becoming the equivalent of a one-shekel note, for example. Bank computers used to be able to handle transactions of fifteen digits, but that number had become hopelessly inadequate.

Israel's economic situation since 1984 has deteriorated more than that of any other country except perhaps Bolivia. The survey, prepared by the International Monetary Fund and World Bank, was based on five factors: inflation, foreign currency reserves, balance of payments, exports, and external debt. Other countries cited were the Philippines, Ghana, and Argentina.

As of September 1984 more than 5.5 percent of Israel's work force has been unemployed, and the figures grow worse. The average family among salaried breadwinners numbers 3.8 people, of which 1.6 are unemployed. The average family income derives 68 percent from the husband's earnings, 17 percent from the wife's, and the rest from other family members' earnings. Only 42 percent of households own a car, and 56 percent of the self-employed own vehicles.

A sobering analysis of the political implications of Israel's inflation was given recently in the *Jerusalem Post* by Dr. Manfred Gerstenfeld, one of the heads of the Euroteam firm of financial consultants. Commenting on whether or not democracy can survive Israel's inflation, he replied, "Possibly, but so far no democracy has survived when inflation ran at more than 100 percent for a long time."

Although inflation ran even higher, Israel managed to stay democratic mainly due to its linkage system by which rises in the cost of living were matched by government benefits given back to workers. In other words, salaries were linked to the cost-of-living index. On the one hand, the linkage system accelerated inflation, sending prices higher and higher. But linkage prevented the distortions between various groups of the population from becoming too significant. According to Gerstenfeld, this imbalance had grown considerably in strength. On the one hand, the average Israeli wanted permanent status at his place of work, as is the rule in Communist countries. But on the other hand, he also demanded the right to strike, as if he were living in a capitalist country. "No democratic government can guarantee employment for everybody in the same job all his life," Gerstenfeld said.

In July 1985 the new so-called "National Unity" government began to tackle the task for which it had been created—to bring down inflation and to improve the economic situation. Among other steps, it effectively froze the value of the shekel at a rate of 1,500 to the dollar. Prices and wages were also frozen and carefully checked, with heavy fines dished out to anyone who tried to effect unauthorized rises. The measures were criticized for being cosmetic and not really getting to the heart of Israel's problems, but subsequent monthly figures began to show a drop in the inflation rate and also brought about the expected rise in unemployment.

For the first time in years, Israelis began to feel what it was like to have prices stay the same for weeks at a time. People stopped checking the papers every day to see what the dollar rate of exchange was. It still fluctuated, but now it fluctuated in both directions, and it always stayed a little bit below 1,500 to the dollar. In August 1985 the government announced that the old shekel would be replaced with a new shekel worth 1,000 of the old. Israel had been through this exercise before when the change was made from the lira (pound) to the old shekel. The change actually went into effect on January 1, 1986. By that time there were good indications that the government's measures were having a positive effect on inflation. In the last months of the year, the inflation ran at a monthly rate of well under 10 percent and the annual rate dropped to under 200 percent. In mid-February 1987 the statistics showed that the monthly index had actually dropped in January by 1.3 percent, the lowest in 17 years. For the previous three months, the annual rate was about 2 percent.

Many are still skeptical that things will stay stable after the tight price controls are relaxed, but a spirit of optimism is certainly discernible from the man on the street. If success in this area should come, Israel will at least have accomplished something that has never been done before.

20

EDUCATION

We should not be surprised if the so-called "People of the Book," with their tradition of high standards of learning, have established in their own state a praiseworthy educational system. Since the early part of the twentieth century, the main language of instruction in Israeli schools has been Hebrew. This fact is primarily due to the efforts of one man, Eliezer Ben Yehudah, who totally dedicated his life to turning the dead Hebrew language into a living instrument for use in the reestablished state.

In 1922, shortly before the death of Ben Yehuda, the British mandatory government declared Hebrew, along with Arabic and English, the official languages of Palestine. With the coming of independence in 1948, the new Israeli government declared Hebrew and Arabic the official languages of the State of Israel.

Education starts with preschool at age three, required kindergarten at age five, and first grade at age six. Children begin to study Bible (the Old Testament) in the second grade, reading Genesis in the original Hebrew. While biblical Hebrew and modern Hebrew are quite different in a number of aspects, the children are able to understand what they are reading with relatively little help from the teacher. Exodus is generally covered in third grade, while fourth graders may move on to the books of Joshua and Judges.

While there does exist a system of more traditional "Jewish" schools, the majority of Israeli children study in secular schools. About 73 percent of Israeli children attend secular schools while the remaining 27 percent receive religious training, of which 6 percent attend ultra-orthodox schools.

The Jerusalem Post conducted a poll asking whether religious studies in state-supported schools should be expanded or reduced. Of those who responded, 57.2 percent said they should be expanded while only 6.1

percent said they should be reduced. The rest voted no change or had no opinion.

Special emphasis is given to the study of the cycle of biblical holidays, both as to their biblical basis and meaning and to helping them understand the present-day customs associated with them. Special biblical passages may be studied for certain holidays, such as the book of Esther for the festival of Purim or Ruth for the Feast of Weeks (Shavout).

Westerners might be surprised in some way by the content of education. Studies are geared primarily to the needs of an Israeli student and certain areas of world history and geography considered important to American educators are covered very lightly if at all in Israeli schools.

Children go to school six days a week, but the school day lasts only four or five hours in primary school and six hours in the higher grades. The shortened school day has been one result of the tight economic situation. Cutting of budgets in all areas of government spending has meant that free education has also suffered through the reduction of the number of hours taught.

More than half of the Arab children from ages six to sixteen in Jaffa do not go to school at all. They are either employed or just wander the streets. Out of 4,030 Arab children of compulsory education age, only some 48 percent go to school. There is little supervision or enforcement of the compulsory education laws among Jaffa's Arab children, but they are very strictly enforced in Jewish sections.

As in the United States, basic education is a twelve-year program, after which students must pass a matriculation exam. Passing this comprehensive state examination allows the student to receive his diploma. Students in high school are required to perform some national service for a week or two each year. Students are allowed to drop out of school at age sixteen.

Adult education of many kinds is available. Programs range from instruction in basic education skills and vocational training to community college programs that offer diploma-level programs. The Open University (established in 1976) offers courses for credit by correspondence and by radio and television. In the mid-1980s, nearly 40,000 adults were engaged in some form of supplemental education program.

Since almost all Israelis complete some kind of military service soon after they finish high school, the men for three years and the women for two, the average age of students entering college is several years older than American students. This seems to have two major effects. For one thing, it gives the young Israeli a chance to think about what he or she wants to do and, if the student isn't planning on college, it gives an opportunity to learn some basics of a trade while in the army that he or she may want to pursue in civilian life. Second, it makes for a generally more mature college student. In Israel, college students have had the discipline of army training, a discipline that can be put to good use in college. Unlike many Western universities in the turbulent sixties, Israel reported not one student revolt of any kind.

Israel before 1948 had three institutions of higher learning. Now it has seven major universities and technical schools:

• Technion—Israel Institute of Technology, in Haifa, began in 1924. In 1984 there were 9,000 students enrolled.

• Hebrew University of Jerusalem, begun in 1925, features medicine and agriculture along with general studies. It had an enrollment of 16,000 in 1984.

• Weizmann Institute of Science in Rehovot is a postgraduate research institute. Begun in 1934, it had 500 enrolled in 1984.

• Bar-Ilan University in Ramat Gan, opened in 1955, features general studies and Hebrew studies with 10,000 enrolled.

• Tel Aviv University features medicine and general studies. Begun in 1956, it had 16,900 enrolled in 1984.

• Haifa University, begun in 1963, has an enrollment of 6,000.

• Ben-Gurion University of the Negev, located in Beersheba, features medicine and general studies, with an enrollment of 5,500.

The academic year in the higher institutions begins after the high holidays of the fall, usually at the end of October or the first week of November. There are short breaks of a day or two for smaller holidays and a longer break of several weeks at Passover time. Classes end in late June, and exams are held during July and August. The cutoff date for submitting papers is usually around the first of October. This system, while spreading out the study year potentially over the entire calendar, has the advantage of not bunching up exams, papers, and the end-of-year activities all in one final hectic week as in some American schools.

Israeli universities are generally fashioned after the European system, where the course of study runs generally for three years instead of four. Another fundamental difference from the American system is that, almost from the beginning, the student chooses his major and concentrates nearly all of his studies in that area.

There are few better places in the world to study the Hebrew language or Old Testament studies than in Israel. All courses are taught in Hebrew, but there is a major emphasis in all schools on science rather than studies in the humanities.

In almost all fields, universities are having to reduce the number of young researchers or faculty due to the economic belt-tightening that has had to take place in all fields. Such problems place a larger burden on older faculty, which in the long run could cause some deterioration of the quality of education in the country.

A UPI reporter once asked an Israeli on the campus of Tel Aviv University if many students cut classes. "Don't you see that our main resource is here, in our heads?" the student replied. A professor at Hebrew University once pointed to his head and said with a smile, "Since we have no natural resources, we are developing supranatural resources here in Israel."

21

ENERGY

Israel currently produces a bit more than 50 percent of its electricity requirements from coal-powered generators. Coal has been found to be 30 percent cheaper than electricity produced from heavy fuel oil. At Hadera, along the coast between Tel Aviv and Haifa, there are four generating units, each producing 350 megawatts. This is Israel's only coal-fired power station, but another is under construction south of Ashkelon. When completed it will have an output of some 1,100 megawatts.

In January 1985 Israel began talking with France about the possibility of purchasing a nuclear power plant. Israel has also begun studying the possibility of wind-powered generators, and at the end of 1984, searches began for those areas best suited for such equipment. Because of its geography, Israel enjoys a fairly predictable wind pattern in many parts of the country. For example, at the Sea of Galilee, it is calm in the morning, while at around noon a light western breeze begins. By midafternoon it has become a stronger wind that whips up sizeable waves on the eastern shore. Toward evening the wind slackens off and by dark it is calm again. In the middle of the night, the process begins again in reverse with the wind coming from the east. It is estimated that a wind energy system in Israel could produce enough power to save about 700,000 tons of oil per year.

Israel's greatest potential for clean power is from the sun. A land that enjoys 300 or more sunny days a year, Israel has already become the world leader in solar energy production. It is true that in absolute terms this percentage is still very low—less than one percent—yet Israel is setting the pace in research and implementation in the solar energy field. Most homes in the country use solar heat for water and new buildings are required by law to use solar water heaters.

Israeli scientists have developed a highly efficient method of collecting solar energy for industrial use. Leading the field in this area is Luz

International, founded in 1979 by Arnold Goldman, an electrical engineer originally from California. The system developed by Goldman and his associates is judged to be 20 percent more efficient than that of its closest competitors elsewhere in the world. The Luz system uses a series of fifty-yard rows of parabolic trough reflectors that reflect and focus sunlight onto selectively coated stainless steel tubes enveloped by vacuum-sealed glass pipes. The reflected sunlight heats oil inside the pipes to temperatures as high as 600 degrees Fahrenheit. The oil is then pumped through a heat exchange system, turning water to steam. The steam can either be used directly in industry or fed through a turbine generator to produce electricity. The system is unique in that microprocessors control sun sensors in the troughs, tracking the sun's east-to-west path through the sky. Through the course of the year, a system is 50 percent efficient, in that it collects half the direct sunlight hitting its curved mirrors into usable energy. At peak efficiency, it can collect 70 percent of the heat. Since December 1984 a Luz system built on 100 acres of the Mojave Desert has been generating 13.8 megawatts of electricity for Southern California Edison.

Israeli scientists have also been working on a method of transferring solar energy to areas far removed from the place of collection. The plan under development will transform the solar energy into energy-rich chemicals. These chemicals would then be piped to industrial regions where, in a transformation requiring special catalysts, the energy would be released as heat for use in manufacturing processes. Until now, solar energy has mainly been used near the spot where it is collected. It can be transformed into electrical energy for transmission, but this means a loss of 75 percent of the energy. Under the new system, the energy loss may be reduced to about 25 percent.

22

ETHIOPIAN JEWS

One of the most exciting—and upsetting—news developments of recent years came with the unveiling of "Operation Moses," the airlift of thousands of Jews from famine-stricken Ethiopia to the land of Israel. Often referred to in Israel as the "Falashas," the Ethiopian Jews call themselves "Beta-Israel," the "House of Israel." They consider the name "Falasha," an Ethiopian slave name meaning "stranger" or "exile," to be derogatory. But the tribe has indeed been perceived since ancient times as a stranger or exile.

Where do they come from—these black-skinned Jews—who seem to have arrived from another world? There are numerous theories about their origin and how they came to be considered Jewish. Leading rabbis over the past five centuries have identified the Ethiopian Jews as the lost tribe of Dan, one of the ten tribes carried away when the Assyrians destroyed the northern kingdom of Israel in 722 B.C. Secular scholars, however, say the Beta-Israel are probably the descendants of converts and that they learned their Judaism from merchants traveling from nearby Yemen to the tribe's home in the mountainous region north of Lake Tana, source of the Blue Nile. According to one Jewish tradition, they came from the union of Moses and an Ethiopian queen. (See Numbers 12: *Cushite* means "Ethiopian.") There is also a theory that they are the descendants of King Solomon and a handmaiden of the Queen of Sheba. Others have suggested that they were converted 2,500 years ago by the Jewish soldiers garrisoned on the island of Elephantine on the Nubian-Egyptian border, some 500 miles from Beta-Israel country.

One fact that might seem to argue for the more ancient dates is the fact that they have no rabbinical tradition, something which developed only after the destruction of the Second Temple in A.D. 70. They have no rabbis but rather a priesthood, which claims its descent from Aaron. These comprise the community's leadership. The Judaism they practice is at its foundation much closer to the kind found in Jesus' day than to present-day Judaism.

For centuries the Beta-Israel had an independent kingdom in the mountains of western Ethiopia. Most of Ethiopia's larger tribes had been Christianized in the fourth century, but the Jews resisted. In the tenth century, led by Queen Judith, they even expanded their territory, conquering the northern part of the country. But that war continued on and off for about 400 years, until the Beta-Israel were defeated and enslaved. At that time, they probably numbered in the hundreds of thousands.

After their defeat and enslavement they were forbidden to own land, a prohibition that remained in force until the overthrow of Emperor Haile Selassie in 1974. Throughout the last five centuries they have been despised by their neighbors, suffering intense persecution. Their numbers dwindled to about 30,000.

It is certain that the tribe has always considered itself to be Jewish. Until the tribe was "rediscovered" by Blue Nile explorer James Bruce in the eighteenth century, and Christian missionaries and Jewish scholars in the nineteenth century, the Beta-Israel thought they were the only Jewish survivors in the world. They found it hard to believe that most Jews were white. There is no dispute over their ancient, mystical attachment to Jerusalem or to their allegiance to the Hebrew Scriptures under the greatest of hardships. Passover was always the most meaningful holy day for the Beta-Israel, who considered themselves to be Jewish slaves awaiting a divine intervention that would take them to Israel.

In 1973, Israel's chief rabbi ruled that the Beta-Israel were descendants of the tribe of Dan. Two years later the Israeli government officially recognized the tribe as Jewish, entitled to citizenship under the Law of Return. However, until 1977, only about 300 Ethiopians had actually immigrated to Israel since the founding of the state in 1948. A program to fly Jews from Ethiopia was begun on the initiative of Menachem Begin in 1977, but a slip of the tongue by then Foreign Minister Moshe Dayan caused the Ethiopian government to break off relations with Israel, and the repatriation plan had to be closed down. Several years ago, still without diplomatic relations, the effort was quietly renewed. With worsening famine, Begin's successors, Yitzhak Shamir and Shimon Peres, stepped up the pace, and by the time the news leaked out some 12,500 Ethiopian Jews had arrived in Israel.

The latest ferrying operation was quite a complicated business. First the Beta-Israel crossed the border into Sudan. Most of the journey was on foot over distances of hundreds of miles. Many had to be carried, and many died along the way. In Sudan they were kept in temporary refugee camps until they could be flown out in aircraft chartered in Belgium. Going by way of Brussels, Basel, or Rome, they were flown to Israel. The roundabout route was necessary, of course, because Israel had no official relations with either Ethiopia or Sudan. Starting in November 1984, the operation took on serious proportions. In the two months until publicity killed it, there were some thirty-five flights ferrying about 7,000 Ethiopians from the Sudan. Sudan had been allowing the Jews to pass through their territory on the grounds that their government was making no distinction of race, color, or religion in helping refugees out of Ethiopia.

In November the Israeli Editors' Committee had agreed to a government request to keep the whole thing out of the media until it was succcessfully completed. The first public disclosure of the airlift came in a fund-raising speech in the U.S. by the head of the Jewish Agency, Arie Dulzin. Unknown to Dulzin, there was a reporter from a Jewish newspaper present, and he published the story. It was picked up by the *New York Times* and given front page treatment. From that point, more and more information came to light in the America media. On New Years Day, ABC-TV broadcast a major story about it.

At about the same time, a very small, bimonthly journal of the Council of Jewish Settlements in Judea and Samaria made an unauthorized publication of an interview with the Jewish Agency's head of immigration. Most Israeli papers chose to ignore the story, but two major papers did print it. Soon after, the government press office called its news conference as a kind of rearguard action. The government justified its official announcement by claiming that it hoped that making the operation known internationally would help to bring enough pressure on Ethiopia and Sudan to allow it to continue.

However, on January 3, 1985, the operation was undermined by its public disclosure. The main carrier, Belgin-based Trans-European Airways, which does a large charter business flying Muslim pilgrims to Mecca, announced its withdrawal from the rescue operation. Sudan officially notified the U.S. that "publicity about the aircraft meant that it could no longer cooperate in the program." This left an estimated 6,000 Ethiopians stranded in Sudanese refugee camps. The drought and famine were no lighter in the Sudan, but now they had no prospect of leaving. As one refugee who did manage to make it to Israel put it,

"Now everyone knows. All the families are stopped on the way. The airlift won't start again. Now they'll die. Only God can help."

Everyone was naturally extremely displeased by the Israeli government's decision to bring up the airlift issue in a press conference. But it was never really clear who was to blame. By the time the press was officially briefed, almost everyone already knew about Operation Moses, and inside Israel it was impossible to hide the increasing number of Ethiopian Jews. In any event, the news conference proved to be an unfortunate miscalculation.

At the point when, as it were, the waters of the Red Sea closed on "Moses," many families were separated. About 10 percent of the children arrived in Israel without their parents. It is not hard to understand the bitterness of many of the Beta-Israel at the disclosure.

Several hundred of the new arrivals were sent directly to hospitals, many suffering from malnutrition. Others were suffering from other diseases, most of them known to Israeli doctors only from their textbooks. Hospitals had to relax many of their rules in dealing with the new patients. Visiting hours were made more flexible and parents were allowed to stay with their children and sleep in their rooms. At one hospital three Ethiopian women waited to give birth in one room. When the first two delivered healthy boys, the third confided that she was relieved that the babies were black. She had been worried that since she was now in Israel her baby might be born white.

This was not the first mass immigration of the Jews of a single country, of course. Right after World War II, large numbers of the survivors of European Jewry had swelled the population immensely. In the next few years, almost all of the Jews of Egypt and the entire community of Yemen had "gone up" to the Land. The latter group had been brought in a mass airlift known as Operation Magic Carpet. Each wave of immigration had been accompanied by its own peculiar difficulties and challenges, both for the immigrants and for those responsible for seeing they were effectively absorbed into Israeli society. This influx of Ethiopians, however, is faced with a set of problems which truly is unique.

The most obvious hurdle, and yet surely the one most quickly and easily overcome, is the cultural and technological leap the Beta-Israel must make. This is also a difficult one to describe objectively, because it naturally lends itself to romanticizing. For the first few days after the operation was publicized, the Israeli media outdid itself in telling about the Ethiopians who thought they were flying inside a big bird, and who had no concept of electricity, money, or cars. In actual fact, this was a case of gross generalization and stereotyping. Most of the new immigrants had seen electricity, cars, and running water. The point that was being overlooked was that the technological thing was only a minor adjustment.

The experience of a group of Ethiopian students in one of the absorption centers illustrates how quickly they adapted. The majority of the children had no previous schooling and even had to be taught what knives and forks are for. Yet within a few weeks they were introduced to computers and after only a few lessons were capable of writing simple programs. It is truly amazing what the children were capable of accomplishing. They were very highly motivated and the older students often stayed up studying until two or three in the morning.

One question that will undoubtedly keep the sociologists busy making observations is that of color. It is a subject difficult to discuss, because Jews are all supposed to be of one race. At the same time, anyone living in the midst of a large community of Jews from all over the world, as in Israel, soon realizes that any generalizations about physical characteristics are sure to be inadequate. In the Jewish society of Israel one can find all colors of hair and eyes, all sizes of noses. And for that matter, every variation of skin color common to humankind can easily be found among the Jews of Israel.

There are not, however, any so-called "racial problems," discernible among the people. As one Israeli explained it, as mentioned in an article appearing in the *Jerusalem Post* in 1985, "When I was studying at the Hebrew University in the late fifties, I was asked to tutor a non-Jewish Ethiopian student who was a recipient of a Foreign Ministry scholarship in the halcyon days of Israel's relationship with black Africa. Yiftah and I became quite close. Towards the end of the year, he would frequently come to my house in Beit Hakerem to cram for exams. My wife later told me that some neighbors had expressed their resentment at the fact that Yiftah was a frequent and welcome guest in our home. When she asked what they objected to, they answered, 'How can you let a goy [Gentile] into your home?' None of these prejudiced neighbors ever so much as mentioned the obvious fact that Yiftah was black."

Nevertheless, there may be a difference between having the occasional dark Indian Jew (who just stands at one end of an infinitely graduated spectrum) and the sudden import of thousands of people who look very much like the stereotypes of the people in the Tarzan movies. Will there be some social reaction? How will intermarriage be viewed? It could be argued, however, that these are questions that only Americans would even think of asking. But Israelis, too, are subject to the images projected by the news and entertainment media, much of which is produced in America.

In the early days after the revelation of Operation Moses, one Israeli expert in the history of the Ethiopian community was asked about the Ethiopian immigrants' potential contribution to Israeli sport. Apparently some were influenced by the media-induced image of the black superathlete and were already having visions of Israel's first Olympic gold medals.

As a matter of fact, soon after the airlift hit the headlines and recriminations were flying about, there were insinuations in some quarters that the Israeli establishment had been dragging its feet where Ethiopian Jews were concerned because of some prejudice against their being black. But it is both instructive and sobering to note that the *first* such criticism came from American Jews or American officials in Israel. That concern was later heard to a small degree inside Israel. But we have to wonder if those initial accusations didn't tell us more about the accusers than the accused.

We are still too close to developing events to be able to say what will happen in the longer term, but it is in order to note some initial reactions in Israel to the new immigrants. The first general response was one of excitement. There really was a feeling of "brethren come home." Several appeals were launched for contributions. People came forward willingly to donate money and clothing. Hospital workers and many others directly involved in receiving the Africans gave time and overtime cheerfully. The emaciated conditions resulting from the famine, the appearance of bloated children suffering from malnutrition, brought back memories of the thousands of Jews liberated from Nazi death camps just forty years ago. The public was sympathetic and wanted to reach out to help.

Even new immigrants from other countries were sometimes able to get into the act. One absorption center near Jerusalem had been established to deal exclusively with immigrants from western countries. As the influx of Ethiopians began to increase, the Jewish Agency and the Ministry of Absorption tried to induce as many of the western residents of the center as possible to move into rental housing earlier than planned. However, when 134 Ethiopians comprising twenty families moved in, there were still quite a few Americans, English, South Africans, Russians, French, and Romanians left in the center. An absorption center is a kind of self-contained complex of temporary housing and other facilities where new immigrants can learn the language and get acclimated to their new homes while they look for work and a place to live. In this center at Mevasseet Zion ("Who telleth good tidings to Zion"), the twenty families had all been "adopted" within a week by the western immigrants. These helped take care of the children, sort and fold the thousands of pieces of used clothing that had been donated by surrounding communities, and just generally help the newcomers learn their way around. Each immigrant family would receive a monthly grant of $175 to cover food expenses. Everything else was supplied free to the immigrants. Food was bought in the absorption center's own store. Many of the Ethiopians needed to be shown around in the store by their helpers, who explained prices and even the uses of the various products. At the time when the airlift came to a halt, it was estimated that the absorption of the Beta-Israel who had arrived would cost around $300 million. Some of this was expected to come from the Jewish people abroad and some from U.S. refugee aid money.

But there was one blot on this bright picture of the homecoming of the brothers from the lost tribe of Dan. Even though, as we have said, one of Israel's chief rabbis had already declared in 1973 that the Ethiopian Jewish community was to be considered Jewish in every way, some religious authorities were now raising questions about the Jewishness of the immigrants. It must be quickly pointed out that even here color had nothing to do with the objections, which were purely on religious grounds. The problems fall into several categories.

Judaism is a religion based on the idea that the injunctions recorded in the Bible can progress with the times. Scriptures such as Deuteronomy 17:8-12 and 30:11-14 are understood to mean that God gave the commandments and also gave the intelligence to adapt these commandments to interpret new cases that may arise. The first passage in particular recognizes the likelihood that questions will arise that are not explicitly covered by Scripture. Over the course of Jewish history, many thousands of such new cases have arisen and been decided by the religious authorities of each generation based on Scripture and the precedents of earlier decisions. Of course, decisions on such cases were made locally, but those same decisions were then passed on to the rest of the Jewish world, and Judaism remained surprisingly uniform in its beliefs and practices.

But Ethiopian Jewry has been cut off from mainstream Judaism for at least two millenia, since long before the first of those traditions had been written down in the third century A.D. While they had the same Bible, our Old Testament, they were not always faced with the same civil and criminal questions. To put it briefly, by the time they were reunited with the rest of their brethren, they were doing a lot of things differently. As we have already noted, they did not even have such a person in their community as a "rabbi." Their leaders were all "cohanim," priests descended from Aaron, while rabbis may or may not be.

Judaism does not have, and never has had, anything that strictly corresponds to a central ecclesiastical authority. It would be a mistake to think of Israel's chief rabbis (there are two) as the Jewish answer to the Pope. However, in Israel the religious authorities, the "rabbinate," has been given a good deal of authority by the successive governments since the foundation of the State of Israel. The cabinet posts of Religious Affairs and Interior, for instance, are traditionally held by coalition partners from the various religious parties.

While most of the religious parties are not directly controlled by the leading rabbis, the decisions of the rabbinate go a long way to determining policies that affect every Israeli. On paper Israel is a secular state, but in practice much is tinted with the dye of religion. Marriage is just one example. While it is true that any Jew can marry any other Jew, it is not the case, however, that any Israeli can marry any other Israeli—or anyone else he or she wants, for that matter. The lay of the land, strictly enforced and overseen by the rabbinate, makes no provision for marriage between a Jew and a non-Jew. So any Israeli Jewess who wants to marry an Israeli Arab will have to go outside the country. This control over marriage is absolute, and marriages can be refused, even on grounds that may not be covered by law. One young couple, in 1974, wanted to get married. Although they were Jewish, they were known to be believers in Jesus. They managed to get their documents signed and the ceremony performed only when they agreed to sign a paper stating that they would never attend a Christian service nor allow Christians into their home.

There are two other categories of Jews who will have to leave the country in order to be married, the most common means being a round-trip flight to Cyprus. Any descendant of a priestly line who wants to marry someone who has been divorced would be forbidden by Jewish law to be married. Although their marriage would be considered as legal once they returned to Israel, their children would be considered *mamzer*, or bastard. The *mamzerim* themselves make up the second class of Jews who cannot get married in Israel except to other *mamzerim*.

Although a former chief rabbi declared that the Jews of Ethiopia were to be considered Jews in every respect, it had been the practice, based on the ruling of an earlier chief rabbi, to have all male Ethiopian Jews undergo a symbolic circumcision, just to be sure. Then they were being listed officially as converts to Judaism. The reason was the suspicion on the part of some religious leaders that Beta-Israel divorces were not as kosher as they should be. Their marriages were in order, but if the divorces were not done properly, it left open the possibility that any marriage entered into *after* that divorce was actually adultery, and the offspring were *mamzerim*. So the authorities required a ritual conversion, the shedding of a drop of blood in circumcision for the men and immersion in a *mikve* (ritual bath) for all. The Ethiopians were naturally deeply insulted by this requirement, for they considered themselves completely Jewish in every way, and in some ways, more observant servants of their Judaism than the Jews they met in Israel. An appeal to the High Court of Justice stopped their being registered as "converts."

Later the chief rabbinate removed the requirement for the circumcisions, but the purification immersion remained. Attempts were made by the authorities to play this down, since ritual immersion is a frequent practice of the religious Jew—not just a part of the conversion ritual. Indeed, among the Beta-Israel themselves, when a person came in contact with a Gentile he would be required to purify himself by just such a baptism. Israeli immigration officials pointed out that the Ethiopians had come in contact with Gentiles during their exodus and hence the necessity of the *mikve*. But the Ethiopians were not buying it. Their priests met with the rabbis and let it be known that if necessary they would even set up their own separate community, thus effectively recognizing the existence of two Judaisms.

A second religious hurdle had to do with the circumcisions already performed by the Beta-Israel within their own community. Israeli rabbis began to question if all of them had been performed with the required degree of completeness. Doubt over this question led to the decision that all male Ethiopian immigrants would have to have their circumcisions examined by a ritual circumcisor. Of course, such a humiliating procedure was not any more acceptable to the Africans than the symbolic conversion. Most Israelis were equally upset by such degrading treatment of their black brethren. In protest at the loss of dignity to which Ethiopian Jewish males might be subjected by this inspection, one American immigrant suggested that the Association of Americans and Canadians in Israel organize a nationwide solidarity rally with the Ethiopians, during which all American and Canadian Jewish males in Israel would present themselves at the Ministry of the Interior and request inspection of their circumcisions to make sure they were valid.

All of this takes on a certain irony in the light of the fact that Ethiopian Jewry is, as a whole, far more orthodox than its Israeli counterpart. The problem is, however, that their orthodoxy is not that of the religious establishment in Israel or, for that matter, of any branch of Judaism in the world. The irony is that precisely because of their centuries-long separation from the outside world, the Beta-Israel have preserved what might be called a more pristine form of Judaism.

Shaare Zedek is Jerusalem's most orthodox hospital. In order to protect the Sabbath, no one will turn a light on or off, no one will pick up a pen or pencil and write so much as one word. Writing is forbidden on the Sabbath. The kitchens, too, are entirely kosher. Stoves stay on throughout the Sabbath in order to keep pre-prepared food warm. In that large influx of Ethiopians, some were brought also to Shaare Zedek for treatment. But they refused to eat the food they were served on the Sabbath. Coming from a technologically underdeveloped area, they had no experience of electric hotplates for keeping food warm, and they were sure that someone had violated the Sabbath. Even the hospital's rabbi couldn't convince them—after all, everyone knows you can't make fire on the Sabbath. The hospital staff had no choice but to take the food off the hotplates and let it get cold before serving it to the devout Ethiopians.

Operation Moses brought to Israel more than 2,200 young Ethiopian children without their families. After careful research by authorities, it was found that 1,600 were orphans. Others were found not to be full-blooded Jews because their mothers were Gentile. Such will be converted to Judaism if they agree. Regardless of status, all will be kept in Israel, and none will be returned to Ethiopia.

Of the approximately 10,000 Ethiopian Jews who were left behind after Operation Moses was cancelled, more than 3,000 died of hunger. Because the number left there is still quite large, there may yet be a sequel to this episode.

And yet another chapter may come from the Far East. A group of Burmese citizens, claiming to be of Jewish descent, are making plans to "return to the land of their fathers." The group calls itself "Masura," claiming to be descendants of the Old Testament tribe of Manasseh.

23

EXPORTS

The so-called "Promised Land" has indeed become a land of promise as a result of an extraordinary show of brain and brawn. Biblical prophecies spoke of it as "a land of wheat and barley and vines and fig trees and pomegranates, a land of olive-oil and honey." To this has been added other produce, such as bananas, citrus fruit of all kinds, avocados, apples, mangoes, pears, guavas, dates, tobacco, cotton, peanuts, and sugar beets. Modern methods of irrigation and cultivation have resulted in some of the finest agricultural production of any formerly arid climate in the world.

For a small, still developing country, and one that is very much isolated from neighboring countries in its own region, Israel has an amazing record in the area of exports. Its markets must be found elsewhere, and about a third of all exports go to Europe, with another 30 percent heading for the United States. Israel's single largest export in terms of monetary value is diamonds. With annual sales of about $1 billion, Israel ranks second in the world to India. Rough diamonds purchased from South Africa are cut and polished by some 8,200 polishers around the country.

Israel's citrus exports amount to about half the annual revenues brought from diamonds. Who has not heard of, if not tasted, the famous Jaffa orange? But this industry is not limited to oranges. The range of citrus fruit includes lemons, grapefruit, tangerines, nectarines, and clementines. Other famous citrus products are the Chamouti oranges, which grow only in the Jordan valley, and the pomelo, which are about twice the size of regular grapefruit and much sweeter. Citrus exports, now about 30 million crates per year, are down from the 50 million crates in the mid-1970s due to strong competition from Spain and Portugal. Because of the drop in exports, about 12,000 acres of citrus groves were taken out of production.

Other agricultural exports are facing the same losses in the last few years, but so far these have not suffered as badly as the citrus exports. Israel, for example, almost holds a monopoly on the European avocado market and almost the same on quality celery.

Wine-making is as popular today as in olden days, and Israeli wines are a major export item, along with olive oil and peanut oil.

Another export industry in which Israel is doing quite well now—third only to Colombia and Holland—is the export of flowers. As with the citrus industry, Spain has started to provide serious competition. In fact, it is rumored that the Saudis were behind the purchase of the 1,500-acre farm in southern Spain, which is already growing 300 acres of spray carnations. The remaining land has been planted with vegetables similar to those exported by Israel. Spray carnations are Israel's biggest seller in Europe with about 400 million stems exported each year.

Saudi Arabia, it would appear, is ready even to lose money and sell the flowers below cost to force the market price down and inflict heavy losses on Israeli growers. This would not be the first Arab attempt to get at Israel through its export market. A few years ago, the Palestine Liberation Organization announced that it had poisoned a number of crates of Israeli oranges bound for Europe, in an attempt to frighten Europeans away from buying them. The attempt failed, as Europeans showed surprising support for Israel and made a point of buying the Israeli oranges. In fact, no poisoned oranges were found.

The land of Israel does not abound in exportable natural resources, so most of what is sold abroad must be a product of ingenuity and human resources. The Jewish people have long had a deserved reputation for good education, and this is certainly reflected in the State of Israel. The nation boasts more than 5,000 scientists, about three times as many, per capita, as France. This helps explain why one of Israel's largest export items is electronics, amounting to about $350 million per year. The range of products being developed and produced is wide, from sophisticated military equipment to orange-picker robots that can identify size, shape, and even color of the fruit, picking the ripe ones and leaving the green ones still on the tree.

From the Dead Sea Israel refines and exports annually about 900,000 tons of potash, giving Israel about 4 percent of the world potash market. A project is underway that will more than double the capacity of the refining plant. The Dead Sea Works have been increasingly profitable over the last two decades.

Israel's ingenuity in developing export markets is phenomenal, and one is especially worthy of mention. Kibbutz Haon, on the shores of the Sea of Galilee, recently entered the business of ostrich farming. Until recently, the export of ostrich feathers, meat, and skins had been monopolized by South Africa. While there is not as large a demand for ostrich feathers as in the days around the turn of the century, the plumes still bring a very high price and are in steady demand, especially in the entertainment centers of Las Vegas, Hollywood, Paris, Rio, and Tokyo. Ostrich meat, while not considered kosher in Israel, is considered a delicacy in Europe, especially for sausage making in Switzerland for German and Scandinavian meat markets. Ostrich skins are in high demand in Italy by high fashion designers and the three-pound eggs for super omelettes.

A shipment of 220 crocodiles from Zimbabwe recently arrived at Kibbutz Gan Shmuel, in the Sharon area, where a crocodile farm is being developed to process and export crocodile skins. This follows the successful cultivation of alligators at Hamat Gader in the Golan Heights to the east of the Sea of Galilee. This profitable venture breeds hundreds of alligators each year in addition to providing a popular attraction for Israeli tourists. There is no worry that the colder winter weather there might harm the alligators, since Hamat Gader is the site of hot springs. The same hot springs that served the Romans in past centuries are now used by the Israelis as a winter playground, and by alligators used to warmer climes.

Israel also exports automotive rubber goods, such as tires and tubes, machinery, plastics, plywood, and pharmaceuticals. Religious items from the Holy Land are sought after worldwide. Israel has few natural resources, so efforts to harness the waters of the Jordan River, desalinate water, and use nuclear and wind power in some ways compensate for this deficiency. Despite all efforts in science, agriculture, and industry, Israel still imports far more than it exports, which is one of the main causes of the struggling economy.

24

EXTREMISM

When the results of a recent election were in, many Israelis were shocked to learn that Meir Kahane of the "Kach" party had received enough votes for a seat in the Knesset. Rabbi Kahane, whom some consider an "extreme right-wing demagogue" had received more than 23,000 votes. Like many so-called "extremists" in Israel, Kahane is from the United States. Now in his early fifties, Kahane was born in Brooklyn, New York, was ordained as an Orthodox rabbi, and later served two synagogues in Queens, New York.

Kahane founded the Jewish Defense League, an aggressive group known for their motto, "Never Again." The Jewish Defense League has been held responsible for bombings and various vigilante actions against targets they consider anti-Semitic, and many of its members have been prosecuted both in Israel and in the United States. In the late fifties, Kahane had been offered rabbinical posts at two locations in Israel, but he did not actually immigrate until 1971. When he did arrive in Israel he was examined and licensed for the rabbinate by the late Isaac Halevy Herzog, then chief rabbi of Israel and father of Israel's incumbent president, Chaim Herzog.

Kahane himself had been arrested more than twenty times since he became an Israeli citizen, but now that he is a member of the Knesset, he enjoys immunity from arrest and prosecution. Kahane and members of his group had run for the Knesset many times without success. Kahane's stand, the complete expulsion of all Arabs from Israeli and West Bank soil, is well known, and he receives much free publicity from the press. More than 700,000 Arabs live in Israel and another 1.3 million live in the West Bank and Gaza Strip. Kach party election rallies were noisy, demagogic affairs, often ending in fights. Most of Kahane's arrests have been for incitement of riots and disturbing the peace.

The bearded leader was usually accompanied by a threatening group of young men wearing uniform yellow shirts on which is sewn a clenched black fist. The Israeli press frequently comments how reminiscent this gang is of the brown-shirted Nazi youth of the thirties, and indeed the parallels do not stop there, for Kahane is a racist of the first degree. He will lose no opportunity to call the Arabs "dogs" or any other demeaning names, even to their faces.

The 23,000 votes were enough to get Kahane elected but not the second man on his list, Yehuda Richter. And it was probably just as well, because only a couple of days after the election Richter was found guilty in a Jerusalem District Court of involvement in the shooting attack on a bus carrying Arab workers some four months earlier. Like Kahane, Richter is an American citizen, from Los Angeles. At the time of the attack, he was serving in the Israeli army.

Election to the parliament of another country made Kahane liable to lose his American citizenship, and shortly after he took his seat in the Knesset, the State Department announced that it was studying his case.

Soon after the results of the election were announced, Kahane led a group of his supporters on a victory march through the streets of Jerusalem to the Western Wall. When they entered the Old City, they took a roundabout route so as to pass through more Arab neighborhoods. At least one automobile was damaged during the march, and several Arab shops were vandalized. Many of the yellow-shirted supporters wore pistols in belt holsters and shouted, "Death to the Arabs" and "Arabs out." In his speech delivered on that occasion, the newly-elected member of the Knesset pledged to open an emigration office in every Arab town in the country. At a press conference on the same occasion, he vowed that his first act in the Knesset would be to propose a bill expelling all of the Arabs. He also told the journalists that he considers the law of the Torah to be above democracy. "I want to do things that today are opposed to the law as the police see it. That is, if there is a law from the Torah and it is opposed to the laws of the state, then I say the law of the Torah is above and beyond the law of the state."

Condemnation of Kahane and shock at his election was almost universal. Every other Knesset faction declared its unwillingness to be identified with Kach or to be in any way politically aligned with it. Even the President of Israel intimated that he might break with tradition and not meet with the newly-elected faction head. When Kahane heard that, he was true to form, declaring that he would force his way into the president's residence. "Those who stand up against Kahane stand up against this," he said, waving a Bible in his hand. Expressions of concern and disassociation came also from Jewish communities abroad. For example, the influential American Jewish Committee called Kahane's election "reprehensible" and called on the Knesset to pass electoral reform legislation that could prevent future repetition of such a negative phenomenon.

The big weapon in Kahane's arsenal was now his Knesset immunity, and he planned to take full advantage of it. One early statement said he would use it to pray on the Temple Mount as a first step in removing the Dome of the Rock and the Al-Aksa mosque from the site. It is the presence of these two mosques that makes Jerusalem one of Islam's holiest places and prevents the building of a Jewish temple there. But Kahane would derive the greatest benefit from his immunity in continuing his program of incitement against the Arabs. This he would do by entering carefully selected Arab communities and arousing tempers and trouble, knowing first of all that he could not be arrested and secondly that the police would be obligated to protect him in what was clearly a dangerous situation.

The town selected for Kahane's first "Arab emigration office" was ideally suited for his purposes. Umm el-Fahm is the largest Arab village inside the pre-1967 borders of Israel, with a population of 23,000. It is also one of the poorer villages, and it is considered to be one of the most radical, in the sense of opposition to the Zionist government establishment. Like residents in other mostly Arab communities, such as Nazareth, Umm el-Fahm tends to vote for the Israel Communist party. In fact, the chairman of the local council was recently elected on the Communist list with a clear majority. Of the more than 200 university students from the village, about half study abroad in Communist countries, maintained partly on Communist party scholarships. Umm el-Fahm tends to be more crowded than other Arab villages, and this is a result of the confiscation of more than 70 percent of its lands in the 1950s for the establishment of Israeli agricultural settlements, kibbutzim and moshavim. The loss of its lands, combined with the growth of its population, has created an overabundance of manpower, so that fully 20 percent of the villagers travel far out of town each day as day laborers. All of this tends to create an atmosphere of dissatisfaction and unrest in Umm el-Fahm, and it was this that Kahane intended to exploit.

Kahane's proposed entry into Umm el-Fahm was announced, causing a flurry of activity. The police mobilized a force of 545 personnel, at a cost of 12 million shekels (then about $40,000), to protect Kahane and to prevent an outbreak of violence. Hundreds of Israelis traveled to the village and spent the preceding night with Arab families as a means of expressing their disgust for Kahane's action and their sympathy for the Arab residents. There were also many journalists, and one of these was to write that "there was a lot of tension, but also that rare thing in Israel—genuine Jewish-Arab solidarity." Several Arabs told the *Jerusalem Post* that the presence of the Jews would "add to the improvement of relations between the Jews and Arabs." Among the overnight guests were about a dozen members of the Knesset.

The morning of Kahane's entry into the village dawned clear and hot. The number of anti-Kahane demonstrators had swelled to about 5,000, and they had organized themselves in coordination with the elders of the village to try to prevent any of the excitable youth from getting out of hand. The police had set up a series of barricades on roads leading to Umm el-Fahm, some of them as far as ten miles away. They might have to let the immune parliamentarian in, but his followers enjoyed no such privilege and would not be allowed near. Kahane's followers had in fact hired three buses to bring them to the event, but their total numbers would hardly have filled even one bus.

Later the government and police decided it would be a threat to security to allow Kahane to enter the city, so he and his group were stopped two miles outside of the town. Rabbi Kahane promised the police that if they would ease up he would not go to the village. But the minute he was released he began marching toward Umm el-Fahm. It was at that point that the police decided not to allow him to go any farther. They put him in a car and took him to a local police station.

Back in the village, however, a rumor was started that Kahane had evaded the police roadblocks and that he was on the way into town. After having waited more than five hours, the crowd became overly tense, and when the police officer arrived in his car to make the announcement that Kahane had been detained, the crowd went out of control and started pelting the car with stones. Knesset members and town elders finally got the crowd under control, but a number of people were arrested, among them five Kahane supporters.

Several days later, the man who caused all the problem, Kahane, left on a fund-raising mission in the United States. When he returned to Jerusalem three weeks later for his party's first national convention, he predictably called for the expulsion of all Arabs from Israel.

One might wonder if people like Rabbi Kahane are one of a kind or if there are others to follow the trend. For over a decade, Kahane has been looked on as just a "sick bigot," never managing to obtain more than a few isolated votes. In fact, the Kach party was almost left off the ballot. Only a last-minute court appeal enabled Kach's name to go on the ballot. And yet, 23,000 voters, 1.3 percent of eligible voters, supported him.

Post-election analyses showed that Kahane did much better in poorer, developing areas of the country, among voters whose origins are in Islamic, Oriental countries. In some ways, this is a continuation of the trend that first showed itself clearly in 1977 when for the first time in Israel's history the Labor parties lost to the right-wing parties of Menachem Begin. Some supporters of the Labor party point out that there is really no qualitative difference between Kach and the other right-wing parties—that their differences are only a matter of degree.

Those with a longer memory recall that the original platform of the Herut party of Begin, Ariel Sharon, and former premier Itzhak Shamir called for the establishment of a Jewish state on both sides of the Jordan River. Perhaps the most sobering fact about Kahane's backers and voters is that they are predominantly from the younger voters. If this trend continues downward into the teenagers who did not have the right to vote yet in this election, then future polls might show an even greater percentage supporting Kach and others on the extreme right.

However, the cloud does seem to have a silver lining. The spontaneous uniting of Jews and Arabs against Kahane at Umm el-Fahm is seen as a very positive development for now. In recent years there have been other such shows of solidarity, but this was probably the largest. Any number of moves are under way, both inside and outside the Knesset, to find ways to limit Kahane's use of his parliamentary immunity. The most likely solution seems to be to limit his freedom of movement, thus not allowing him to enter Arab areas for the purpose of incitement.

Perhaps the most significant move of all to stop Kahane's efforts will be a proposed antiracism law, now under consideration from several different areas of government. Such a law would impose penalties for "incitement to deny another person's rights on the basis of race or nationality." The Knesset has already introduced new house rules empowering the Speaker of the Knesset to strike racist remarks from the record, to expel a member who utters such remarks, and to prevent racist draft legislation from being tabled. The antiracism law would not penetrate Kahane's immunity as long as he stays in the Knesset, so the possibility of racial unrest remains.

25

FUND-RAISING

Few nations in the world have been the object of philanthropic gifts as has the State of Israel. Except for government property, almost every public building or park bears signs and inscriptions of donors. For example, an ambulance in Jerusalem will have painted on its sides not only the fact that it is an ambulance, but the names of individuals and organizations that may have contributed to the purchase, usually donors from the United States, such as: Friends of Magen David; in memory of so and so, given by a brother-in-law or a child from Milwaukee, Wisconsin. One public vehicle was described as having more inscriptions on it than a Chinese wall-poster.

Gardens, park benches, even forests are planted, with each tree contributed by donors, whose names may be memorialized on plaques nearby. Such gifts have been pouring in since Israel became a state, but during the times of war, even more gifts were coming in. Fund-raising by all kinds of organizations for the benefit of Israel has in recent years been developed into an art.

26
GOVERNMENT

The government of the modern State of Israel was based on the British model, with just a touch of ancient Jewish tradition. There is a head of state, the president, who corresponds to the queen in England. He is a figurehead, who provides a certain amount of continuity when there is an election and a change of governments. He is not involved in politics, although he could well come from a political background. When he becomes president, through an election of the Knesset, he is expected to leave behind all political leanings, and generally all of Israel's presidents have managed this fairly well.

Unlike England or the United States, Israel has only one legislative house, the Knesset. Like the so-called "Great Knesset," of which Ezra the scribe was said to be the head, the Knesset consists of 120 members. Technically they are elected in a popular vote of all adult citizens of at least once every four years. In actuality, Israelis do not vote for individuals but for parties. Each party puts forward a list of candidates, up to 120, and then the ballot contains the name of the party. The candidates on a party's list are in a numerical order of priority, so, for example, if a party receives enough votes for ten seats in the Knesset, number eleven on its list goes looking for another job.

The total popular vote is calculated in terms of percentages. To get any candidates into the Knesset, a party must have received a minimum of one percent of the vote. Those parties that have achieved at least that minimum divide up the Knesset seats proportionately. If one party were to receive 50.9 percent of the vote, that would be enough for sixty-one seats and an absolute majority in the Knesset. As a matter of fact, that has never happened in the history of the State. When no party receives a majority, the bargaining begins between the big parties and the small ones. A party with fifty-three seats might have one natural partner with another of five seats, bringing their combined total to fifty-eight. This is still not enough to "form a government," so they must try to woo some other party to join a coalition with them. This is when the smaller parties make hay. So far, in the history of the State, the smaller parties, with anywhere from one to twelve seats, have been the religious factions. Since no party has ever won an outright majority, Israel has always had coalition governments. No Israeli government has ever been without a religious faction helping to make up its majority. But this has come at a price, for the larger parties have invariably had to make concessions—some minor and some major—in order to convince the smaller party to agree to join the coalition.

The number one man on the winning party's list will be the prime minister. This is the real head of the government, which consists of a cabinet of ministers. This cabinet is not of a fixed size and can be increased or decreased in number as political necessity may dictate. The present "government of national unity," for example, is the largest in Israel's history with some twenty-five ministers. Some of these men do not even have a specific job—ministers without portfolio—but political exigencies made it necessary to include them in the government.

A cabinet in such a parliamentary system is not like the cabinet of an American president. The story is told that when Abraham Lincoln proposed emancipating the slaves in 1863 he went around the table to get the reactions of his cabinet. One after another of his secretaries said, "Nay." Lincoln was last and said, "Aye." He then announced, "Gentlemen, the ayes have it."

Such a situation could not occur in an Israeli cabinet, where most decisions are taken by a majority vote of the ministers. The prime minister can bring pressure and prestige to bear, but he cannot ignore the majority. In fact, he cannot usually safely ignore a disgruntled minority, because if even one member of the cabinet submits his resignation, then new elections are mandatory.

The prime minister has the option of calling elections at any time he sees fit for no other reason than that he might think it an opportune time for his own party to improve its position in the Knesset. If no election has been held for four years, then it is automatic that one be held. If the prime minister does decide the time has come for elections, he "goes to the president," which means he submits the resignation of his entire cabinet. At that point new elections are not certain. First the president must see if the leader of one of the other parties can muster enough support for a majority in the Knesset. If enough bargains can be struck for this to happen, then elections will not be held, even though there will now be a new prime minister and cabinet.

If in the end elections are held, then there is a period of as long as three to four months from the time the cabinet resigns until voters actually go to the polls. During that time the old cabinet will stay on in a caretaker role. This long delay between the fall of a government and new elections has been the target of reformers on several occasions. Until now, however, no one has succeeded in getting enough support to change it. Reformers would prefer something more like the two to three weeks, as in Britain, between the resignation of the government and elections.

Another area where reform has often been suggested is in the minimum required percentage for gaining a seat in the Knesset. This was discussed particularly after the last election in which Meir Kahane, representing a fanatical right-wing fringe, got a seat in the Knesset with less than 2 percent of the popular vote. Raising the minimum would also affect the number of little parties that can pull so much weight in coalition negotiations.

It is not likely, however, that either proposed reform in the method of electing Knesset members will be changed any quicker than efforts in the United States to reform the electoral college system of electing a president. If any government in Israel, which itself depends on the small factions to stay in power, would try to effect legislation to raise the minimum, those very same splinter groups would resign, leading to the fall of that government. And the party that made such a proposal could be quite sure of not getting the support of those small parties later.

27

HOSPITALS AND MEDICAL CARE

There are 145 hospitals in Israel, with 9,000 doctors and 20,000 nurses. The doctor-to-patient ratio is among the world's highest—1 to 500. No less than twenty-one specialized schools exist—five medical schools, two schools of dentistry, a school of pharmacology, and fourteen nurses training schools.

All permanent residents of Israel, whether they are citizens or not, employed or self-employed, are members of a compulsory national health insurance plan. A small percentage of monthly wages of all workers goes to the National Insurance Institute, similiar in many ways to Social Security in the United States. When the worker retires he will receive a monthly check as well as certain insurance coverage during his working days.

Special compensation is given for the time people spend in the compulsory military reserve service, usually thirty days a year. Wives giving birth receive hospital coverage plus a $100 bonus when they leave the hospital and a further monthly child allowance. The more children in a family the more the child allowance will be. At present the child allowance amounts to about $50 per month. Workers covered through the National Insurance Institute pay nothing for the delivery of a child.

Other routine medical expenses are not covered by the National Insurance Institute, but almost all Israelis belong to some kind of medical insurance program similar to health maintenance organizations in America. The law stipulates that an employer must pay half of his employees' sick fund payments, so that the expense of the member may be about $20 to $30 a month. Membership in a sick fund makes him eligible for free visits to a doctor for just about anything except dental work and cosmetic surgery. Medicines prescribed by a sick fund doctor are also highly subsidized. This program has the interesting psychological side effect of causing people to visit doctors more frequently than they would otherwise. Statistics show that the average Israeli visits a doctor about twice as often as his American counterpart.

The level of medical expertise available in Israel is second to none in the world. In fact, with the tradition of Jews entering the medical profession in whatever country they live, and with the influx of immigrant doctors, it is understandable why the doctor-patient radio in Israel is so high. On the other hand, there is a serious shortage of nurses, since Israeli nurses are not paid especially well. Even doctors cannot expect to earn anywhere near the salaries of their counterparts in the Western world.

28

JERUSALEM

According to an old Jewish tradition, God in the beginning created ten portions of love, joy, peace, and beauty and poured nine of them upon the city of Jerusalem. But the traditions says also that God also created ten portions of hatred, pain, anguish, and bloodshed and that nine of these portions were also poured out upon the city of Jerusalem.

The more one understands the history of the city, the better one can understand the truth borne out by this old saying. To walk the streets of Jerusalem is literally to walk on top of what has been called "the world's largest cemetery," considering the tens of thousands of people who have left their bloodstains on the streets of the Holy City, either attacking or defending it.

It is true that there have been periods during the past few years when bombings or attempted bombings were almost daily occurrences. This experience has created a public alertness such as can be found nowhere else in the world, except perhaps Beirut or the cities of Northern Ireland. Bombings are now a relatively rare phenomenon in Israel, because no object—car, briefcase, suitcase, or shopping bag—can be left unattended anywhere without arousing suspicion. This fact, combined with policy considerations by the terrorist organizations, has actually caused a decrease in the number of attempted bombings in Jerusalem. In fact, it would be no exaggeration to say that Jerusalem is now a safe place to live and the rest of Israel even more so.

Taking all factors into consideration, Jerusalem must be considered safer than many American cities of comparable size. A person who goes for a walk in the city at night need have no fear of mugging, and even single women are more secure than they would be in many other cities of the world. Even children feel safe in Jerusalem. The fear of child stealing is practically nonexistent in Israel. In the history of the State of Israel, there have been only two or three instances of kidnapping, the first of them not coming until the late 1970s. Parents think nothing of letting their eight- or nine-year-olds go across town alone by bus to visit friends.

Unfortunately for Israel's largest industry, tourism, foreign travelers sometimes gain a different image of the security atmosphere in the land. In recent years, many tours have had to be cancelled as tourists hear news of unsettled events in Lebanon or elsewhere in the Middle East and drop out of a tour. Those who have been brave enough to go anyway have invariably been impressed with the general tranquility of the land.

29

JORDAN AND ISRAEL

In October 1984 King Hussein of Jordan resumed diplomatic relations with Egypt. Jordan, along with almost all other Arab countries, had broken off relations following President Sadat's visit to Jerusalem in 1977 and the subsequent peace treaty signed in 1979. Jordan became the first of seventeen Arab nations that broke off relations to restore them.

It will be remembered that Sadat's decision to visit Israel in 1977 followed a public invitation from then Prime Minister Menachem Begin. Sadat had earlier said that he would be willing to go anywhere, even to the Knesset in Jerusalem, in order to achieve a solution to the Palestinian problem. It was perhaps with Begin's invitation and its results in mind that Israel's later prime minister, Shimon Peres, issued an invitation to Jordan's King Hussein to visit Israel to begin negotiations for peace. The results of this invitation were not, however, as satisfying as Begin's invitation, almost seven years earlier. Hussein rejected the call, saying that it was a "subterfuge and a deception." Hussein further stated that he would not give an iota of the territory of the West Bank, the Gaza Strip, or the Golan Heights, nor would he forfeit one small stone of the mosques, churches, or holy places, no matter how long it would take or how great the sacrifice.

Many observers in Israel have felt and hoped that Hussein's decision to renew relations with Egypt might signal a new willingness to get involved in some sort of peace process with Israel. However, the king's statements toward Israel have continued to be precisely what they have always been, with no particular indication of any softening of his line.

Only toward the end of 1985 did it begin to appear that some progress might be made in peace talks between Jordan and Israel. Several factors have made this difficult, however. For one thing, the king wants to have the endorsement of the PLO in steps that he takes, and this has been impossible to obtain. And despite Hussein's dramatic divorce of himself from the PLO in February 1986, it will be extremely difficult for him to go it alone. Right after this announcement, he was still reiterating his refusal to enter peace negotiations with Israel.

On the Israeli side, the coalition National Unity Government has made little progress on the peace initiative. Shimon Peres has followed the traditional desire of his Labor party to engage in talks with Jordan and has made frequent overtures. But members of the Likud party, who spent the first twenty-five months of the coalition agreement waiting their turn to lead, have always been far more extreme in their demands and have dragged their feet on anything that might resemble concessions to the Jordanians, or anyone else, for that matter.

30

KABBALAH

Without doubt, the most mysterious branch of the Jewish religious community is the Kabbalah. The name literally means "tradition," specifically relating to the tradition of Jewish mysticism. The term came into prominence during the twelfth century. The Kabbalah differs from rabbinical Judaism in several aspects. It views the Creator God of the Bible as a limited God who is subordinate to a yet higher, limitless and unknowable God, called the En-Sof. It also teaches that the universe was not created out of nothing but is rather the result of a complex operation performed by the emanated attributes of En-Sof and the Sefiroth (bridges connecting the finite universe with the infinite God).

There are two main subdivisions of Kabbalism. One is speculative, dealing with philosophical considerations, and the other is practical, having to do with the magical, stressing the mystical value of Hebrew words and letters. An example of this is the *Testament of Solomon*, which lists the names of the demons responsible for a variety of illnesses, along with the cures.

Some Kabbalists believe the entire Torah, the first five books of the Old Testament, is the single holy and mystical name of God. Others claim the Torah existed originally as an incoherent jumble of letters and that the phrases, sentences, words, sections, and chapters that now exist came into existence at the time that the events described took place. For example, the written passage describing the creation of Adam automatically arranged itself into its present form as his creation took place. If any of the events that happened in the creation of Adam had been different, the written account would have been different as well. Historical events, in other words, were not predetermined by God. What was predetermined, however, were the number of letters contained in the written Torah.

Because not so much as a vowel point can be added to or subtracted from the Torah, and because it is thought of as a living organism reflective of the secret life of God himself, what we have is a receptacle for divine energy. The Torah thus has been alloted a divine spirit, and this spirit aspect is the feminine principle of God. It is also held that there were 600,000 different meanings and aspects in the Torah.

Advocates of Kabbalah teach that by fasting and the repetitious recitation of hymns and prayers a believer can go into a trance and send his soul upward to pierce the veil surrounding the Merbabah, the throne chariot of God. It is held that the twenty-two Hebrew letters created all things, the most important being the letters aleph, mem, and shin. These three were the "mothers" of the remaining nineteen letters of the alphabet. Man's head was made by the letter shin, his stomach by mem, and his chest by aleph.

By using seven other Hebrew letters—beth, gimel, daleth, kaph, pe, resh, and tau—God created the planets, days of the week, and seven gates of the soul, which are man's eyes, ears, nostrils, and mouth. Through the remaining twelve letters, everything else was created, including such things as love, work, anger, and laughter. The Kabbalist claims that beneath the words of Scripture there is a hidden meaning that must be discovered. As God is hidden, so is his Word. This method of discovering his Word is known at Gematria and is based on the fact that every Hebrew letter has a numerical value to it.

When one knows the numerical value of a word, one may then find a correspondence between the original word and another with the same numerical value. In this way one number can become representative of several ideas, all of which are thought of as being interpretive of each other.

Perhaps the most bizarre belief of all has to do with the Golem traditions. It is taught that after saying certain prayers and observing certain fast days, one could make the figure of a man from clay or mud, and actually bring this lump to life by pronouncing the miraculous name of God over it. The living mud figure would not be able to speak, but could be used as a servant.

31

KIBBUTZ

In 1948, A. D. Gordon, a Russian born to a well-to-do Jewish family, arrived in Palestine with a number of other "pioneers." Although he had no background in farming, he started an agricultural project and enlisted many of the newcomers to join him. Reacting to the negative aspects of Marxism, yet convinced that physical toil was fundamental to human existence as the remedy for society's problems, he began to attract other newly arrived pioneers, the so-called *halutzim*, to his ideas of communal work.

Work, Gordon believed, was a psychological as well as a spiritual necessity for the development of the Jewish personality. Rather than try to change the mechanics of economic life, as Marx suggested, Gordon wanted to develop and nurture a new attitude toward work and negate the power struggle inherent in communism.

Gordon put into practice exactly what he was advocating, and the result of his efforts was first the *kevutah*, the collective enterprise, and later the *kibbutz*. The word *kibbutz* (plural, *kibbutzim*) means "gathering." A kibbutz is a collective unit of which each member owns an undivided share of the whole.

The kibbutz movement, then, was actually an offshoot of early failures to establish communism in Russia. The first kibbutz, Deganya, was founded in 1911 on the shores of the Sea of Galilee. Today it is one of the most idyllic settings in the land, but then it was only swampland, full of mosquitoes and malaria. They began by draining the swamps and planting farms.

The ideal kibbutz would have everyone own everything in common. Each person works according to his ability and receives the same as everyone else. Housing facilities are the same, food is prepared in a large kitchen and eaten together in a common dining hall. Each member is expected to work eight hours a day, six days a week, and one Shabbat (Saturday) per month.

The material welfare of the individual is directly dependent on the welfare of the entire kibbutz. On some long-established and successful kibbutzim, each member might have a color TV and be able to make a trip abroad once or twice in his lifetime, all paid for by the community. There is no permanent leader on a kibbutz. Administrators are elected for a set period of time and usually cannot be reelected repeatedly. Decisions are taken at regular meetings of all members, usually once a week. At these meetings, any problem or issue, no matter how small, can be discussed and a decision taken. That decision is binding on all.

In the unrealistic extremism that often characterizes movements based on the writings of theoreticians, some early kibbutzim held that even the children born to a kibbutz couple belonged to the entire membership. Marriage was recognized, but children were to be raised by the community. While no kibbutzim in today's Israel still holds to that theoretical extreme, many kibbutzim still have the children live separated from their parents. Even nursing babies are kept in a special home and are visited at nursing times by the mothers. The rest of the infants' needs—including diaper changes—are taken care of by those women who specialize in child care. The child is considered to be a member of the physical family into which he was born, but he will live with his peers.

This setup seems strange, even mean and inhuman, to many outsiders, but some things need to be said in its defense. First of all, the fact that children sleep and eat two meals a day separated from their parents does not necessarily mean that they have less contact with their parents than an average American child might have. Though in recent years some have moved away from the practice, kibbutzim which have this arrangement will always designate a certain time of the day when parents are expected to be with their children. This will usually be a couple of hours in the evening including supper when there are no activities scheduled so families can be together.

In a study done in the United States several years ago, researchers hooked a representative sample of American fathers to portable tape recorders in order to find out how much time they spent in meaningful exchange with their children. The shocking results showed that the average American father spends only a matter of seconds per day talking with his child. If that statistic is anywhere near accurate, then kibbutz parents are far ahead of their American counterparts.

Anyone who has spent even a few hours on a kibbutz will have noticed the many playgrounds scattered all over the place. The kibbutz is usually extremely children-oriented, and there is never a lack of things for a child to do. Many kibbutzim, for example, have built their own little menageries, where the children themselves take care of all sorts of animals.

In the children's houses, the boys and girls are not separated until quite a late age, a practice which has led some to suppose that all sorts of illicit relationships must develop. Sexual promiscuity, however, is no higher among kibbutz children than in other areas of Israeli society. Interestingly enough, marriages between peers on a kibbutz are quite rare. It would seem that the children see each other more as brothers and sisters than as potential marriage partners.

The kibbutz idea began as an agricultural movement, and a major part of kibbutz production is still in the area of agriculture. However, in recent years, kibbutzim have moved more and more into industry, producing anything from shoes to plywood to plastics or irrigation systems. While the kibbutz population makes up only about 3 percent of the total population of the country, industrial output as well as agricultural output of the kibbutzim is many times higher than 3 percent of the total output of such products.

Since the kibbutz movement at its roots was a labor movement, its kibbutzniks have had a disproportionately high profile in the various Israeli governments since 1948, all of which were formed from the labor parties until 1977. In fact, until the Likud party won the election in that year, no less than 33 percent of all government ministers had come out of the kibbutz movement.

Although former kibbutz members comprise only 3 percent of the total population of Israel, they make up a large portion of the military. Nearly one-fourth of all army officers are kibbutzim members, and during the Six-Day War, 200 of the 778 fatalities, and 25 percent of all casualties were from the kibbutz system.

32

MEDITERRANEAN–
DEAD SEA CANAL

The idea of a waterway going across Israel east and west goes back a long way. Sixteenth- and seventeenth-century maps often showed the Sea of Galilee and the Mediterranean connected by a water link, perhaps an erroneous depiction of the Kishon River.

The Old Testament prophecies speak of such a waterway: "On that day living water will flow out from Jerusalem, half to the eastern sea and half to the western sea, in summer and in winter" (Zech. 14:8). In these words the prophet described an event which, in his account, will come soon after the Lord returns and "his feet will stand on the Mount of Olives, east of Jerusalem, and the Mount of Olives will be split in two from east to west, forming a great valley, with half of the mountain moving north and half moving south" (Zech. 14:4).

About 1850 a British Royal Engineers officer proposed a Mediterranean–Galilee canal as part of a larger water system, which would include the Dead Sea. A couple of decades later, General Charles Gordon, discoverer of the Garden Tomb in Jerusalem, saw the canal idea as part of Britain's strategy to keep the Russians from invading the Holy Land and as part of a defense line for the Suez Canal. In 1899 a Swiss engineer, Max Bourcart, submitted to Theodor Herzl a written proposal for *two* canals. One of these would carry sweet water south from the Sea of Galilee. Its water would be used for irrigating farmland on the western plateau. A system similar to this, but far more extensive, has been in use in Israel for more than twenty years now. Bourcart's second canal would bring sea water from Haifa in the north through the Jezreel valley to the Jordan River and would be used to drive electricity-producing turbines.

It was not until 1974, however, that Israel's Ministry of Development began to study the idea seriously. Other studies were commissioned, and in late 1977 the Mediterranean-Dead Sea Committee was formed to review more than two dozen suggestions. The basic idea was to exploit the drop in elevation of more than 1,300 feet between the two seas to produce hydroelectric power. The first detailed study of the proposals was completed in April 1980. Out of all the proposals, three major candidates remained. One in the north would run, much as Bourcart had suggested, from a point near Haifa to the Jordan River. The middle route would run into the northern end of the Dead Sea from a point opposite on the coast. The southern route would start from a point within the Gaza Strip, pass south of Beersheba, and cascade into the southern end of the Dead Sea. It was this last entry that eventually won out, despite the objections of some that the start of the canal would run through occupied lands.

The proposed project would build an open canal of almost fourteen miles running inland from the Mediterranean Sea. This would then go underground to a tunnel some 17 feet in diameter and fifty miles long, ending on the plateau to the west of the southern end of the Dead Sea. Here the water would flow into a series of seven lakes or reservoirs before dropping through four turbines to the Dead Sea. The whole thing was estimated in August 1980 to take four to six years at a cost of $700 million.

There was, of course, the expected protest of the Arab countries, reaching even to the United Nations, and a few environmentalists raised their voices on behalf of the ecology in the region. But generally there was a good deal to recommend the program. The Dead Sea is the lowest spot on the face of the earth. It is fed from the north by the Jordan River and by small springs that burst out of the surrounding higher ground. The surrounding territory is high in mineral content, and the Sea is consequently high in minerals. In the Bible, and in the Hebrew language today, it is known as the Salt Sea. In fact, it is ten times saltier than the ocean and half again as salty as Utah's Great Salt Lake.

Only a few basic life forms manage to survive in its water. Until the end of the first half of this century, the Jordan was putting 1.2 billion cubic meters of water into the Dead Sea annually. The extremely high rate of evaporation off its 1,000 square kilometer surface exactly balanced the inflow. Since there is no outlet the Sea maintained its level of 393 meters (1,289 feet) below sea level. For centuries, farmers on both sides of the river had irrigated their fields in a hot valley where rain rarely falls. But civilization and population growth has taken its toll on the flow of the waters of the Jordan and consequently on the Dead Sea's main source of replenishment. Israel has made the Sea of Galilee its primary reservoir and annually pumps off about half of the water that would have gone into the Jordan and southward. To the east, the kingdom of Jordan annually takes some 300 million cubic meters of water from the Yarmuk River, a major tributary of the Jordan. In addition, a high dam built by Jordan will take off another 100 to 150 million cubic meters. This leaves between 150 and 200 million cubic meters of water actually reaching the Dead Sea by the Jordan River, about one-sixth or less of the amount needed to keep up with the relentless evaporation. By 1981 the size of the Dead Sea had shrunk from 1,000 square kilometers down to 800, and its surface level had dropped by about 30 feet. Estimates are that it will drop another 30 feet by 1990.

One clear advantage of such a canal, then, would be that it could be expected to restore the Dead Sea to something like its original size and depth. The plan, finally officially approved by the Israeli government in April 1981, envisioned an initial inflow of Mediterranean water of some 1.5 billion cubic meters per year. Within thirty years, the Dead Sea could be back to its original size and depth. Then the flow would be reduced so that this level would be maintained. Of course, the primary reason for considering the canal was not the Dead Sea's level, but to generate electricity.

The canal was to be dug if it could be shown to be financially feasible. With the rising price of oil in world markets and Israel's dependence on imported oil, the electricity that could be generated by the water flow provided the only real justification for such a huge outlay. Various studies were commissioned to find out if the initial optimistic predictions were accurate. It was a complicated business. Reasonable estimates said that Dead Sea hydroelectric power could be expected to supply about 15 percent of Israel's power needs. This, of course, was free electricity, once the canal and turbines were built. But cost estimates for the project kept going up, and in less than three years after the first estimates had been made, the government found itself talking in terms of $1.5 billion, more than twice the original figure. Would it pay itself off or not? One study said yes, one said no, but most seemed to indicate that it would about break even.

But there were too many factors to weigh to make accurate guessing easy. For one thing, those seven lake-reservoirs might prove ideal places to build hotels and a large tourist complex. Tourism is Israel's biggest business, and this might add a lot to national income. But how much? Another intangible was oil prices. Estimates could fluctuate widely depending on how one projected future oil prices. Would they stay at present levels, or might they drop back to what they had been a few years before? It made a lot of difference.

One of the biggest considerations was the effect such a rise in the level of the Dead Sea, and a diluting of its relative mineral content, would have on the potash industry of the Dead Sea Works. Israel as a major producer of potash depends on it heavily for its balance of trade, as more than 84 percent of it is exported. Total Dead Sea-related exports in 1981 were $148.7 million and it has steadily increased since then. Raising the water level might cut potash production.

It could be argued also that the very inflow of the lighter Mediterranean water would create a situation that could be exploited for energy. The ocean water does not mix easily with the heavy Dead Sea water and tends to float on the surface. When the sun shines on the surface, it creates a kind of greenhouse effect, which heats up the water underneath to a very high temperature. This heat could then be harnessed to produce electricity. A trial project of exactly this type is already in operation on the northern end of the Dead Sea.

Another possible plus to offset the $100 million annually that the Dead Sea Works estimated it would lose was the canal's possible usefulness for cooling nuclear power plants. Israel has long planned to build several nuclear power plants, and undoubtedly will, in time. Such a plant requires great amounts of water for cooling. Building nuclear plants alongside the canal would get extra use out of the flowing water and would save a good deal of money that would otherwise be needed to pump water to the plants. And then someone suggested that after the water has flowed through the plant, it comes out several degrees warmer and could be used for raising seafood, such as shrimp, for export, of course (shrimp are not kosher). The possibilities seemed endless. But turning these ideas into money estimates for feasibility studies were highly subjective.

It could not be forgotten that it was not only Israel's potash industry that would be impaired. The water level of the Dead Sea would not only rise on Israel's side of the border. Jordan continued to complain loudly that its own potash and tourist industries on the shores of the Dead Sea would be injured. It made no difference that when the Israeli government had approved the project they had invited Jordan to join. Jordan had naturally spurned the offer. But if there was any doubt in anyone's mind as to why Jordan opposed the project, these doubts were laid to rest in August 1981 when Jordan announced at a United Nations energy conference that they were planning their own canal from the town of Aqaba on the Red Sea to the southern end of the Dead Sea—a Red-Dead Canal! In opposing Israel's plan, the Jordanians were simply trying to protect their own interests.

The canal Jordan proposed would be much longer than the one proposed by Israel, by about 118 miles, but it would require far less tunneling and could conceivably be completed in a shorter time at a lower cost. Only a few months later, Jordan also announced the opening of a $465 million potash refinery on the southern tip of the Dead Sea. The estimated power output from Jordan's proposed canal was about half of what Israel was projecting for its own, but the lower amount was still about two times what Jordan needed, even during its peak consumption hours. Israel uses seventeen times more electricity per day than Jordan. It is hard to see how the Jordanian canal could be justified except as a political reaction. And its route straight up the fault line of the Syrian-African Rift would make it extremely susceptible to damage from earthquakes.

One thing was clear, however: there could not be two canals pouring large amounts of water into the Dead Sea. Now more than ever the feasibility of Israel's own canal was brought into question, and it seemed highly unlikely that Israel would even come close to completing a canal before the Jordanians.

There was a well-publicized ceremony by Menachem Begin to launch the project in May 1981, but everyone knew it was mostly a gimmick preceding the upcoming elections. As yet no actual work had begun anywhere and the costs of just the many studies were in the millions of dollars. Optimistic estimates were saying that it would take until the early 1990s to complete the Israeli project.

In the intervening years, Jordan has shelved its canal plans as being too expensive and unrealistic. But Israel's canal was to find itself faced with even bigger hurdles. A canal from the Mediterranean Sea to the Dead Sea is a kind of romantic, exciting idea that grabs people's interest. In the first couple of years after it was approved, the Israeli government went looking for donors. They were not too hard to find. Final economic engineering feasibility studies were now showing that the whole thing would make a profit—not a big profit, but perhaps $400 million over a period of fifty years. It was enough to convince people to donate or invest their money. By the start of 1983 some $100 million had been raised just from the sale of Israeli bonds. Construction would start in 1984 or 1985 and finish in 1992.

But during that time, the Israeli government was finding itself more and more strapped for funds as Israel's enconomic difficulties deepened. Certain officials in the government began to use the canal money for other needs. Strictly speaking, they were within their rights, but when the news broke there were a lot of unhappy donors who had purchased bonds for the sole purpose of supporting the building of the canal. This did not help the fund-raisers abroad, and it wasn't too long before they stopped mentioning the Med-Dead Canal in their speeches.

But there was a far more ominous cloud on the horizon. In 1982 world oil prices began to drop and with them the feasibility of such a grandiose scheme. In January 1983 the Energy Minister, Yitzhak Modai, one of the strongest supporters of the project, announced that plans for the actual power plant were being put on hold for several years while it proceeded on the canal and tunnel. Now talk was more about the side benefits of the canal rather than its original purpose of producing electricity. No work had yet begun on site beyond feasibility studies and planning.

During the spring of 1983 tension began to build up between Modai and Finance Minister Aridor, who was looking for ways to cut government spending and the Canal project looked to him as less and less a necessary expense. Modai said he needed another $7 million right away to cover expenses. The money was, in fact, earmarked for the canal, but Aridor was not ready to hand it over. Modai threatened to liquidate the Med-Dead company if he didn't get the money. Finally, at the end of May, he got his money, and the planning continued.

But the economic situation was getting worse. Oil prices continued to drop, and the canal was looking less and less viable in an economy that could ill afford the expense. There was talk of a two-year halt even in the planning, pushing the project's completion date back to 1994.

Following the elections in the summer of 1984, who should become the new finance minister but Yitzhak Modai, the knight defender of the Med-Dead Canal! The main task facing the new government of national unity was to heal Israel's floundering economy, and the man with primary responsibility for finding ways to do that was Minister of Finance Modai. In September 1984 he proposed and got a large budget cut, including about $1 million from the planning budget for the canal project.

Up to that point about $14 million had gone into all the studies and planning with not a spade having been turned. The new Energy Minister did his own reassessment of the whole project, and in the first week of November announced that he was at least cutting a sizeable amount from the canal budget. Then a few days later, the State Comptroller reported to the Knesset on the progress of the project. It had been impeded by the wrangling between Modai and Aridor, he said, but it didn't really matter. In the opinion of the Comptroller, the project should be put on ice until such a time as Israel's situation improved or until the price of conventional fuel for the power stations becomes so high that the Med-Dead Canal becomes strongly feasible. So, for the moment, the canal project is on hold.

Might a canal from the Mediterranean Sea to the Dead Sea be a fulfillment of Ezekiel 47 and Zechariah 14? Perhaps it would be more correct to ask if the prophets, when they were describing water flowing out of Jerusalem to the east (Ezekiel) or both east and west (Zechariah), could have been describing a vision of something like the proposed Med-Dead Canal. In the end, the answer will have to depend on how literally one wants to take the words of the prophets. Both of them describe the source of the flow as being in Jerusalem—not in the western sea. In fact, no canal plan that has yet been proposed would even come near Jerusalem. And the prophet Zechariah, who is the only one who described something that could connect both seas, seems to indicate that it would come about supernaturally. It is difficult to imagine that the hassles and infighting of a ten- or twenty-year man-made project could be the same thing as the beautiful, simple, but powerful event described by the prophets.

33

NATURAL RESOURCES: MINERAL, ANIMAL, PLANT

The problem of Israel's natural resources seems to be improving as time goes on. Although there is not a tremendous amount of the basic forms of mineral wealth, the Israelis have developed a number of methods for extracting them from the land and sea or producing them through artificial or enhanced methods of agriculture or animal husbandry.

MINERAL WEALTH

Among the chemicals produced are potassium salts, which go into fertilizer manufacture. Magnesium salts from the Dead Sea are used in metals for the aircraft industry and sodium salts are used in many different kinds of manufacturing. From the Negev comes silica sand or quartz for glass-making.

Building materials—stone, cement, lime, and marble—are available in many places and especially in the northern part of the country. Some copper and manganese are found in the southern Negev desert, but only a limited quantity of oil and natural gas have been discovered, despite Israel's close proximity to some of the largest oil-producing nations in the world.

The most important, and often the most scarce natural resource in Israel has been fresh water. Much of the countryside is near desert and at least a third cannot be irrigated.

FAUNA

Though the climate and geography has changed in many ways since Bible times, many of the animals and birds mentioned in the Bible still live in Israel. Some seventy different mammal species have been seen in Israel. On the coral reef, at the Gulf of Elat, more than 500 tropical marine species have been identified. Gazelles, hyenas, jackals, shrews, lynx, wild boars, porcupines, badgers, cheetahs, and an occasional wolf can still be seen in the countryside. About 475 species and subspecies of birds have been identified, among them eagles, wild ducks, quail, hoopoe, storks, cranes, pelicans, herons, kites, vultures, gulls, and ubiquitous sparrows. The snakes, scorpions, spiders, grasshoppers, locusts, and other insects mentioned in the Bible still live there. Bees are a welcome sight because of their economic value.

A stretched economy and limited resources have resulted in the appearance of a number of exotic animals, imported and cultivated for their economical value. Alligators, crocodiles, and peacocks, for example, are now grown on special farms, adding thousands of dollars to the economy each year.

Because of its geographic location, Israel is a favorite stopping-off place for birds migrating between Europe and Africa. Some who used to pass through have started staying the whole winter in the warmer valleys around the Sea of Galilee. Pelicans, for example, numbering as many as 7,000, began staying several years ago in a nature reserve in the Hula Valley, north of Galilee. Experts thought they would be there only a week or two, but they chose to stay and were soon wreaking havoc with the fish breeders in the area. Local people tried everything, finally shooting several of them, but nothing moved them until a frost came the next December, convincing the pelicans to continue their journey south.

Israelis were surprised several years ago to see a number of European swans show up. An unusually heavy winter in Europe may have been what sent the huge birds south. One of them, in fact, collided with a light plane, causing considerable damage. Evidently, the agricultural development and reforestation changes the wildlife patterns as well.

One would not think that wild gazelles in Israel could cause a problem to farmers. A most unusual method has been developed to keep the animals from grazing in cultivated fields. Someone thought of the novel idea of ringing the planted fields with the droppings of lions. The scent of the predatory lions is apparently enough to keep the gazelle herds off the farms. Conservationists are as happy as the farmers, because it solves the problem of protecting the endangered gazelles as well as the farms. When the farmers discovered how effective the lion droppings were, even though they have to be replaced every two weeks or so, they began contacting the Safari Park at Ramat Gan, near Tel Aviv, for more of the droppings. The curators began exchanging the droppings for a regular supply of food for the lions. The forty lions there, however, could not produce enough to meet the growing demand, so the Agricultural Research Organization is working on the development of a synthetic substance to replace the spoor.

FLORA

The climate and geography largely control the flora of Israel. In the north and along the Mediterranean during the moister seasons, there is an explosion of color in the flowers, trees, and shrubs. Further south, one might see only scattered date palms.

During earlier days, the country of Israel was covered with forests of oak and pine trees, where now only a few remain. The tamarisk, carob, poplar, oleander, fig, grapevine, pomegranate, and olive flourished, but dryer climates have turned parts of the country into literal desert land. As in other parts of the world, many of the older forests were destroyed by an increasing population looking for wood for cooking fuel. Since the establishment of the State of Israel, nearly 150 million trees have been planted on some 120,000 acres, mostly pine and acacia. Highly profitable citrus, banana, and other fruit orchards are now in production in Israel.

The bees, the cows, and the hyssops that share the Ephraim and Manasseh Heights in ecological balance are now being disturbed by intrusive men. The Nature Reserves Authority (NRA) complained in a recent bulletin that a growing number of illegal harvesters from the nearby Jenin and Tulkarm areas are denuding the hills of the hyssop, an herb that is used both as the popular za'atar spice and for making fragrant attar oil. The small plant is a protected species, and the NRA recently took Tel Aviv Magistrates Court judges on a tour of the affected area to impress them with the importance of cracking down on harvesters with deterrent punishment.

The NRA believes that most of the hyssop is smuggled across the Allenby Bridge to neighboring Arab states, where it fetches high prices. It has proposed that local farmers start growing it commercially to save the natural crop. Women and children from the Jenin and Tulkarm areas pick large quantities. Once they were observed taking away fifty sacks of the herb on a truck. The herb is also very important for beekeepers because it blooms late, when other plants have wilted, and its nectar tides the swarms over until the rains come. Bees feeding on the hyssop not only provide a lot of extra honey but also ensure pollination, which is crucial for the ecology.

Cattle breeders who graze herds on the plateaus of the region are happy to keep hyssop out of their pastures, since the cows don't like its pungent taste. But the illegal harvesters, often several hundred at a time, spread the seeds as they cart off their loot, much to the breeders displeasure. In addition to lobbying for legal measures, the NRA has also started a large-scale information drive in the Arab community against the illegal harvesting.

There are more than 3,000 species of plants in Israel, 150 of which grow only in that land. The British Isles, with an area two and a half times the size of Israel, can boast of only 1,800 plant species. Egypt, ten times larger than Israel, has only 1,500 plant species. No other land in the world has such a wealth of plant life in so small an area.

34

OIL EXPLORATION

Israel currently uses almost 60 million barrels of crude oil per year, or about 160,000 barrels per day. Of that amount, the country's handful of producing oil wells provides perhaps 2 percent. The remaining 98 percent is imported—25 percent from Egypt, 45 percent from Mexico, and the rest is bought on the international spot market. The cost of imported oil runs to nearly $2 billion annually, a heavy expense for such a small country already beset with severe economic problems.

An obvious solution to the problem would be for Israel to discover its own oil reserves and become self-sufficient. To date this has not happened, even though most of its antagonistic neighbors are floating on oil, figuratively speaking. As Golda Meir once remarked in jest, "When Moses crossed the Red Sea, he turned in the wrong direction."

Ever since the formation of the State of Israel in 1948, Israel has been searching for oil. More than 330 exploratory wells have been drilled, but only a few have even yielded enough to pay the expense of the drilling.

The largest deposit within the borders of Israel so far lies in the Heletz field, just north of the city of Ashkelon. This field has been producing since 1955 and by now is almost dry. The search for oil has intensified in the past few years, and international experts have been invited to assess the results of seismological studies and other data in an attempt to narrow down the theoretical areas where oil might be found. The three most promising regions are the coastal plain, near Heletz, the Jordan Rift Valley, and some shallow gas wells in the Hula Valley in the north and the Negev in the south.

In the late 1970s the former chief geologist of Shell Oil, James Wilson, came to Israel and estimated that the country has oil reserves of some 300 million barrels not including the area of the Dead Sea, which he thought might contain billions of barrels. The first number is modest by international standards; the latter figure is large by world standards. But most geologists do not accept Wilson's assessment, at least not for the Dead Sea region. For the rest of the country, they tend to agree more or less with Wilson, estimating that Israel probably has a number of commercially viable fields, each containing several million barrels of oil. Again, this would not be exceptional—certainly nowhere near enough to make of Israel any kind of world power. But it needs to be said that seismological tests and discussions by experts do not determine where oil actually is—only drilling a well does that. And until now, the number of wells drilled is extremely small. Indeed, many areas of the country have hardly been explored at all.

Israel has its own oil research and drilling company, Lapidot ("Torches"), which owns all of six rigs and employs less than 700 people. Even those six rigs are only about half utilized, and their utilization is likely to drop in the next year or two. After the new government of national unity took over in the fall of 1984, the new energy minister ordered a study done on the state of Israel's oil exploration and drilling. The results of the study reached the minister in October 1984, and he immediately recommended to the government that all oil and gas exploration be halted for two years while present projects are reexamined. The study showed that in the past nine years some $250 million had been invested in oil research, including 131 test drillings. In 1984, $65 million went into oil prospection, $45 million coming from the government and the rest from private firms, with about 30 new wells being drilled.

It was the private investors who usually provided the more interesting stories and there have been quite a few of them. American Jewish oil magnate Armand Hammer visited Israel in the fall of 1984 and announced that he was initiating a syndicate for extensive oil drilling in Israel and was showing his good faith by laying down $1 million of his own money to get it started.

Another venture, the King David Oil and Gas Corporation, is owned by Jewish investors from the United States and Australia and has been drilling north of Ashkelon, not far from Heletz. But it would probably be safe to say that the widest press coverage has not been given to Jewish drillers but rather to a Bible-believing Christian from Texas. Andy Sorelle was born in 1920 into a well-to-do Texas family. In World War II he was a hell-raising fighter pilot with the Army Air Corps. One day over Normandy his plane was hit and he lost control, but instead of crashing, the aircraft performed some inexplicable maneuvers, righted itself, and took Sorelle safely back to his base. He says he became an instant believer and soon began to sense that God had some special purpose for his life. After the war he went into the oil business and is now the co-owner of the Houston-based Energy Exploration, Incorporated. One reason for his success has been the development of a magnetic device for detecting oil reserves.

In 1968, Sorelle and his wife made their first visit to Israel and fell in love with the country. He wanted to help the young state and felt that his specialty of oil exploration would be a welcome contribution. In 1975, he wrote to the Israeli government, proposing that they allot him some land so that he could come and drill at his own expense and give Israel any oil that was found. Surprisingly he got little response until he sat down and wrote an angry letter, deploring their lack of interest.

Finally, his letter did elicit a response. In 1977, Sorelle was visited by a government representative who wanted to check out his operation. He received a formal invitation that same year, and in September he came with some equipment to investigate likely sites. The most promising areas seemed to be in the northern Sinai, and he was all ready to negotiate a drilling site. But a week later, Egyptian President Sadat came to Israel, setting in motion the whole process that ultimately led to the return of the Sinai to Egypt. Israeli officials asked Sorelle to wait to see how things developed. While he was waiting, one day in 1979, a friend came and showed him Deuteronomy 33:24 and a Bible map of the tribal division of the Promised Land. The verse says, "Let Asher . . . dip his foot in oil" (KJV), and the map showed the allotment of Asher looking like a leg with the heel of the foot in the area of Mount Carmel near Haifa.

Neither Andy Sorelle nor his friend knew enough Hebrew to realize that the word oil meant olive oil and not petroleum. Excitedly, he recalled that one of the regions he had not explored was the Carmel. When he contacted the appropriate Israeli officials, they admitted that they too had left that area unchecked. At Christmas of 1979, Sorelle was back and his equipment gave readings that indicated worthwhile oil reserves in the Carmel region.

Drilling began at the Carmel site in 1981. It needs to be said that Andy Sorelle was not the first born-again Christian to drill for oil in Israel. Gilman Hill, a Denver-based oilman, had been drilling in the Carmel region for almost two years before Sorelle got started, but Hill's project, costing $12,000 a day, had run out of money. Sorelle actually got some of his equipment and personnel from Hill's failed project.

Until now, Sorelle's well has not shown appreciably more success than Hill's. The new drilling, on the site of the old Crusader fort at

Atlit, has encountered numerous difficulties, and scientific know-how has often been supplemented with prayer to get stuck equipment freed many thousands of feet beneath the surface. In 1983, the equipment got stuck at a depth of 22,000 feet. A stretch of oil-bearing limestone was found near the bottom, but after expenses of about $12 million the operation has had to be suspended until the stuck drill bit can be freed. Sorelle, however, remains optimistic, convinced that God led him to this site and that it contains sizeable amounts of oil. Pointing out that Atlit is not far from the plain of Megiddo (Armageddon), he suggests that it could be the bonanza from this very well that would cause the Russians to invade Israel.

There is an ironic side to the story of Israel's search for oil. After the Six-Day War in 1967, priority was given to searching for oil in the Sinai Peninsula. In the mid-1970s, a large field was discovered at Alma on the Gulf of Suez as well as a natural gas deposit at Sadot along the northern Sinai coast. Twelve drillings were begun at Alma, and seven of them were completed, even though it began to be clear that Israel's new-found relationship with Egypt would certainly result in the handing back of the Sinai. The extraction and distribution systems at Alma were actually completed after Camp David, and in November 1979, Israel gave to Egypt a newly developed oilfield complex that was at that time supplying 20 percent of Israel's energy needs. This explains in part why Egypt today is one of Israel's main oil suppliers.

Perhaps the most tantalizing prospect for oil discovery in Israel is in the Jordan Rift Valley. The Jordan Valley is the northern end of the world's longest fault lines, the Syrian-African Rift. The special geological characteristics of this rift line, and especially the area around the Dead Sea, the lowest spot on earth, have created favorable conditions for trapping oil and gas and preventing its escape. Just about everyone agrees up to that point. However, on the question of whether there actually is oil under the Dead Sea, expert opinion is sharply divided. Either there is none there at all or the deposit is huge; there seems to be no middle ground.

Jordan began to drill on their side of the Dead Sea as early as 1978, so far without success. Israel has been slower to get going, partly because of the special emphasis on the Sinai in the late 1970s. In 1983, the government approved $50 million, the largest ever for a single project, for survey and drilling in the Jordan Valley. A sizeable area of some 400,000 acres was set aside for the concession, and attempts were begun to raise additional funds from private investors. By the end of 1984, drilling had still not begun in the area, and it remains to be seen how the energy minister's moratorium on new wells will affect what could be Israel's best chance to become self-sufficient in oil. In the meantime, the Israeli-based Teroil Exploration International has been granted permission to drill for oil in, of all places, Virginia!

35

ORTHODOXY

Many American Christians have little contact with Jews. Some do not even know one personally. What they think they know about Jews is a kind of stereotyped image gleaned from their Bibles and their newspapers. So, it may come as a shock to learn that perhaps half or more of the Israelis are atheists or at most agnostics. And most of those who do profess some belief in God would not be classified as orthodox, that is, strictly observant Jews.

Admittedly, it is difficult to arrive at an accurate figure for the number or percentage of orthodox, observant Jews, but it may not be much more than 15 to 20 percent, and it may be even less. In lieu of actual census material, which in itself would lose some accuracy by the fact that most strictly orthodox would refuse to cooperate with questioners, voting statistics might serve as an indicator. Politics and religion are closely related in Israel, and about 10 percent of the members of the Knesset belong to the religious parties. The ratio of religious to nonreligious varies widely from place to place in the country. In a largely secular area such as Tel Aviv, the figure would be much lower than the national average, while in Jerusalem there might be as many as one-third who are orthodox.

But we have a difficulty of definition here. As in Christianity, there are may levels of being "religious." However, Judaism is different from Christianity in that there is an immediately visible outward evidence of a committed and observant Jewish man. He will be wearing a special head covering, the small skullcap called a "kipa" in Hebrew. To the untrained eye, an equally religious Jewish woman is harder to pick out. When we say "observant," we mean that the person is committed to the commandments of the Jewish religion as laid down in the Bible and interpreted in the centuries of authoritative decisions and developments that have intervened. It will be seen then that the essence of being a "religious" Jew is less in what he believes than in how he lives. Judaism has no "born again" experience corresponding to that which properly makes a person a Christian. Since the days of Jimmy Carter, of course, everyone uses the term, but in Jewish parlance, it signified a person who has "repented" of his secular, nonobservant ways and has started to live according to the commandments and requirements of the religion. Again, it is not so much what one believes as what one does.

Some years ago, a pastor was studying Hebrew in a daily *ulpan*, a study center for newcomers. One day the class was discussing Christianity and the teacher asked, "What is the difference between Judaism and Christianity?" One Jewish girl answered, "I don't know much about Christianity, but from what I see, it seems that for Jews it is important what you do while for Christians, it is only important what you believe."

Sadly, for us Christians, she may not have been far off. If a Christian were asked if someone he knew was a Christian, he would probably reply more in terms of what the person believes than whether or not he cares for orphans or widows or keeps himself unspotted from the world (James 1:27).

Within the group considered orthodox in Israel may be found a number of different kinds. One group might be completely secular—those who pay no attention to the sanctity of the Sabbath, who do not fast on the day of Atonement, or ever attend synagogue, and who do not keep the laws of kosher. Sanctifying the Sabbath has mostly to do with not using electrical appliances or traveling. There is a sizeable number of Israelis who keep kosher kitchens and attend the occasional synagogue service. A kosher kitchen basically entails having two complete sets of dishes and utensils, one for meat products and one for everything else. Girls who can prove that they keep the laws of kosher and the Sabbath can gain exemption from military service.

Most Israelis who would be considered orthodox attend synagogue daily, fast on the several designated fast days in the year, strictly observe the laws concerning the Sabbath, and generally try to live according to the precepts of the religion. At the far end of the scale are those who are often known as "ultra-orthodox." These have a much stricter level of kosher rules, eating nothing that was produced during the seventh year, when the fields were supposed to lie fallow, and nothing from which the tithe of the produce has not been taken. The men in this group will touch no woman other than their own wife, whether that means shaking her hand or sitting next to her on a bus. They will refuse to have pictures taken because of the biblical injunction against making images.

While Israel has universal conscription, the young men of the ultra-orthodox generally do not serve in the army, and some extremist groups even oppose the existence of the state on the grounds that only the Messiah can reestablish the Jewish people in their land. One of these latter groups is the *Naturei Karta*, an Aramaic title meaning "guardians of the city." These are so outspokenly opposed to the state, from which they do not hesitate to accept financial support, that their leaders have often issued declarations of encouragement to the PLO.

Naturally enough, it is easiest for people with strict religious require-ments to live in the same general area, and many of Israel's cities have exclusively orthodox neighborhoods. In Jerusalem there are several such neighborhoods, including, of course, the Jewish quarter in the Old City. The oldest such neighborhood outside the walls is that of Mea Shearim, founded by pious European Jews from the Old City in about 1874. At that time, Jerusalem had only a total population of 16,000 to 20,000, about half of whom were Jews. Those who moved to the new settle-ment to the north of the Damascus Gate chose the name from the words of Genesis 26:12, "Then Isaac sowed in that land, and received in the same year an hundredfold [*mea shearim*]: and the Lord blessed him" (KJV).

A visit to Mea Shearim is a fascinating experience for someone from abroad. There people still dress the way Jews dressed in Poland in the nineteenth century. On the street the language you are most likely to hear is not Hebrew but Yiddish. When Friday evening brings the Sabbath, roadblocks are set up, dividing the neighborhood from the rest of the city for twenty-five hours. Not a vehicle moves, no sounds of a machine are to be heard. All is quiet except for the voices of children playing and groups of men singing. The impression is one of peace and, for many orthodox Jews, living in Mea Shearim or a similar neighbor-hood elsewhere in the land is the fulfillment of a centuries-old dream.

The peace of Mea Shearim, however, is conditional. No secular Israeli would even consider driving his car into Mea Shearim during the Sabbath, but it happens regularly that some unsuspecting tourist drives his rented car past one of those barricades and suddenly finds himself in the most unpleasant situation imaginable. People will block his way, shouting violently, and then possibly throwing stones. A broken wind-shield is a likely result. Even a pedestrian can expect the same reception if he strays into the forbidden area smoking a cigarette. In some shops in

Jerusalem, outside of Mea Shearim, it is possible to buy a T-shirt that reads "I got stoned in Mea Shearim."

On weekdays it is still necessary to enter the neighborhood with caution. No one should enter in shorts, and women who sport bare arms are setting themselves up for verbal or even physical abuse. It is not unusual to read in the papers of women who have had ink thrown on their summer blouses. Community leaders try to prevent such incidents by posting signs around the neighborhood that read:

> DEAR VISITOR: You are quite welcome to Mea Shearim, but please do not antagonize our religious inhabitants by strolling through our streets in immodest clothing. Our Torah requires the Jewish woman to be attired in modest dress. Dress sleeves reaching below the elbow (slacks forbidden), stockings, married women having their hair covered, etc., are the virtues of the Jewish woman throughout the ages. Please do not offend our residents and cause yourself any unnecessary inconvenience. We beg you not to infringe upon our way of life and "holy code of law." We beseech you to use discretion by not trespassing our streets in an undesired fashion. The men are requested not to enter bareheaded. Thanking you in advance for complying with our request and wishing you blessings from above for your good deeds. Signed, Committee for guarding modesty, Mea Shearim and vicinity, Jerusalem, the Holy City.

Such strict observances of dress codes and Sabbath observance would be considered "zeal for the Torah." The patron saint of all such guardians of the Torah is Phinehas, the son of Eleazar. In Numbers 25 is recorded the story of Phinehas, who killed an Israelite man and a Midianite woman for having sexual relations contrary to God's Law. For this action he was highly praised by God and he became an example for violence to many religious zealots after him. However, unlike Phinehas, most zealots who resort to violence in defense of God are misguided and acting contrary to the precepts of their own religion. So, for example, while stone throwing is the most common response by young orthodox Jews to what they perceive as a desecration of the Sabbath, Jewish law expressly forbids the throwing or even lifting of stones on the Sabbath. This has been repeated frequently by Israeli religious leaders, but to no avail.

In recent years, there has been a marked increase in the use of violence by some zealots. In 1983 Jerusalem's mayor, Teddy Kollek, was one day physically assaulted because of a stand he had taken on an issue. Shortly before the elections in June 1984 an ultra-orthodox Knesset member was attacked in a synagogue by a dozen young men belonging to a rival ultra-orthodox faction opposed to his candidacy. Two years before, members of the same group had broken into the same rabbi's house and beaten him up.

The road that leads from downtown Jerusalem to the outlying neighborhood of Ramot is regularly the scene of stoning cars on the Sabbath. The road does not pass through a religious area, but can be seen from a nearby orthodox neighborhood. On occasion, Ramot residents have launched counterattacks, and police have had to be called in to break up battles between secular and religious. Some would say that there is an increasing polarization in Israel between religious and secular Jews. Clearly, there has been a rise in the number of incidents in which secular residents have met violence with violence, and police have occasionally expressed concern that things could get out of control.

One issue that has sparked off a great deal of controversy and violence has been the construction of a new wing on a Tiberias hotel. The city of Tiberias was first constructed by Herod Antipas in honor of the emperor Tiberius in about A.D. 30. In its first centuries, it was always a mostly Jewish city and many famous rabbis lived and worked there. Over the years, many pious Jews came to live and die there, and the city is the site of numerous cemeteries. In fact, it would hardly be an exaggeration to say that most of the present-day city is built over ancient Jewish graves. Today's population is largely religious, many of them, no doubt, dwelling in buildings built over ancient graves.

However, when the Ganei Hamat Hotel began to construct its new 140-room wing, the Burial Society, *Atra Kadisha*, protested that there was fear of desecrating some ancient grave sites. Israel's largest bank, Bank Leumi, controls a subsidiary company that owns the hotel, and bank officials began to negotiate with *Atra Kadisha* in an attempt to preclude the problem. More than 150 major architectural changes were requested by the Society and carried out by the bank at an extra cost of some $1.5 million. But the Society was not satisfied and began to arouse orthodox ire against the bank. A boycott of the bank was declared, causing religious investors from Israel and abroad to close accounts and withdraw tens of millions of dollars. All this came *after* one of Israel's two chief rabbis inspected the construction plans and approved them.

Somehow, the issue became a major cause for the zealots. Boycotting the bank was not enough; they began to go on a more violent offensive. In the bank's branches in Mea Shearim, customers were threatened and in one incident even stoned as they stood in line at tellers' windows. The bank's mail to its customers was opened, the envelopes stuffed with warning notices. Swastikas and slogans were smeared on windows and walls of branches, and several of the branches were subjected to arson attacks. One branch was completely gutted; others were severely damaged. Shortly after several of these fire incidents, one Mea Shearim leader, who did not directly condone the attacks, said that the perpetrators were out of the control of the rabbis. These people, he said, were committing such acts in order "to appease the wrath of God, and to protect God's honor."

Israel's mixed secular and religious society is a complicated one. In a country fighting for its life economically, it goes without saying that every dollar must be used as efficiently as possible and natural resources exploited to the fullest. It would be simplistically logical that the energy and manpower efficiency to be saved by daylight saving time would make this an annual event. However, it has actually taken court action to force the country's Interior Ministry to institute summer time.

The opposition to summer time has been on religious grounds. An orthodox Jew is required to go the synagogue for prayer every morning after sunrise. Turning the clock back makes it more difficult for him to complete his prayers and still get to work on time.

A second, and perhaps more serious objection to summer time, is that indirectly it can cause a desecration of the Sabbath. Israelis work five and a half days a week. In the middle of Friday afternoon everything begins to close down, and about an hour before the start of the Sabbath the buses stop running. Except in some of the more secular areas, like Tel Aviv, there is little nightlife on Friday nights. That leaves only Saturday night for the young people to get out and walk. Sidewalk cafés and restaurants do as much as half of their business on Saturday night. According to a seldom-enforced law in Jerusalem, businesses may not open until half an hour after the close of the Sabbath. When daylight saving time is in effect, this can mean as late as 9:00 P.M. Opening that late, however, would mean a considerable loss in income for many businesses. So, in practice, the kids are out, the businesses are open, and all before the Sabbath has actually ended.

In 1984 the Supreme Court ruled that summer time must be instituted. Optimally, it should run for about seven months, but by way of compromise, it now lasts five months, from immediately after Passover until the day before the start of the Jewish New Year, Rosh Hashanah. And in the meantime, bands of black-clad orthodox young men roam the downtown area of Jerusalem, using whatever method of persuasion is most effective to prevent shopowners from opening too early.

In June 1984 the foundation was laid for what will reportedly be the largest synagogue in the world. Situated in a northern neighborhood of Jerusalem, the Belz Great Synagogue will be able to accommodate up to 4,500 worshipers. It will cost about $12 million to build, and it is expected to be completed sometime in 1987. The Belz community traces its roots to a small town in Galicia in Poland more than 170 years ago. It is a Hassidic community that suffered greatly during the Holocaust. There are about 10,000 Belz families living in Israel. About 5,000 Belz Jews from Europe, the United States, and Australia came to Israel for the groundbreaking ceremony. The Belz community expects that the Messiah will stop over at the new synagogue on his way to the rebuilt temple.

36

PEACE NOW

Only a few months before, Israelis had been totally elated by the visit of Egypt's President Sadat, and now the government was engaged in its first peace treaty negotiations with an Arab neighbor. These negotiations were being carried out for the Israeli side by the newly-elected Premier Menachem Begin, and things were moving fairly slowly as spring approached in 1978. For reasons of political ideology, Begin's Likud party was not at all eager to give up the Sinai Peninsula as part of a peace arrangement.

In 1956 Israel had captured the large peninsula in eight days and then been forced to return it under pressure from the United States and the Soviet Union. Again in the Six-Day War of 1967, Israel had overrun the Sinai, and even though the time needed to take it was short in both wars, the cost in lives had not been small. It was not hard to understand the reticence of the new government and indeed of many Israelis to return again a piece of desert for which so many young soldiers had died. Begin was soon to meet with U.S. President Carter about the negotiations, and he was saying that his position represented an almost complete consensus of Israeli opinion.

It is true that there had been a few voices raised in favor of peace even if it cost the Sinai. Some schoolboys had written to Begin, and there were those far to his political left who opposed his negotiating tactics, but he had not seen fit to take these objections as representing any serious segment of Israeli public opinion.

Then on March 8, the prime minister received a letter signed by 350 reserve officers and soldiers from combat units. These were young men, many of whom had fought for the Sinai. Many had been wounded in combat, and the list included men who had won Israel's highest awards for valor. And they wanted the government to know that they were not part of its "consensus." Among other things, they wrote, "A government that prefers the establishment of settlements across the Green

Line to the ending of the historic conflict . . . will raise questions about the justice of our cause. A government policy that will lead to the continued rule over one million Arabs is liable to change the Jewish democratic nature of the State."

Certain religious-nationalist groups, especially one known as *Gush Emunim,* had been pushing hard for the establishment of numerous new settlements in areas that were under negotiation with Egypt, and Begin's Likud party was inclined to go along with them. Even more at issue, of course, was the program of settlements in the West Bank, or, as the new government insisted it be called, "Judea and Samaria."

One of the signers of the letter to Begin was Yuval Neriya, a young tank officer who had received the *Itur HaGvura,* Israel's equivalent of the Congressional Medal of Honor. He explained it this way: "Our idea was to show the prime minister that he did not have the nation behind him when he refused to negotiate over Judea and Samaria to get peace. We also wanted to show him that we, the combat soldiers, would be placed in a very difficult moral position if the chance to achieve peace is lost and another war breaks out. It was a problem of conscience. If we have to fight again, we have to be sure that everything possible has been done to avoid war and get peace, that there really is no alternative."

It would not be accurate to say that the reserve officers had the majority of Israelis with them any more than it was for Begin to claim almost complete consensus for his negotiating stance. But overnight Israel's largest, longest-lived, and most successful protest movement was launched. In Hebrew it was called *Shalom Achshav,* "Peace Now," and within three or four weeks it had snowballed to include thousands of adherents with branches all over the country.

The Peace Now movement had what was basically a two-plank platform: (1) Israel must not rule over a million-plus hostile Arabs and must not try to absorb them; and (2) while trading territory for peace, defense and security needs must be guaranteed.

Their posters included such slogans as "Peace is preferable to the whole land of Israel" or "Better a land of peace than a piece of land." In a rally barely two months after the movement got started, they displayed a mock golden calf, which they had made and labeled, "The Land of Israel" (i.e., the territories of the West Bank). The intention was clear: Those who refused to negotiate over land were in effect idolizing that land. Throughout its seven-year history, Peace Now has been especially active in opposing the setting up of new settlements in the territories that Israel captured in 1967. They have organized some of the largest mass demonstrations that Israel has ever seen.

One of the peculiarities of Peace Now (some would say one of its attractions, but certainly one of its weaknesses) is in its lack of organization. In many ways it is a classic grass-roots movement. It has no formal membership and only three officials (none of them paid), a spokesman, a person responsible for foreign contacts, and a treasurer. The treasurer may not have all that much to do, because the organization is run on contributions and has a very small budget. Volunteer workers are not even reimbursed for phone calls or travel expenses. One of the right-wing members of Israel's Knesset once charged that Peace Now was financed by the CIA.

Unlike peace movements in other countries, adherents of Peace Now do not hesitate to serve in the army. Not a few of them died in "Operation Peace for Galilee" or, as it is otherwise called, "The War in Lebanon." During the initial fighting in Lebanon, Peace Now made no public statements either for or against the operation. However, after the cease-fire had become stable, they began to demonstrate and to speak out against continued Israeli presence there. They strongly opposed the entry of the Israeli army into West Beirut in the summer of 1982. In September of that year, after the massacre carried out by "Christian" Falange forces in the Sabra and Shatilla refugee camps, a huge rally organized by Peace Now and others stimulated the Israeli government to set up an official inquiry into the affair. When the results of the inquiry were published, Peace Now activists pushed hard for the resignation of Ariel Sharon.

Perhaps because of their lack of organization, perhaps because of the relative youthfulness of their members, Peace Now stumbled rather badly in late 1979 when some of its representatives spoke out against the government. This in itself would not have raised any eyebrows, but the antigovernment statements were made on trips in the United States. One hallowed principle of politics, not always observed in our day and age, is that you do not criticize your government in front of foreigners. Israelis are especially aware of this because of all the criticism Israel generally gets from the foreigners themselves. Peace Now spokesmen seem to have learned the lesson and have not since earned rebuke for the same offense.

It would probably be accurate to say that most Israelis do not identify themselves with Peace Now, at least not with its methods of protest. A poll conducted in the summer of 1983 showed that just over half objected to Peace Now's methods of opposing government policy. About 30 percent justified some of their methods and objected to others, and 13 percent were completely supportive. A breakdown of those opposed showed that they came from the eighteen-to-twenty-two-year-old age group, had only a partial high school education, came from Israel's Oriental communities, and tended to be more observant of their Judaism.

It was a young man quite close to this profile who caused Peace Now's first martyr. On February 10, 1983, Yona Avrushmi tossed a grenade at a group of Peace Now demonstrators outside the prime minister's house. The explosion killed one and wounded nine. The dead man was Emil Greenzweig, himself almost the representative Peace Now supporter, in his early thirties, of European background, and a reserve paratroop officer. It was a sobering moment for most Israelis as the prospect of brother against brother suddenly became a reality.

In what must be seen as one of the ironies of history, four Swedish parliamentarians in early 1984 nominated Peace Now for the Nobel Peace Prize. The irony lies in the fact that Israel's only winner of the Nobel Peace Prize was Menachem Begin, the man whom Peace Now's founders had so opposed.

37

POPULATION

According to 1986 figures, Israel has a combined population of 4.2 million. Of this number 82.9 percent are Jews, 13.5 percent Muslim, 2.3 percent Christian, and 1.3 percent Druze. Israel's population is small compared to all of her fourteen Arab neighbors, who have a combined total of nearly 160 million. Compared to 4,578,000 square miles of her neighbors, Israel's land area is only 7,992 square miles.

Populations of some of Israel's towns and cities are as follows:

- Tel Aviv Jaffa (330,400)   The New York City of Israel
- Haifa (227,900)   One of Israel's three deep-water harbors
- Beersheba (110,800)   The city where Abraham once lived
- Hebron (65,000)   The city where Abraham was buried
- Bethlehem (20,000)   Where David and Christ Jesus were born
- Jerusalem (431,800)   The Holy City; capital of Israel
- Nazareth (44,800)   Where Jesus grew up
- Tiberias (28,200)   City on the shores of the Sea of Galilee
- Metula (590)   Israel's most northern city
- Elat (18,900)   Israel's most southern city; on the Red Sea
- Ashdod (65,700)   Ancient Philistine city
- Shechem (85,000)   Located between Mt. Ebal and Mt. Gerizim

There are 92 towns and cities in Israel with a Jewish majority and 36 with Arab majorities. More than 85 percent of Israelis are city dwellers. Seventy-seven percent of the Arabs are Sunni Muslims, 13.5 percent are Christian, and 10 percent are Bedouins. There are two communities of Samaritans with a total population of approximately 600. One community is located near Tel Aviv, and the other at Shechem, near Nablus.

It has been interesting to watch the population shift in the city of Jerusalem in the past 150 years:

Year	Jews	Muslims	Christians
1844	7,120	5,000	3,390
1876	12,000	7,560	5,470
1896	28,112	8,560	8,748
1922	33,971	13,413	14,699
1931	55,222	19,894	19,335
1948	100,000	40,000	25,000
1967	195,700	54,963	12,646
1970	215,000	61,600	11,500
1983	300,000	105,000	15,000

There has been a growing Arab population in the north of Israel. By the year 1993, one out of two Galileans will be an Arab, according to some studies. At that time there will be 1.1 million Israeli Arabs, half of which will live in Galilee.

The Israeli population passed the 4 million mark in 1982. Israeli Arabs are increasing annually at the rate of 3.4 percent, about twice the natural growth rate of the Jewish population. The average Arab family is eight. Some 60 percent are under the age of nineteen. The average life expectancy has jumped from fifty-two years in 1958 to seventy in 1980.

Israeli experts predict that by the year 2010 the Jewish population will reach 6 million, about the number who died in the Holocaust. More than a million Jewish settlers will live on the West Bank by the end of this century.

The Arab population is growing faster than any other group of the world. At its current annual rate of 3.4 percent, the number of Arabs will double in twenty-three years. Arabs also have the world's highest fertility rate. There are presently 185 million Arabs in the world. The birth rate of the Arab world is 45 per 1,000 as compared with the world average of 27 per 1,000. The birth rate for developing countries is 31 per 1,000, and for the developed nations it is 15 per 1,000.

Births to Arab women average 6 to 7, compared with 3.5 for women in the world, 2.0 in the developed regions, and 4.1 in the less developed regions. Eighty-one percent of the total Arab population—145 million people—live in countries with inadequate resources. The remaining 19 percent live in oil-rich countries. At present rates of growth, Cairo will have a population of 20 million by the year 2000, Baghdad 12 million, Alexandria 7.2 million, Beirut 3.5 million, and Damascus 3 million.

38

PREJUDICE

Beneath Israel's economic, religious, and social problems lies a hidden social and political issue, another cause for concern. A visitor to certain places of work in Israel will often discover a smouldering hatred between the Jews who migrated from Europe in the past two centuries, the *Ashkenazim*, and ones who came later, originally from Spain and Portugal and then from northern African countries and from the Middle East, the so-called *Sephardim*. There seems to be a growing political unrest among the two groups as profound as the orthodox-secular conflict.

Jewish immigrants who came with their children to Israel from Morocco, Algeria, Tunisia, and Libya since the end of the 1940s number today around 800,000. This influx of North Africans makes them the largest single ethnic subdivision among Israel's 3.5 million Jews. These and other Sephardim constitute a clear majority, amounting now to about 55 percent of the total Israeli population.

The problem arises primarily from the fact that the Israeli upper class, the Ashkenazi Jews, make up the majority of the Knesset. Despite Israel's high literacy rate of 97 percent, the Ashkenazi are among the better educated and the Sephardim among the lowest. The Ashkenazi Jews usually hold the better jobs in the country. For example, only 15 percent of Israeli university students are from the Sephardim community.

The division between these Central European Ashkenazi Jews and the Oriental Sephardim parallels in many ways the secular and orthodox division in Jerusalem. Under the laws of immigration, any Jew from anywhere in the world desiring citizenship was granted it. But once the Sephardim began arriving, they met with much more difficulty in many ways and perhaps more prejudice than any of their European or North American peers.

An uninformed visitor to Jerusalem, seeing the Sephardim Jews, dressed as Middle Easterners, eating Middle Eastern foods, living in crowded sections of the city, large families crowded together in a few tiny rooms, might not even recognize them as Jews. Many of them, when they first arrived in Israel, were tent dwellers, living and looking much like Bedouin. Their growing numbers in such cities as Jerusalem, where they already are in the majority, almost certainly promise to them decidedly more political influence in the future.

39

QUALITY OF LIFE

While the landscape, architecture, and some of the dress in Israel is definitely Middle Eastern, in most other ways Israel looks more and more like a European country.

Israelis live mostly in apartment buildings, not in single-dwelling houses. They work in offices and shops, usually on a five-and-a-half-day per week schedule. A day off is often the occasion for a family picnic. The standard of living is higher than most other countries of the Middle East, with an average annual income of $5,000, comparing favorably with Spain, England, and Greece.

Apartment rentals for a three- or four-room flat run around $200 a month, but to buy the same apartment would cost perhaps $60,000 or more.

Travelers from overseas might be surprised to learn that almost anything they could want or need around the world can be bought in Israel if they are willing to pay the price. Even peanut butter is now available, and some of it is even cheaper and certainly more healthful than the American brands.

Automobiles are common, despite their high cost and exorbitant tax and import duties, now around 200 percent of the purchase price. Sale prices and taxes make even small cars go for $15,000 or more.

Israel is a produce exporter, importing very few produce items. This means that fruits and vegetables are plentiful in the corner grocery stores, supermarkets, and street sellers, but only when the produce is in season. Local produce and vegetables are cheap and are grown to full ripeness, making them not only more healthful but better tasting.

40
RABBINATE

In March 1986 Rabbi Moshe Feinstein died in New York. A Russian-born Talmudic scholar, he spent many years in Russian prisons for religious activities. In 1937 he was brought out of Russia through international intervention and settled in America. For many years he was looked to as the guiding light for questions of Jewish law and morality, perhaps the world's foremost spokesman on practical application of Orthodox Judaism in America and Canada. As important and as revered as he was, his function was as a spiritual and moral advisor.

In Israel, however, the rabbinate and functions of the rabbi are different from other places in the world. Because of the laws of Israel, which established the *halakhah* (Jewish religious law as it has developed through the centuries by precedent and tradition) as state law, all matters affecting personal status, such as marriage, legitimacy, divorce, and conversion are judged by the Ministry of Religious Affairs. The Ministry itself is controlled by the (Orthodox) National Religious Party, having the effect of making Orthodox Judaism the "state religion."

The rabbinate in Israel consists of two chief rabbis, who are state-appointed. One is from the Ashkenazim (European Jews) and the other from the Sephardim (Oriental and North African and Middle Eastern Jews). Similar twin rabbinates have also been established in all the larger cities. A powerful force within the system are the *rashei yeshivot*, the heads of the seminaries, who are constantly scrutinizing the National Religious Party for any signs of heterodoxy. The Ashkenazi rabbinate holds as firmly to the tradition of Eastern European Judaism as the Sephardim hold to their traditions, making for great stability within the system.

The rabbinate then, for all practical purposes, functions as the civil court within the land. Under the chief rabbis are the *dayyanim*, the judges of the Supreme Bet Din of Appeal, followed by the *dayyanim* of the district courts, men who serve only the courts and have no pastoral function. Next in importance are the rabbis who serve as religious functionaries with specific and limited duties, such as inspectors of dietary laws and Sabbath observance laws. Marriages are conducted by appointed officials and funerals and burials are performed by others of the *hevra kaddisha*, the "burial society."

Since there is such a close relationship between religious and civil functions in Israel, the rabbinate becomes a somewhat closed society. Foreign-trained rabbis have a hard time finding a place of service in Israel. Most of them end up finding their livelihood in some other field of work.

41

SEXUAL MORES

A recent survey of Israeli youth caused great concern for their parents. In a study of eleventh and twelfth graders in Haifa schools, the survey showed that one-third of the girls and one-half of the boys were having sexual relations on a regular basis. A similar poll conducted at Hebrew University in Jerusalem showed that only 35 percent of all undergraduate women had not had sexual relations.

The researchers in the schools of Haifa also found that many of the high school aged young women were especially ignorant about sex. Nearly 40 percent of the girls questioned said they couldn't recognize the first signs of pregnancy. As in other parts of the world, Israeli youth find it difficult to discuss sex with their parents.

Prostitution is a problem worldwide, but recently it is reaching troublesome proportions in certain cities in Israel. The police in Tel Aviv estimate that some 300 call-girls are operating a sophisticated prostitution ring, working through a chain of contacts in bars and hotels. Many of them are from Ashkenazi origin. Unlike the more numerous streetwalkers, they do not usually have underworld contacts. But the street girls, of whom a high proportion are from Oriental background, are generally involved with pimps and crime syndicates.

42

SMOKING

A report of U.S. Surgeon General C. Everett Koop, based on his visit to Israel, showed that 70 percent of all Israelis smoke, compared to 30 percent of Americans. A study by Jerusalem-based Society for the Prevention of Smoking puts the figure slightly lower. The Society sets the figure at 65 percent of all Israelis above the age of eighteen as having the habit. As a result, according to recent reports of the Ministry of Health, 5,500 Israelis die annually from smoking-related illnesses, such as lung cancer, emphysema and other obstructive lung diseases and cardiovascular illnesses.

The statistics bear out also among Israeli doctors, as some of them have been observed smoking even as they lecture their patients about the harmful effects of the habit. Less than 5 percent of American doctors are now smokers.

There are already laws banning smoking in specified public places, such as the Knesset plenum, city council meetings, public buses, taxis, and medical facilities, but a recent attempt was made by the Israeli Minister of Health, Shoshanna Arbeli-Almoslino, to ban smoking in all workplaces, meeting rooms, sports facilities, and hospitals. His efforts have been met with strong opposition. The health minister tried to extend the ban after reading about successful antismoking legislation in several American cities. Ora Namir, chairman of the Social Affairs Committee of the Knesset, was quick to block the attempt. Namir said the ban went too far.

Another member of the Social Affairs Committee, a four-pack-a-day smoker, Binyamin Ben-Eliezer, reportedly issued a warning that extending the ban on smoking would make instant criminals of all Israeli smokers and that such a move would lead to widespread civil disobedience. He further vowed to organize a lobby to fight for smokers' rights in Israel.

Israelis smoke almost everywhere, despite laws against smoking in public buses and taxis. Oblivious to complaints and the health hazards, they smoke in movie theaters, gas stations, doctors' offices, and even between courses in restaurants, which, in Israel, do not provide non-smoking areas. Premier Golda Meir chain-smoked her Chesterfields until she died of cancer in 1978. Shimon Peres and Yitzhak Rabin are also heavy smokers. Although the laws banning smoking in specified public places are punishable by fines as high as $156 for each offense, the laws are rarely exercised. It is reported that in Jerusalem's City Council, thirteen members, including Mayor Teddy Kollek, break the law every time the council meets.

"It's an intolerable rule, and I know that the mayor feels the same way," one councilman recently said. Yet this same councilman, ironically, doesn't touch cigarettes on the Sabbath, when smoking is forbidden.

Another approach to stop people from smoking is being tried by the ultra-Orthodox Rafa organization. The organization has announced that the two most prominent rabbis in the country, both nonsmokers, will walk out of any wedding, bar mitzvah, or circumcision ceremonies to which they are invited if they see any of the other guests smoking. Since it would be considered a shameful experience to have a rabbi walk out of such a ceremony, it is hoped that this move will do something to curtail smoking in public places and to call attention to the problem throughout the country.

43

SOVIET-SYRIAN COOPERATION

Arab leaders visiting Russia have invited thousands of Soviet military advisors and technicians into their countries in recent years. Great quantities of weapons have been purchased from Russia by the Arab nations—more than $90 million worth since the Yom Kippur War of 1973. Batteries of long-range antiaircraft missiles line the border between Israel and Syria, a move to which both the United States and Israel have attached great importance. The missile batteries pose a serious threat to Israel's early-warning and communications capability.

More serious than the threat from outside the borders may be the growing sentiment among Arabs toward Palestinian-Soviet alliances. A recent poll taken among Arabs on the West Bank and Gaza strip, most of whom were under forty years of age, gave some alarming results.

Arabs were asked, "Do you support the activities and goals of the PLO?" The answers were 90 percent, yes; 7 percent, no; and only 3 percent had no opinion. The pollsters also asked, "Do you support a Palestinian-Soviet Alliance?" To this the answer was 60 percent, yes; 33 percent, no; and 7 percent had no opinion. This growing sentiment could continue to trouble the State of Israel in years to come as long as the Arab question in Israel remains unsettled.

44

SPORTS

Israel sent its first team to the Olympic Games in 1952 and, with the exception of the 1980 Moscow Games, have participated regularly since then. No one can forget the tragedy that befell the Israeli Olympic Team in the 1972 Munich Games, when PLO terrorists attacked and murdered eleven team members.

While Israel has yet to win its first Olympic gold medal, its athletes have made impressive showings in such events as sailing and shooting. Many remember sprinter Esther Roth, who finished fifth in the Olympic 110-meter hurdles. One of the most consistent good showings of sportsmanship has been made by the members of Maccabi Tel Aviv basketball team, who have several times won the European Cupwinners competition in Europe, defeating such teams as the USSR, Spain, Yugoslavia, and Czechoslovakia. The year that the Washington Bullets won the NBA title, they were rewarded by their coach with a trip to Israel. In a friendly game, the NBA winners were defeated by the enthusiastic Maccabi team.

Football (soccer), basketball, swimming, tennis, volleyball, track-and-field games, gymnastics, sailing, weight-lifting, and fencing are among the most popular sports in Israel. Horseback riding, snorkeling, wind surfing, and hang-gliding are rapidly gaining enthusiasts.

League football (soccer), basketball, and volleyball teams, organized at local, regional, and national levels, play full schedules before enthusiastic crowds all over the country.

45

SYNAGOGUES

There are 6,000 synagogues in Israel, each cared for and supervised by one of the more than 400 officially appointed rabbis. Jerusalem alone has 800 synagogues. With few exceptions, the synagogues in Israel are neither built nor maintained by local communities but by the government.

The idea of a rabbi who serves as a pastoral minister is virtually unknown in Israel. The rabbi's main function is to teach and study Torah and the Talmud. He does not visit nor deliver sermons. He conducts funerals and weddings only if asked.

There are no seminaries to compare with those in the western world, but there are *yeshivot* schools, which are the traditional sources of Jewish learning. These schools are financed through the Ministry of Religious Affairs, costing the Israeli government nearly $35 million per year.

46

TECHNOLOGY

In 1899 Mark Twain wrote an essay entitled "Concerning the Jews." The essay was written a full eighteen years before the Balfour Declaration of 1917 and nearly fifty years before the State of Israel came into being. Twain's essay, in retrospect, seems to have been prophetic in many ways. Twain wrote:

> If the statistics are right, the Jews constitute but one percent of the human race. It suggests a nebulous dim puff of star dust lost in the blaze of the Milky Way. Properly the Jew ought hardly to be heard of; but he is heard of; he has always been heard of. He is prominent on the planet as any other people, and his commercial importance is extravagantly out of proportion to the smallness of his bulk. His contributions to the world's list of great names in literature, science, art, music, finance, medicine, and abstruse learning are also way out of proportion to the weakness of his numbers. He has a made a marvelous fight in this world, in all the ages; and has done it with his hands tied behind him. He could be vain of himself, and be excused for it. The Egyptian, Babylonian, and the Persian rose, filled the planet with sound and splendour, then faded to dream-stuff and passed away; the Greek and the Roman followed, and made a vast noise, and they are gone; other peoples have sprung up and held their torch high for a time, but it burned out, and they sit in twilight now, and have vanished. The Jew saw them all, beat them all, and is now what he always was, exhibiting no decadence, no infirmities of age, no weakening of his parts, no slowing of his energies, no dulling of his alert and aggressive mind. What is the secret of his immortality?

There is, of course, a simple answer to this secret mentioned by Twain. Both the intelligence and immortality of the Jew came directly from God's hand, not as a reward for any personal or corporate merit of the Jew, but because of the divine plan that called for the nations of the world to be blessed through Israel.

It is a curious irony that Israel, the subject of scorn and abuse by so many Third World countries, possesses the key to many of their most pressing problems. Not even big countries have been able to supply the kind of know-how that has solved the agricultural and water management problems as Israel has. In one generation, Israel has increased its agricultural production twelvefold, six times more than the rosiest prognosis for similar semiarid zones. It has become a leader in developing such sparsely populated zones, both in water management and plant genetics, and is in the forefront of dairy-cow breeding and milk production, as well as cotton growing.

Many countries see Israel as a model to copy, an inspiration, a natural laboratory, because they have a semiarid area without enough arable land or water, and this is the predicament of most developing countries.

The technical achievements, a few of which are mentioned here, are examples of how the world has been "blessed" through the Jews.

METHANE GAS PRODUCTION

At Kibbutz Zikkim, located on the Mediterranean coast between Ashkelon and Gaza, a cheap source of energy has been found in cow manure. The farm collective has opened a modern plant for converting cow manure into combustible methane gas. The plant processes three tons of waste each day—enough to make the kibbutz independent of other sources of fuel. A side benefit of the process is that it also produces fertilizers and soil conditioners that can be used on the kibbutz or sold commercially.

GREENHOUSE TECHNOLOGY

Scientists at the Sde Boker campus of Ben Gurion University have developed an energy-saving greenhouse that keeps hot during winter nights without the use of electric or gas heaters. The greenhouse is covered by narrow channels containing a specially developed pale gray dye that absorbs the sun's heat rays while allowing the light energy necessary for photosynthesis to reach the plants within. The dye is pumped into a storage tank once it has been heated to 92 degrees Fahrenheit. At night, it is returned to the greenhouse roof to heat the air within. The channels containing the dye are sandwiched between two thin sheets of plastic. Added cost is 20 percent more than conventional glass greenhouse materials, but the extra expense is paid for in six months by the savings on fuel. Because the greenhouse does not require ventilation, it can be sealed from the outside. This allows for the introduction of carbon dioxide into the atmosphere, which boosts the yield of the plants.

SUGARCANE ENERGY

Dr. Menachem Zur, director of the Department of Introduction of Agriculture Research Organization, has been working since 1977 to exploit Israel's ideal conditions for sugarcane cultivation as an energy source. Sugarcane produces sucrose, which can be converted easily into ethanol, an alcoholic fuel.

By 1983, three million cars in Brazil were powered by commerically produced ethanol, produced from sugarcane at a yield of 1,600 to 2,400 liters per acre. Israel's sugarcane yields as much as 4,000 to 6,000 liters per acre, nearly three times as much as Brazil's product, even though Brazil has been committed for much longer to ethanol production.

High performance ethanol can power a vehicle 20 percent farther than gasoline for an equivalent quantity of high octane gasoline. Furthermore, sugarcane is a replenishable product while gasoline, a fossil fuel product, is not. Cost of ethanol production also compares favorably with gasoline. It costs $1,250.00 to produce an acre of sugarcane. Given an average of 5,000 liters of ethanol per acre, the cost per liter is about 25 cents per liter (or $1.10 per American gallon). In Israel today, the cost of a liter of gasoline is about $3.00 American.

SOLAR ENERGY

Enough sunlight falls on the earth every fifteen minutes to supply its energy needs for one full year. The problem is in harnessing the power. Israel, which has 250 to 315 sunny days a year, has been a world leader in solar-related research.

Dr. Yirmiyahu Branover has developed a system to provide electric power at one-half the cost of conventional electricity by liquid metal heated by the sun through a large magnetic field. The liquid metal, such as sodium potassium alloy, is heated rapidly by being circulated through a solar collector. It is then mixed with droplets of a volatile liquid. The droplets heat up, vaporize, and expand, driving liquid metal at a high velocity through a metal pipe surrounded by a high-intensity magnet. This interaction generates an electric field and the current produced is picked up by electrodes on either side of the pipe. The mixture then flows into a separator for recycling, the liquid metal running to the solar collector and the vapor condensed in a tank to produce hot water, which can be used in the home or factory.

The benefits are many. The system can be used with relatively low heat source, even geothermal, it provides maximum use of the industrial waste heat, it does not pollute the atmosphere in any way, it can be built to any size or specifications, it needs no outside energy source to set it in motion, and it has no moving parts.

PLASTIC SHEETING

Israeli scientists have made two rather amazing advances in the plastic sheeting used by farmers in their fields and hothouses. One discovery increased the heat trapped under the plastic by 50 percent. The other allows the sheeting to dry up and disappear when it is no longer needed.

Researchers at Weizmann Institute of Science at Rehovot have found that by the simple expedient of adding salt to polyethylene sheeting, 50 percent more heat is retained, thus cutting heating costs at night and providing for faster growth of crops. The new material, called Infrasol-266, was invented by Professor David Vofsi and Dr. Yael Allinghan in research at Weizmann, sponsored by the petrochemical industry. Kibbutz Ginegar is developing and commercializing the material with cooperation of the Ministry of Agriculture.

Meanwhile, scientists Dan Gilead of Kibbutz Hazorea and Professor Gerald Scott of the Aston Institute of Birmingham, England, have developed a plastic sheeting which is photo-degradable, that is, it disintegrates in sunlight. The material, called Plastor, has a stabilizing element that can be timed to hold the sheeting together for anywhere from one to seven months. At the end of its planned life, the plastic flakes into dust and eventually dissolves into harmless water vapor and carbon dioxide. This kind of sheeting spares the farmers the nasty problem of plastic clogging their harvesting equipment and littering the landscape.

ROBOTICS

Robotics is still an infant science in Israel, but experts here say that robots will soon increase in production and use in Israel. About a dozen companies in Israel are already engaged in planning and developing robots. Their tasks will include the picking and packaging of agricultural products, including Israel's Jaffa oranges, welding, driving tractors and other farm tasks, polishing gems, manufacturing machine tools, sewing shoes and clothing, and assembling automobiles.

Arie Lavie, chief scientist at the Ministry of Industry and Commerce, sees a big future for robots in Israel, predicting that their addition to the labor force will not affect employment. Israel is moving rapidly into more high-tech and computer-based industries, and a compact, super-efficient Israeli-made computer is already selling well abroad.

Lavie and Israel's bent toward modern techology will be accelerated with the opening of branches of two international associations in Israel, CASA-Computers and Automated Systems Association, and SME, the Society of Manufacturing Engineers.

AUTO SPEED GOVERNOR

An Israeli-invented speed governor for cars that doubles as an antitheft device made its international debut at Frankfurt's Auto Mechanica trade fair in September 1983. The ingenious device, about the size of a small transistor radio, can be set at any speed by flicking some switches in a certain combination. It can be used also as a fuel-saving device and to assure drivers that they won't exceed speed limits on roads if they set the maximum permissible speed on the regulator. The regulator can be used to thwart thefts by setting the speed to nearly zero when leaving the car parked. Unlike other speed-governing devices, such as cruise control used on many American cars, this one requires constant foot pressure on the gas pedal. This, say safety experts, keeps drivers more alert than when the foot is not required to be on the accelerator to keep the car moving at a given speed.

AGRICULTURAL FOOD PRODUCTION

Israelis are highly optimistic about their future on the agricultural front. Their degree of plenty in agricultural surpluses have created a healthy kind of problem for them. Approximately 50 percent of the Egyptian population is still living on the land but producing only about 30 percent of their food requirements. By contrast, Israel has about 6 percent of its population on the farms but they are producing more than 100 percent of the food requirements of their population.

KIBBUTZIM PRODUCTIVITY

The record of productivity in kibbutzim is considerably better than one finds in both public and private enterprises. A worker in a kibbutz industrial plant produces 20 percent more than his counterpart in other sectors of the economy. He produces goods to the value of $63,000 annually compared with $51,000 by a worker in other sectors. The reasons for this disparity are found in the fact that the kibbutzim have more modern equipment and due to the absence of strikes in kibbutz-owned plants. In the year 1982, the Israeli economy lost more than 1.8 million work days due to strikes in both public and private companies. According to Israeli press reports, all of the country's kibbutzim together account for no more than 3 percent of the population. And yet they produce about 45 percent of all agricultural products and nearly 6 percent of all industrial goods.

ORGANIC CHEMICAL PRODUCTION

Scientists at the National Oceanographic and Weizmann Institutes have discovered rare single-cell organisms living in brackish ponds along the Dead Sea that convert solar energy into three valuable industrial products: glycerol, used as an industrial solvent and plasticizer; beta-carotene, a natural food color; and a residue of high protein feed for animals, all at minimal cost. Koor Foodstuffs, Ltd., is now building large shallow ponds for growing the unique rosy algae cells near Elat. The company will be raising, harvesting, and marketing the algae products, from makeup to medicine. Meanwhile, in their labs, Professor Mordhay Avron and Dr. Ami Ben-Amotz continue to conduct research into the best condition for growing the profitable cells, each cell able to reproduce once each day. The scientists theorize that such algae may be raised in any arid zone where brackish water is found, turning otherwise unusable land into highly economical algae farms.

BACTERIA CULTIVATION

Agricultural researchers at Hebrew University have developed a method of using bacteria to increase grain crop yields and reduce the need for high cost nitrogen fertilizer. The Axospirillum bacteria fix nitrogen while attached to grain roots, and in turn the bacteria are nourished by secretions from the roots. The advantages are: it saves energy, lessens the degree of pollution of ground water by nitrogenous wastes, requires a smaller outlay for equipment, is cheaper than nitrogen, is locally available, and actually increases the dry weight of the grain by 10 to 15 percent with increased nitrogen content.

IRRIGATION METHODS

British irrigation experts, sent to Palestine at the time of the Mandate, declared after detailed study that no form of irrigation could be successful, except at such cost as to make agriculture prohibitively expensive. One look at today's lush, green fields is enough to make them drink their words. The Negev Desert and the Arabah are blooming with flowers and exotic fruits and vegetables. Their crops are exported to Europe and other countries, as Israel has taken the worldwide lead in the development of irrigation methods.

Israel invented the system of drip irrigation that revolutionized agriculture in arid areas all over the world. The system consists of dripping water through a perforated pipe to reach the roots of the plant. It was drip irrigation that made the Arabah region cultivable, after experts had predicted it would never be fertile.

Today Israel uses 95 percent of its available water resources, which means that if there is a drought in one year, several years of good rainfall are needed to make up the loss.

New irrigation systems to conserve water have also been pioneered in Israel, especially the computerized control method developed by

Motorola Israel, a subsidiary of the American Motorola company. These systems led to a 23 percent increase in crop yields per unit of water from 1965 to 1970, and another 35 percent increase in 1978, a total increase of nearly 50 percent in thirteen years. Israeli water technology has been exported to more than twenty foreign countries.

COMPUTERIZED GARDENING

Now anyone can have a green thumb, as long as his thumb can operate the switch of a pocket-sized computer. Michzur Ltd. of Kfar Givton is marketing a computer-controlled home gardening system that promises dramatic results for even the least experienced gardener, and even for those who don't like to sweat or to get their hands dirty. The system is based on a computer-regulated flow of water and liquid fertilizers carried through plastic drip-lines to plants either in the ground or bedded on the roof or patio in troughs of special absorbent volcanic pebbles. Developer Noam Blum says that the system brings about spectacular growth in everything from fuchsias to fruit trees, and that the computer regulation means no waste in water or fertilizer. Prices for the system begin as low as $700. Blum's method has proved successful in Israel and he has his eye on the export market.

NONALCOHOLIC WINE

It looks like wine, tastes like wine, smells like wine, is grown on a vine, and gives every sign of being wine—but it isn't. It is a new nonalcoholic drink that was developed by Tel Aviv University Authority for Applied Research and Industrial Development. The spiritless wine is expected to be welcomed by those who must restrict their alcoholic intake for health or religious reasons. The wine comes in dry and semisweet varieties and is produced by a completely organic but nonalcoholic fermentation process. It is made from a hitherto unused grape by-product and a fermenting agent, after which it is filtered, pasteurized, and bottled. Because it requires no aging and few man-hours to produce, the product costs about one-fourth of the cost of ordinary wine.

INSTANT YOGURT

Professor Moshe Trop, a scientist at Ben-Gurion University's Research and Development Authority, has come up with some startling innovations for one of man's oldest foods, yogurt. He has developed an instant yogurt for drinking and freezing in powder form. Just add milk (or powdered milk and water) and in a few moments you have a delicious treat. He has also created a thicker powdered yogurt for eating, which takes forty minutes to set. The new product has the same taste, texture, and bacterial culture as regular yogurt, but has more protein, is nonallergenic, and can stand repeated freezing and thawing better than natural yogurt. Dr. Trop also believes his powerhouse powder will make yogurt cheaper to produce.

SALT-WATER FISH CULTIVATION

Ten years of intensive scientific work ended recently with the successful domestication of an edible salt-water fish that can be raised in salt-water ponds in the Arabah or in huge cages anchored off Elat. The director-general of the Oceanographic Research Institute in Haifa said that the fish, which is very tasty and in high demand in Europe, brings $16 to $18 a kilogram and is the first salt-water variety to be domesticated. Known as the "dennis," the fish is native to Bardawil lagoon off the Sinai, and breeds rapidly in captivity.

COMMUNICATION WITH THE DEAF

A machine that makes it possible to communicate with the deaf and blind even though the user doesn't know Braille was demonstrated at Ramat Gan for the first time. It was developed by David Abrahamoff, a yeshiva student. The computerized machine consists of a light-weight miniature typewriter keyboard and a box on which the deaf and blind user places a fingertip. The person who wants to communicate with him presses one of the typewriter keys, which causes the proper Braille letter to rise under the deaf and blind person's finger. This one-letter-at-a-time system is very slow, but it is a great improvement over standard Braille typewriters.

LASER SURGERY

A version of the YAG lazer system, used in eye surgery, was developed by Laser Industries in Israel. The miniaturized device, which sells for about $25,000 enables the eye surgeon to perform certain repairs to the retina of the eye by aiming the lazer beam through the pupil.

EAR SURGERY

One form of deafness can now be relieved because of the work of Professor Ya-acov Sadeh, at the Nose and Throat Department of Meir Hospital. His work provides a solution to those who are deaf because of the destruction of the stirrup, one of the small bones in the middle ear. Successful surgery on these people can restore their hearing. The procedure replaces the destroyed or malfunctioning stirrup with one made of an artificial material, which the body does not reject.

RELIEF FOR EPILEPTICS

A new delivery system for one of the most effective anti-epileptic drugs, valporic acid, has been perfected at the Hebrew University. Despite its great effectiveness, valporic acid was seldom used in the past since it had to be given three times a day, and stable plasma levels were not always maintained. The new delivery system will allow one pill a day to be slowly released throughout a twenty-four-hour period, which will eliminate the peaks and valleys in serum levels resulting from multiple doses.

ELECTROCARDIOGRAPH DEVELOPMENT

A new electrocardiograph, 100 to 500 times more sensitive than the conventional EKG, was invented by a Tel Aviv University physician and a computer engineer, giving physicians a powerful weapon to detect potential heart attacks in seemingly healthy patients.

The new device, designed to diagnose heart defects that would go undetected by ordinary EKGs, was developed by Professor Yoram

Lass, vice-dean of Tel Aviv University's Sackler Faculty of Medicine, and Gideon David, a computer engineer from the Ligad Company in Ramat Gan. The inventors report that their EKG may be added to any conventional EKG recorder at a relatively low cost.

PREGNANCY TEST

A pregnancy detection kit developed by the Teva pharmaceutical firm is reported to be the quickest and most accurate in the world. The company was producing nearly a million kits in 1983 with much of its production going to the United States. The device gives a color indication. If the liquid turns blue, the woman is pregnant, and if it remains white, she is not. The test is not affected by sunlight, temperature variations, vibrations, or other external factors.

ARTIFICIAL KIDNEY

The world's smallest artificial kidney device was developed by Ramot Plastics Ltd., a subsidiary of Tel Aviv University's Applied Research Authority. The device offers two distinct advantages to kidney dialysis patients, who are normally dependent on hospitals for treatment. The briefcase-sized device is portable and, unlike other dialysis machines, this one runs on tap water.

Currently being tested in Israeli hospitals, the artificial kidney features a computerized control system and a unique reverse osmosis purification system that filters everything from salts to bacteria. Although not yet on the market, the device has already won international recognition as a major technological innovation. The device was developed by a team headed by Dr. Moshe Frommer.

BIOFEEDBACK MONITOR

An energetic Israeli, trained in the United States, has developed a computerized biofeedback monitor that promises to net his company $1 million in exports annually. Dan Atlas, of Atlas Researchers, produces devices that are attached by electrodes to the periphery of a wound or incision and, by subtle measurement, can determine the healing process going on without removing surgical dressings. The monitors can also measure the effectiveness of physical therapy for sufferers of migraine headaches, epilepsy, speech problems, and a wide range of muscular disorders. Atlas' products have been approved by the USDA for sale and use in America.

MOSQUITO CONTROL

The mosquito, though just an annoying pest in America, in many parts of the world is a deadly disease carrier. Their bites can spread malaria, yellow fever, dengue fever, and encephalitis. When synthetic pesticides, such as DDT, were first introduced in the 1940s they were very effective on the insect and were considered harmless to other forms of life. It is well known today that these strong chemicals are not only harmful to the environment, but they have actually caused stronger strains of the insects to produce, some of which are so resistant to other insecticides that malaria and other diseases are on the increase around the world.

A solution to the problem may have been produced by an Israeli biologist, Joel Margalit, who isolated a bacillus in a pool of stagnant water in the Negev desert in 1977. The tiny bacillus, Thuringiesis Israelensis, produces a crystalline protein substance during spore formation that acts as a poison to the mosquito larvae by paralyzing their digestive systems soon after they eat the bacteria. Dr. Margalit has now succeeded in producing the protein substance in powdered form with a shelf life of at least one year. Because the bacillus seems to harm no other form of animal life, is easily shipped and applied in powdered form, and is comparable in cost to other insecticide production, it is expected to yield far-reaching benefits to the entire world.

47

TEMPLE MOUNT

Twice in the Bible a place called Moriah is mentioned. In Genesis 22, Abraham was told by God to go to the land of Moriah and there to sacrifice his son. In the description of the building of the Temple by Solomon in 2 Chronicles 3:1, we are told that it was on "mount Moriah, where the Lord appeared unto David his father, . . . in the threshing floor of Ornan the Jebusite."

Solomon's Temple stood for just under 400 years until it was destroyed by the Babylonians in 586 B.C. When some of the exiles were allowed to return to the city, the temple was rebuilt. The second one was a pretty dingy affair, but it lasted longer than Solomon's, until it was completely renovated and expanded by Herod the Great and his successors in the time of Jesus. The final touches were put on only seven years before it was destroyed by Titus in A.D. 70. From that time until this, no Jewish temple has stood on that spot. There were attempts to rebuild—one only a generation after it was destroyed and one under the Emperor Julian in the middle of the fourth century—but no attempt ever succeeded.

In the seventh century, the caliph Omar built a wooden mosque on the mount, and this was subsequently expanded to the beautiful building that stands there today, still called the Mosque of Omar or the Dome of the Rock because of the large protruding piece of bedrock that is its central feature. Except for a century interlude, when Jerusalem was in the hands of the crusaders and the mosque became a church, the Temple Mount with its mosque has remained under control of Muslims. It is a holy site of Islam, although the degree of this holiness has been much played up by Muslims for political reasons since 1967. At the hour of prayer, each Muslim on the Mount demonstrates dramatically what is truly important to him by turning his back on the mosques next to him to face south toward Mecca as he prays.

On June 7, 1967, the Temple Mount came under Jewish control for the first time in 1,897 years. In actual fact, Israeli authorities are only responsible for maintaining public order on the thirty-acre site on the eastern edge of the Old City. Under the arrangements whereby the status quo was to be maintained in all holy places, oversight at the Mount remains the prerogative of Muslim authorities. For their part, the Israelis maintain a small police station near the Mosque of Omar.

Right from the start of Israeli control over Jerusalem and Mount Moriah, it was evident that there would be much tension and disagreement over the question of whether or not Israelis would be allowed to go up onto the Mount to conduct their prayer services. Two months after the reunification of Jerusalem, the question was tested practically. The occasion was the ninth day of the Hebrew month of Av, which that year fell in mid-August. It was on the ninth of Av that both the First and the Second Temple had been destroyed. It was on that same day that the Bar Kochba revolt had finally been put down, leading to a Roman ban on Jews entering Jerusalem. Only on one day, the ninth of Av, were they allowed to come into the city to pray and weep at the western retaining wall of the temple compound. Ever since, that day has been a day of fasting for Jews, a day when the Book of Lamentations is read by all with loud mourning. There could be no more appropriate day for a prayer service on the Temple Mount than the ninth of Av.

But there was a serious difficulty. According to Jewish law, all human beings are unclean and in need of ritual cleansing. Since no Jew was permitted to ascend to the Temple Mount until he had undergone the appropriate purification, many had ruled that prayers could not be conducted by Jews until such a time as a bona fide prophet would appear and sort things out. Not everyone agreed completely with this view, however, and among these was the then chief rabbi of the Israeli army, Shlomo Goren, later to become chief rabbi of Israel. On the afternoon of the ninth of Av 1967, Goren and some fifty followers prayed on the Temple Mount. Goren, an amateur archaeologist and historian, claimed to have determined that certain areas were definitely not part of the temple area in the first century and that to pray in these areas was permitted. He was criticized by both his military and religious superiors. One week later, signs were posted at all entrances reading, "Notice and Warning. Entrance to the area of the Temple Mount is forbidden to everyone by Jewish law, owing to the sacredness of the place. The Chief Rabbinate of Israel." According to the expanded interpretation of this ruling, it was even forbidden to fly over the area, since its holiness extends to the heavens.

But this was not the end of the story. Far from it! Over the years that have intervened, many groups of Jews have attempted to hold prayer meetings on the Temple Mount. On a few occasions they have succeeded. More frequently, they have been stopped in midservice or simply refused entrance to the compound. After one such attempt, eight young men were taken to court for disturbing the peace by trying to pray. In the ruling, delivered in January 1976, the judges declared that Jews are legally allowed to pray on the Temple Mount. The youths were acquitted. However, five months later, that acquittal was overturned by the Jerusalem District Court. This court was not willing to take a clear stand on the question of the legality of Jewish prayers on the Mount, but it did say that public order should take precedence over that right.

But the question of small groups praying on the Temple Mount was only a minor matter compared to the desire of many Jews to see the temple itself rebuilt on the spot where it once stood, where now two mosques stand. Mainstream Orthodox Judaism has never relinquished the hope that someday the Messiah will appear and rebuild the temple, and some people are doing what they can to prepare for the big event. Ancient sources such as the Bible, the Talmud, descriptions of contemporary historians, and even coins that have been dug up can all aid in arriving at the proper building dimensions and floor plans. In fact, the visitor to Jerusalem today can see an impressive scale model of the Second Temple designed from these very sources along with some archaeological discoveries. But Jewish tradition says that the actual groundbreaking will have to be done under the supervision of an authentic prophet. It is pointed out that David mistakenly tried to start work on the First Temple without proper prophetic guidance, and this mistake must not be repeated.

One small Jewish seminary (yeshiva) inside the Old City not far from the Temple Mount is dedicated to the study of those things that the priests will need to know when the temple is rebuilt. The fruit of their research includes such things as detailed descriptions of the step-by-step movements to be taken by the High Priest on the Day of Atonement. Scattered around Jerusalem are several small workshops where religious artisans are at work faithfully crafting many of the articles that would be required in the daily service of the rebuilt temple. One dedicated weaver, for example, has been working for years weaving the special linen that would go into the clothing of the priests. It cannot be just any linen but must be made according to the strict dictates of traditional sources.

We cannot resist at this point recalling a persistent rumor that tells of some Christians busy quarrying and labelling stone somewhere in Indiana or Arizona for a kind of prefabricated temple. If such a thing does exist, they are wasting their time. No stone but that quarried locally in Jerusalem would be acceptable.

Of course, if the temple is to be reconstructed, one obvious difficulty is that its place is presently occupied by two mosques. There can be no suggestion that the temple would be built anywhere else than on that expanded hill to the east of the Western Wall, so what about the mosques? Some have thought that they will be brought down by some act of God, such as an earthquake or a stray Arab rocket in time of war. But wherever an act of God can be conceived, there will always be someone who feels called to be God's instrument.

Since the Israeli takeover of Jerusalem in 1967, there have been several attempts by such misguided fringe elements to hasten the coming of the end by destroying the Mosques of Omar and al-Aqsa. The first of these happened on August 23, 1969, when an Australian "Christian" tourist named Dennis Michael Rohan entered the Temple Mount carrying two cans of kerosene. He succeeded in dousing an area of the southern al-Aqsa mosque and setting it alight before he was caught. Damage to the mosque was extensive, and tensions between Arabs and Israelis reached new heights. Many Arabs were convinced that Rohan was nothing more than an Israeli agent. In court, however, Rohan declared himself to be a member of the "Church of God," acting as the Lord's agent in accordance with a biblical prophecy. In the end the court decided that he was insane and shipped him back to Australia.

The early 1980s have seen several such attempts, and these all by Jews. On Good Friday, 1982, an immigrant from the United States tried to take the temple area by storm. Alan Harry Goodman was serving in the Israeli army and so was carrying his rifle when he entered the Mosque of Omar and began shooting. Before he was finished, Goodman had killed one and wounded three. At his trial he explained that he was "liberating the spot holy to the Jews," and that for this action he was expected to become "the King of the Jews." He was subsequently convicted and sentenced to prison terms of life plus two twenty-year terms.

Some three months later, the police arrested Joel Lerner, one of the lieutenants of Rabbi Meir Kahane. In the legal proceedings that followed, it was determined that Lerner, who had already served a prison sentence for plotting to overthrow the government and replace it with one based on religious law, had been planning to blow up the Mosque of Omar. He was sent away again, this time for two and a half years. In March 1983 the police caught four armed young men attempting to break into the Temple Mount through an underground passage. This led to the immediate arrest of some forty others at the apartment of a rabbi, himself a member of Meir Kahane's election list. A search of the apartment uncovered weapons and diagrams of the Temple Mount.

On a rainy night in January 1984 one of the Muslim guards on the Mount heard some strange noises and went to investigate. Several times he called out, "Who's there?" in Arabic, but no one answered. It was four Jews, who were carrying out what they considered to be divine instructions to destroy the mosques. They had been living in a kind of commune in an abandoned village just outside of Jerusalem. They called their leader, "the most high," and considered themselves to be charged by God to carry out a "redemptive act" by liberating the holy mount from its domination by foreigners. On the day before the planned attack, they prayed together that as a final confirmation of God's approval of their plan he would cause it to rain to cover the sound of their movements. The next night it poured. But when they were accosted by the guard, they fled, leaving behind a grenade and other weapons. These subsequently led to their arrest. One of them managed to escape and leave the country, and the others were put on trial. Their statements to the court were replete with quotations from the Bible, and in the end they too were declared to be insane.

In April 1984, Israel was rocked by the arrest of some twenty young orthodox Jews who were accused of belonging to a terrorist underground that was planning acts of reprisal against Arabs. Indeed, it was alleged, they had already been successful in several such attacks. The immediate event leading to their arrest was the sabotaging of a number of Arab buses. Police had been watching some of the men for some time as they gathered evidence against them, but now they moved in so as to prevent the disaster that would surely occur if the buses were blown up. In the unfolding events of the weeks that followed, it came to light that this Jewish underground had also made elaborate preparation for blowing up the Temple Mount mosques. Using explosive material from fifty old Syrian mines they had found, they had constructed a number of bombs that were being held ready for use against the mosques. They had actually begun to think about the action some four years earlier, seeing their action as a way of "purifying the Temple Mount from Muslim possession, in order to bring about the redemption of Israel and the establishment of the promised Kingdom of Israel."

While their preparations were careful, they had not yet carried out the attack because they had not yet been able to come to agreement on the best method to use. They had succeeded in obtaining detailed aerial photographs of the Mount and had even weighed the options of bombing the Mosque of Omar from the air. One of their members, an Israeli Air Force pilot, reportedly advised them that such a raid would likely endanger the Western Wall, so that idea was shelved. Later, using the explosive devices they had made, they actually made test explosions. The plan that was developing was a direct assault on the Mount, using silencers on their Uzi submachine guns. When it was found that silencers did not work well on that model, they obtained tear gas for the purpose of overcoming the Muslim guards around the mosque.

One aspect of the whole Temple Mount rebuilding question that repeatedly appears in the Israeli press is the rumored connection of certain Christian fundamentalists in the financial backing of various Israeli groups pushing for the rebuilding. These groups, including the Faithful of the Temple Mount and the Temple Mount Foundation, are small and unimportant in Israel. To the degree that Israelis even know about them, they are considered weird and marginal. The former has been behind numerous attempts to conduct prayers on the Mount, and the latter was founded by a man who was once jailed for complicity in the murder of a U.N. diplomat. The other five members of the board of directors of the Foundation are American fundamentalists.

One of the main objectives of these groups seems to be to get Israelis excited about the idea of rebuilding the temple, because it must be stated frankly that most Israelis are quite uninterested. Neither of these organizations, it should be noted, endorses violence as a valid means of achieving their end, although certain media articles have appeared both in Israel and in the United States, attempting to connect the Foundation indirectly with one or the other of the groups most recently trying to blow up the Muslim shrines.

A CHRONOLOGY

June 1967—Mordecai Gur, mounted on a half-track, takes the Temple Mount on the third day of the Six-Day War.

June 28, 1967—Prime Minister Levi Eshkol meets Muslim and Christian leaders from both sides of the prewar border and pledges free access to all holy places and the government's intention to place the internal administration for the holy places in the hands of the respective religious leaders. The same day the barriers come down between East and West Jerusalem.

August 1, 1967—Jerusalem police take on the maintenance of public order at the holy places in the Old City at the request of Muslim and Christian authorities, who complained of unseemly behavior by visitors at the Church of the Holy Sepulchre and in the Harim-e-Sharif compound.

August 14, 1967—A committee headed by Minister for Religious Affairs Zerah Warhaftig is given cabinet responsibility for holy places in Jerusalem and the West Bank.

August 15, 1967—IDF Chief Chaplain Aluf Shlomo Goren and fifty followers, including other army chaplains, hold a *mincha* service on the Temple Mount. Goren contends that some parts of the compound are not part of the Temple Mount and therefore the halachic ban against Jews stepping on the Temple Mount until the temple is rebuilt does not apply. He says his conclusions were reached after measurements based on Josephus and archaeological evidence. He also declares that the Rock is not the site of the Holy of Holies.

August 22, 1967—The chief rabbinate puts up signs outside the compound noting the halachic ban on visiting the Temple Mount area.

July 15, 1968—The president of the Muslim Court of Appeals turns down a request by an American Masonic Temple order, who asked for permission to build a $100 million "Solomon's Temple" on the Temple Mount.

December 19, 1968—Hanukkah prayers by a group of nationalist Jews are held on the Mount.

August 21, 1969—A fire at the al-Aqsa guts the southeastern wing. Brigades from West and East Jerusalem fight the blaze together for four hours while an angry Muslim crowd chants, "Down with Israel."

August 23, 1969—A non-Jewish Australian tourist, Dennis Michael Rohan, identifying himself as a member of the "Church of God," is arrested as a suspect in the arson.

August 27, 1969—Rohan tells the court he acted as "the Lord's emissary" in accordance with biblical prophecy. The Temple Mount is closed to non-Muslims for two months.

December 30, 1969—The Court convicts Rohan but declares him not criminally liable by reason of insanity.

January 1, 1976—Magistrate Court Judge Ruth Or rules that Jews are permitted to pray on the Temple Mount, as she acquits eight youths accused of disturbing public order by holding prayers at the site against police orders.

March 17, 1976—Security forces use tear gas in the Old City and troops quell riots in West Bank towns. Curfews are imposed due to violent demonstrations against Or's decision.

July 1, 1976—Magistrate Or's ruling overturned by Jerusalem District Court. The court rules that eight Betar youths who attempted to pray "demonstratively" on the Temple Mount were guilty of behavior "likely to cause a breach of the peace." The court also rules that Jews have an "unquestionable historical and legal right" to pray on the Temple Mount, but these rights could not be exercised until the authorities had adopted regulations fixing the time and place for such prayers. Such regulations were necessary, said the court, in order to maintain public order. The court noted that the Religious Affairs ministry had "good reason" for not yet setting the rules.

August 14, 1979—Rumors that followers of Meir Kahane and yeshiva students would attempt Temple Mount prayers cause a general West Bank strike and bring 2,000 Arab youths with staves and rocks to the compound. They disperse after police intervention.

August 10, 1981—Religious Affairs Ministry workers are found digging a tunnel under the Temple Mount. The work began secretly a month earlier when water began leaking from a cistern under the Temple Mount and had to be drained. Chief Rabbi Shlomo Goren closes the dig because of the issue's sensitivity.

September 2, 1981—Jews and Arabs clash with stones and fists in a tunnel north of the Western Wall. The Arabs had attempted to seal the cistern. A group of yeshiva students, under orders from Rabbi Meir Yehuda Getz, rabbi of the Western Wall, knocked down the wall. The two groups were separated by police after a scuffle. The next day the cistern was sealed. Goren is quoted as saying that the cistern was a tunnel that could lead to temple treasures, "including the lost Ark."

September 4, 1981—A strike called by the Supreme Muslim Council closes shops and schools in East Jerusalem to protest against excavations under the Temple Mount.

September 10, 1981—The Wakf (Muslim council) seals the cistern from the other side to prevent Jewish penetration. Meanwhile archaeologist Dan Bahat discounts theories that the cistern was connected to the temple.

April 11, 1982—Israeli soldier Alan Harry Goodman, a U.S. immigrant, goes on a shooting rampage on the Temple Mount, killing one and wounding three. The incident sets off a week of rioting and strikes in Jerusalem, the West Bank, and Gaza, and angry reaction against Israel internationally. At his trial, Goodman told the court that by "liberating the spot holy to the Jews," he expected to become the "King of the Jews." A year after the incident, Goodman was convicted and sentenced to life, plus two terms of twenty years.

July 25, 1982—Kach activist Yoel Lerner is arrested under an administrative detention order signed by Defense Minister Ariel Sharon for allegedly planning to sabotage one of the mosques on the Temple Mount.

October 26, 1982—Lerner is convicted of planning to blow up the Dome of the Rock. He had previously served a three-year sentence for heading a group that plotted to overthrow the government and establish a state based on religious law. He was sentenced to two and a half years in prison. Police arrest more than forty people suspected of planning to penetrate the Temple Mount. Police had found four armed youths trying to break into the underground passage known as King Solomon's Stables.

March 24, 1983—A request to revive the ancient sacrifice of a lamb on the Temple Mount on Passah Eve (Easter) is made by the Faithful of the Temple Mount group in letters to Prime Minister Menachem Begin.

September 17, 1983 (Yom Kippur)—Police try to prevent former Chief Rabbi Shlomo Goren from holding prayers in a room beneath the Temple Mount. Police then relent, allowing the Yom Kippur prayer to take place.

TEMPLE MOUNT

January 1986—Several members of the Knesset Interior Committee decide to visit the Temple Mount to investigate rumors that illegal building has been taking place in Solomon's Stables below the surface and that perhaps this is also being used for storage of weapons. Several other Knesset members, from some right-wing opposition factions, decide to go along, even though they are not members of the committee. These had long campaigned for the assertion of Jewish sovereignty over the Temple Mount and saw this as an opportunity for making political hay. They invite photographers to come along to record the visit of Knesset members to the Mount. The Muslim authorities had not objected to the visit and welcome the group at the entrance to the Mount. However, when they see the photographers, accompanied also by other individuals who had long records as troublemakers where the Temple Mount was concerned, they demand that only the Knesset members proceed with the visit. When the right-wing members insist that the entire party be given access, a near riot ensues, and the Israelis have to be escorted out under police guard.

48

THIRD TEMPLE

The Third Temple may be a dream for some people, but for others, many of them non-Jews, the rebuilding of the Jewish temple, on the site now inconveniently occupied by a Muslim shrine, is an imminent reality.

An American sensationalist journal recently claimed that Henry Kissinger and the Mafia were involved in a plot to rebuild the temple on its ancient site. As doubtful as such information may be, there are Christians who long to see the temple rebuilt and they are in contact with Jews in Israel.

Among their main contacts is Stanley Goldfoot, an investment advisor, one-time publisher, and former Lehi member, originally from South Africa. Goldfoot is an activist in *Ne'emanei Har Habayit* (the Faithful of the Temple Mount), a group known primarily for their repeatedly unsuccessful attempts to pray on the Temple Mount.

As Goldfoot points out, many Christian fundamentalists, especially in America, see in Israel the fulfillment of biblical prophecy. They are the real Zionists in the U.S., not the American Jews, he says. These Christians feel that the world is coming closer to a critical period in history and they want to help the Jews to fulfill prophecies and thus hasten the second coming of the Messiah.

It is for this reason that they are so adamant in opposing territorial compromise, such as the Reagan plan, which would give the Arabs control over much of what Israel considers its own lands. Before the redemption of Israel can occur and the Messiah appear, they say, the Jews must hold all the Land of Israel.

But although Goldfoot is happy to accept fundamentalist support, both moral and financial, he does not go so far as to talk of mutual understanding.

"I tell them there is no dialogue," he says. "I make it clear that I can't accept their views, and they can't accept mine. If they're prepared to help us openly, then we're prepared to accept it. The Christians have not yet redeemed themselves for what they have done to the Jews," he adds. "They have a lot to do before we can accept them."

Goldfoot is regularly asked to address evangelical groups visiting Israel. At one session at the Jerusalem Hilton, a group from Santa Ana, California, listened with enthusiasm as Goldfoot told them that they must help Israel carry out the divine plan for that country. He noted that the group had obtained a document from the U.S. Internal Revenue Service, making any donations tax-deductible. Among the institutions that his groups supports, he told them, is *Yeshivat Torat Cohanim,* a school dedicated to the study of the temple ritual, to enable its students to step in whenever the temple is erected.

There are significant, and to some minds, worrisome, links between a handful of American evangelical leaders and right-wing Israelis such as Goldfoot. Some of the personalities on his board are important men. One of them, physicist Lambert Dolphin, heads a key section of the world's most massive research conglomerate, the Stanford Research Institute, a $200-million-a-year concern whose main clients are the U.S. government and corporations such as Bechtel. Board member Terry Risenhoover is received at the Reagan White House, and chaired the 1987 "national prayer breakfast in honor of Israel."

Their real interest, and that of fellow evangelical and fundamentalist preachers and laymen, is the Temple Mount. They believe that Jesus cannot come again until the Temple Mount is restored to the Jews and the temple is rebuilt and destroyed again for the third time. "It was in the Second Temple that Jesus worshiped, taught, and threw out the moneychangers on two occasions. It was in the Temple Court that the Christian Church was born," reads an official Stanford Research Institute International brochure put out by Dolphin.

Goldfoot frequently speaks to groups of evangelicals touring Israel about the importance of the Mount, and has toured America on the evangelical circuit. When he spoke at the Reverend Chuck Smith's Calvary Chapel in Costa Mesa, California, the church's lavish 3,000-seat auditorium was filled to overflowing.

Goldfoot says he plays the tape of his speech every night before going to bed, "just to hear the applause." They loved him there in Costa Mesa, as he recited Jewish prayers that implore the Almighty to "Build thy temple speedily." To the wild applause of the believers, he said, "Jerusalem is not truly liberated yet—its heart is still under alien control.

There is no freedom of worship on the Temple Mount, not for the Jews and not for the Christians."

It is difficult to ascertain just how much money Risenhoover has given Goldfoot. One reliable Christian source told me that the sum far exceeds $50,000.

Risenhoover describes himself as a Southern Baptist, whose ventures include drilling for oil in Israel. He and his colleagues believe that they have been stirred up by God to prepare for the Messiah's return. They quote Revelation 11, saying that a final spiritual battle will take place over the temple site and that Israel and the Church will together triumph. The evil king of the North has transformed himself into the USSR in their eyes. A major war is coming, one that will also involve Egypt, and Damascus may be destroyed. Israel on the millennial maps of the evangelicals includes great chunks of Egypt, Lebanon, and Syria.

The link between this small group of individual evangelicals and Israelis is indicative of a much broader alliance between the reborn Christians and American Jews. The traditional alliance between American Jews and liberal Christians is over, mainly because the liberal churches are seen as anti-Israel, while the conservative evangelicals and fundamentalists are down-the-line pro-Israel.

AIPAC, the Israel lobby in Washington, has taken on a full-time Christian liaison, whose main task is to deal with the conservative Christians. Some major Jewish organizations now devote a great deal of attention to emerging alliance, with hardly a second thought about what it means to team up with the fundamentalist movement.

Dr. Charles Monroe, president of the Jerusalem Temple Foundation in Los Angeles, California, of whom Terry Risenhoover is chairman, explained in a recent letter his biblical reason for supporting Christians cooperating with Jews in the construction of the Third Temple. Monroe writes:

> According to the Holy Scriptures, Gentiles or strangers were involved in the erection of the First Temple in Jerusalem (2 Chronicles 2:17-18). It also seems apparent that strangers who came to Israel for the sake of the name of the Lord were to be privileged to have the temple as a focal point of prayer and worship (1 Kings 8:41-43). Because of these and other pertinent Scriptures, the Jerusalem Temple Foundation, U.S.A., has been established by Bible-believing Christians to make the Church aware of its mandated responsibilities related to Israel, and in

particular the Temple Mount and the preparation for the construction of the Third Temple on Mount Moriah.

Lambert Dolphin, a member of the Jerusalem Temple Foundation who works with the archaeology and science team in the radio physics laboratory at Stanford Research Institute, has devised methods that he claims can survey beneath the surface of the earth without actually excavating. He was trying to make soundings in order to draw an underground contour map of the Temple Mount, believing that it would remove some of the mysteries about the place, to show where the actual Temple stood, and might even locate the Ark of the Covenant, which some think was buried in some of the passageways beneath the Temple Mount. Israeli police, however, asked Dolphin to discontinue his work in the Temple Mount area "for his own protection."

Israeli courts have generally denied the right of Jews to pray on the Temple Mount, but there are signs of change. The fact that the courts in 1983 declared prayer on the Mount to be legal but not yet properly regulated so as to maintain order probably means that someday pressures will cause such rules to be formulated.

In the Old City of Jerusalem a few years ago, a group of young scholars continued their studies about the Messiah's appearance. One of the young scholars, Motti Hacohen, was reported as asking, "What is the sense in asking for the Messiah to come if we are not really ready to meet him?" In this yeshivah, fifteen students studied the Talmud and works of Maimonides dealing with the *Bet Hamikdash*, the Holy Temple. From their studies the students have put together a model replica of the Temple. Almost every student has a framed photo in his room with a rendering of the temple as it might have appeared in its days of glory.

This yeshivah is only a few hundred feet from the Temple Mount, and the roof of their building affords a breathtaking view of the area where it is thought Abraham readied Isaac for the sacrifice. One can see the group where the two ancient Jewish temples stood and where today the Muslim structures stand.

A few years ago, anyone in Israel who talked about rebuilding the temple, or advocated freedom of prayer on the Mount, was considered to be a lunatic. Today, according to a poll published in the newspaper *Haaretz*, 19 percent of the Israeli public believes there should at least be freedom of prayer on the Mount. The chief rabbinate has created a special committee to "prepare a theological, archaeological, and architectural report concerning the location of the Holy of Holies on the Temple Mount," and some members of the committee—Rabbi Dov Lior from Kiryat Arba and Rabbi Mordechai Eliau, the Sephardic chief rabbi—are known to support the building of a synagogue on the Temple Mount. Other committees, studying temple rituals and the preparation of priestly garments and the training of priests, all add to the growing pressure to open the Temple Mount for Jewish worship.

Some of the members of the committees, however, are simply interested in the historical or scientific aspects of the Temple Mount. But many, and the number is growing, are working for a Jewish presence on the Mount and eventually the rebuilding of the temple. Some of these people are highly orthodox and firmly believe that the Messiah will soon arrive. Others are primarily Israeli nationalists, who view Muslim control of the Temple Mount as an insult to the Zionist dream. But, in the end, the religious and nationalistic themes are hard to distinguish from each other, and the effect is the same—Arab control over the Temple Mount is being challenged.

49

WAR

Jesus said there would be "wars and rumors of wars . . . but the end is not yet" (Matthew 24:6). Since that time, many thousands have died attempting to conquer and defend the soil considered sacred to three major world religions—Christianity, Islam, and Judaism.

On May 14, 1948, the British flag was lowered in Tel Aviv for the last time. At 4:00 that afternoon, Israel was declared to be a nation again, amidst the singing of the Jewish National Anthem, the *Hatikvah*. While it was the beginning of the nation, it was also the beginning of a number of wars fought to maintain not only their nationhood but their very territory and lives.

THE WAR OF INDEPENDENCE

The day following their declared independence, Israel was invaded by Egypt, Jordan, Iraq, Syria, and Lebanon. Nearly 45 million Arabs went to war with 64,000 Jews. Britain's Field Marshall Montgomery predicted that it would take the Arabs but eight days to drive the Jews into the sea. Nine months and four days later, Israel had not only survived, but had come out much strengthened, with 23 percent more territory than they had been allotted in the 1947 partition plan.

The Arabs, outnumbering the Jews almost forty to one, had a very simple battle plan. Egypt was to attack from the south with 10,000 men, sweep up the Negev toward Tel Aviv with half the force, and the rest would move toward Jerusalem. Lebanese, Syrian, and Iraqi forces would move down from the north, through Galilee, into Haifa, and on toward Tel Aviv, where they would join up with Egyptian forces. From the East, Jordan would send 10,000 men to occupy the West Bank, capture the Old City of Jerusalem, and lay siege to the new city.

The outcome of the war was probably determined more by the

attitude of the two sides. To the Arabs it was a war of expansion and revenge; for the Jew it was sheer survival, a fact that is known to make people fight harder than for those who are fighting simply to gain more territory.

The Israeli battle plan was much more complex. The first goal was to defend to the utmost every Jewish settlement in the path of the invading armies, a task made difficult by the fact that the Israelis had 10,000 rifles, each with fifty rounds of ammunition, four ancient artillery pieces, and thirty-six submachine guns. The second goal was to piece together a navy to lift the blockade and bring in men, munitions, and immigrants by way of the sea. The next goal was to lift the siege of Jerusalem, and then to turn the tide of battle from defensive to offensive moves.

Each one of these goals was accomplished, perhaps the most dramatic being the rescue of Jerusalem. Since all the roads into Jerusalem were Arab-controlled, several thousand Israeli citizens carved out a road over the limestone hills through which food and weapons were brought in to defend the city. Banners displaying the words of Psalm 137:5 were flying from the vehicles bringing in the supplies and weapons: "If I forget thee, O Jerusalem, let my right hand forget her cunning."

The heaviest fighting occurred between May 15 and June 11, after which time a four-week truce was arranged by the United Nations. During the lull, huge amounts of weapons were purchased from Czechoslovakia, and when fighting began again, Israel inflicted heavy casualities on the Arabs on all fronts. During the next lull, a group of Jewish radicals, calling themselves the Stern Gang, murdered one of the U.N. mediators, Count Bernadotte, causing a great loss of image for the Israelis. Finally, on October 15, the war broke out again, and Israeli troops, by now well supplied, literally threw the Egyptians out.

THE SINAI WAR

In October 1956 Egypt, Syria, and Jordan prepared themselves again to encircle Israel. At the same time, Egypt had seized control of the Suez Canal Company and had occupied all of the Sinai. The British and French, moving against Egypt in retaliation for closing the Suez, made sudden air attacks, knocking out Egyptian air power. Israel seized the moment to launch an attack, overrunning and clearing the Sinai Peninsula, destroying or dispersing about a third of the Egyptian army, and capturing huge quantities of Russian-built equipment. Israel took about 5,600 prisoners and killed somewhere between 2,000 and 3,000 Egyptians while suffering 171 killed and 600 wounded.

The situation in the Middle East at that time became so tense that many feared Armageddon was just around the corner. When Britain and France attacked Egypt, Egypt sank every ship and barge in the Suez Canal in an attempt to close it to western shipping. Russia threatened to come to Egypt's aid and the United States quickly promised to back Britain if Russia did jump in on Egypt's side. By December, however, the U.N. troops were able to restore order and to persuade Israel to pull its troops out of the Sinai, a decision it would later regret.

THE SIX-DAY WAR

All during the early 1960s minor border skirmishes and Arab terrorist attacks came, followed by reprisals by Israel. In 1966, Nasser made a pact with Syria in the event of an Israeli invasion. In 1967, terrorist attacks and Syrian bombardment of Israeli villages in the north continued. In retaliation the Israelis shot down six Syrian MiGs, while continuing their warnings to the Arab nations that Israel might have to take further reprisals if the attacks continued. Nasser began amassing troops in the Sinai, at the same time forcing the U.N. peace-keeping force to withdraw, and threatening this time to completely destroy Israel. Finally, Nasser closed the Straits of Tiran, threatening to blow up any shipping vessel bound for Elat.

When another war with the Arab nations seemed inevitable, Israel decided to seize the advantage. With several lightning air raids, beginning on June 5, Israeli Mirage and Mystere jets succeeded in destroying most of the air power of Egypt, Jordan, Syria, and Iraq before the planes could even get off the ground. Israeli armored columns then cut through the Negev and into the Sinai, overrunning more than 100,000 Egyptian forces stranded there without air cover. In a matter of hours, hundreds of armored vehicles were destroyed or captured.

By June 7, Egyptian resistance in the Sinai had collapsed. In the north, after serious fighting, Nablus and Jericho were captured, and at 8:00 P.M., Israel and Jordan had accepted a cease-fire called for by the United Nations.

For two days, Syrian artillery had been bombarding Israeli villages in Galilee, but the Israeli air force and infantry units by June 9 had overrun the gun implacements. By the next day, Israeli forces were twelve miles into Syria, capturing villages as far north as Kuneitra. A cease-fire was arranged for 4:30 on the afternoon of June 10.

Egyptian losses in both men and equipment were very heavy, although casualty figures were never released by the Egyptian government. Jordanian casualties were listed as 6,094 killed and missing, 762 wounded, and 463 taken prisoner. Israeli losses were given at 679 killed and 2,563 wounded.

THE YOM KIPPUR WAR

Tensions between Israel and the surrounding nations have never been completely tranquil, but in the fall of 1973 the situation became worse. Finally, on a day when they thought Israelis would be least prepared to defend themselves, Egypt from the south and Syria from the north attacked. The assault was planned for 6:00 P.M. on October 6, which was Yom Kippur, a day when Israelis would have been observing a fast—their most holy day of worship. Russian satellite intelligence warned the Syrians that Israel was beginning to expect something and was making preparations, so the attack actually took place four hours earlier than scheduled.

The amassing of troops and armor was said to be the largest since the close of World War II, some 5,000 tanks and more than one million men—838,000 Arabs and 275,000 Jews. Egypt alone was said to have thrown 3,000 tanks, 2,000 heavy guns, and 600,000 men against the Israelis.

Considering just the strength of forces alone, it should have been the annihilation of the State of Israel that followed in the next nineteen days. Being caught so terribly off guard and outnumbered, Golda Meir later confessed, "For the first time in our twenty-five year history, we thought we might have lost."

At one time only a few dozen tanks stood in the way, both in the north and the south, of oncoming Arab forces. But during an unexplained two-day lull in the fighting Israel was able to regroup and, on October 19, a tank battle of unprecedented magnitude took place in the Sinai. When the dust cleared, Israel had won a tremendous victory and began pressing on into Egypt, conquering territory west of the Suez. In the north, Israel began pushing the Syrians back, and by the time a cease-fire was arranged Israeli troops were within twenty miles of Damascus.

During this war Arab casualties were more than 15,000 and Israeli losses were more than 4,000.

WAR IN LEBANON

Over the years, Israel's border areas have always been vulnerable to attack. In the early 1980s there had been numerous rocket and mortar attacks on the section of northern Galilee that bordered on Lebanon. These attacks came primarily from Palestinians who had set up operation in the southern part of Lebanon. In the year prior to June 1982, more than 400 rockets and shells had fallen inside Israel. Even though these had resulted in only two deaths, the Israeli government decided the time had come to clear southern Lebanon of this threat. On June 6, 1980, the Israeli Defense Force launched what they called "Operation Peace for Galilee," with the objective of removing PLO presence from all the areas twenty-five miles north of Israel's border.

This initial objective was reached within a matter of days, but it became quickly evident that, once started, the operation would not stop there. In the areas captured by the Israeli forces dozens of armed caches were found, some small and some large. The arms were usually situated near a mosque, a school, a hospital, or a church so as to deter the Israelis from hitting them with air or rocket attacks for fear that civilians would be injured. The amount of arms captured was staggering, some ten times what even the efficient Israeli intelligence had estimated was in the area. Just in the southern area of Lebanon it took 1,000 men and 150 trucks about five weeks to evacuate the many tons of arms captured. For unknown reasons, the amount of arms captured was overwhelmingly more than the PLO could have needed for its own troops.

The invasion continued on toward Beirut, where the Israelis found themselves engaged in a war of a much longer term than the few weeks the politicians had promised. The PLO had its headquarters in Beirut, and there the Israeli Defense Forces concentrated their attention, including air strikes on PLO headquarters and weapons dumps. Finally, in September 1982, all PLO troops were evacuated from Beirut. Many left the country, but others simply made their way to the north of the country.

Still, Israel was not able to extricate itself from the quagmire of Lebanon. As casualty figures mounted, public support for the operation dwindled. In a poll taken in June 1982, 84 percent felt it was the right action to take, but by the time Israeli troops withdrew in June 1985, 40 percent felt that it had been the wrong step to take, and 75 percent felt the operation had been a failure. Never before in the history of Israel's wars had there been such a wave of antiwar protest. Even numbers of soldiers chose to go to prison rather than participate in the war.

In mid-June 1985 Israel completely withdrew from Lebanon. Even then, there was a declared buffer zone that would continue to be patrolled by Israeli troops to prevent the return of PLO troops. By the time of the withdrawal, more than 650 Israeli soldiers had died. On the day of the final pullback, two shells fell on northern Galilee, and such attacks continued periodically in the months that followed.

50

WATER

Israel takes advantage of 95 percent of its scanty supply of annual renewable water, perhaps the most efficient in the world. It consumes 50 billion cubic feet of water each year, 82 percent for agriculture, and 15 percent for urban and domestic use. Irrigated farmland has jumped from 75,000 acres in 1948 to 425,000 in the 1980s.

One study conducted by Thomas Naff of the University of Pennsylvania's Middle East Research Institute indicates that there could be increasingly tense days ahead for Israel and Jordan because of the problem of water resources. At present rates of growth and consumption, both countries could run out of renewable fresh water in ten years. With Israel's current use of 95 percent of its annual renewable water, the Institute's study concluded that in sixteen years, Israel will fall short by 800 million cubic meters of annual renewable water, about 210 billion gallons.

Jordan will have a deficit at that time of 170 million cubic meters. The water shortage is likely to complicate the political and social problems of these two nations. The problem is so far-reaching that it could lead to increased hostilities, even a war over water. On the other hand, it could force the countries in the region to overcome their differences and begin to cooperate to solve their problem jointly.

The study concentrated on the Jordan River, which forms the present boundary between the two countries. In theory, Israel could deal with the crisis by restructuring its economy to reduce the role of agriculture, which uses most of the available water each year. Such a move would be difficult, not only because of the country's current economic problems but because of the ideology of an agricultural economy being so deeply rooted in Zionism.

Water has been a problem in Israel from early days, when Jacob's men fought the local inhabitants of the land over the wells in the area. The Old Testament shows Israel has always been hit with droughts and famines because of the marginal rainfall the country receives each year. By the time the rains come each year, the countryside appears almost like a desert. Jerusalem receives about the same amount of rainfall as London or many American cities, about twenty inches per year. However, almost all of the rain comes in a period of about five months, between late November and April. When rain does come, it comes violently, and runoff is so fast it hardly has time to soak the soil. The heavy runoff cuts deep wadis through the countryside, favorite trails for hikers in cooler weather. Sometimes unsuspecting hikers, trekking the wadis, may be overrun by runoff water from a heavy rainstorm. Despite many warnings broadcast regularly, hardly a year goes by without someone being swept away by a wall of water crashing down the high-walled wadis and rushing toward the Dead Sea.

51

WEST BANK

When Israel took over the land granted to them in 1948, they met with the strong opposition of nearly all the Arabs of the world, but especially those of Palestine. When the State of Israel came into being, it was cause for great joy and celebration for the Jews of the world, but it brought despair and anger to the Arabs and, forty years later, the controversy still rages.

In 1967, as a result of the Six-Day War, Israel laid claim to those portions of the ancient regions of Judea and Samaria west of the Jordan River that were formerly occupied by Jordan, now known as the West Bank. Shortly afterward, the State of Israel approved certain areas of the West Bank as open territory for Israeli settlement. Few observers of modern Israel would disagree that this move was among the most controversial action ever taken by that nation. In the eyes of the world, what Israel did goes far beyond just being controversial to being condemned. Much of the criticism has come from Americans, who have generally been sympathetic to the State of Israel and their overall aspirations.

Despite what the United States government can do to mediate the problem, it seems that the West Bank settlements are going to remain a major roadblock to ending the controversy and bringing about a final settlement to the Arab-Israeli conflict.

It is true that some of the occupation and resettlement in West Bank and Gaza Strip territory had military goals of security for the rest of the country. But by 1977, it was clear that the settlements went far beyond just providing military security to the area. Security is no longer the main issue. Israelis, under Prime Minister Begin, were using the Bible as their title deed. They believed God made a biblical promise to the Jews of the ancient Eretz Yisrael (Land of Israel), which includes Judea and Samaria—today's West Bank. Thus, Jews will be settled anywhere and everywhere, and never mind the claims of Arabs who have owned the land for centuries.

Almost at every turn of the road through the hills around Jerusalem one can now see settlements, most of them only a few years old, some surrounded by barbed wire, trenches, and watchtowers. Pressure was exerted by the government to get people to move to West Bank homes, even to the neglect of buildings in old Israel. At one time, Israelis were taken on extensive bus trips through new territories in the West Bank in an attempt to encourage more people to settle there.

The usual method of establishing a settlement was that the military would first arrive without warning, set up boundary markers, and warn farmers to stay off the land. An announcement would be made that the land would be needed for military purposes. A few weeks later, after the area had been bulldozed, the soldiers would disappear and the area would be taken over by civilians. Soon a cluster of ten to thirty buildings would appear, often looking much like a collection of holiday trailers without wheels. Soon the houses were connected with water, electricity, and telephone service.

Sometimes it was the settlers themselves who did the expropriating. In 1975, the Israelis made a settlement at Ophra out of the old Jordanian army camp. Within a few years the settlers were wanting more land, so they drove up with rolls of barbed wire and cordoned off a section of an Arab bus driver's one-acre home site, and took three-fourths of his property, cut down his fruit trees, and quickly erected a dozen prefabricated homes. His pleas for help from the local Israeli miliary governor were ignored, so now he lives on a tiny plot big enough only to park his bus and grow a few vegetables.

The Israelis argue that they are not seizing private land but acquiring "state land," property formerly owned and controlled by Jordan. In some cases that is true, because land ownership laws were vague and complicated. The villagers' right to their land was traditionally implicit in their inscription on local Jordanian tax registers, and everybody knew where one man's property stopped and another's began. The Israelis simply took advantage of this informal arrangement to make their claim to whatever land they wanted for the new settlements.

Twenty years later, the controversy remains, the settlements are still there, and the Jordanians and the Palestinian Arabs, many of whom left the area when it was overrun by the Israelis, are still angry over it. Though the future status of the occupied area remains unresolved, the Israelis have established more than 100 settlements, in defiance of the

United States and most of the other countries of the world. The figure of Israeli settlers in the region was expected to reach 100,000 by 1987, and they boast that the West Bank, by the year 2010, will be home for 1.4 million Jews alongside 1.6 million Arabs.

Some think that the war with Lebanon, aimed primarily at the PLO, was an attempt by Prime Minister Begin and the Likud party to crush all hopes for the Palestinians that they would one day reoccupy the land that they left. Since many of the PLO were those who left the West Bank in protest to Israeli occupation, some might think that settling the PLO question once and for all would settle the West Bank problem as well.

The Israelis have never made a secret about their plans for the West Bank. To reach the goal of 100,000 Jewish settlers in 1983, the State of Israel was prepared to spend $610 million over a period of two years. All of these plans were made in direct contradiction to the Begin-Sadat agreement forged by Jimmy Carter at Camp David, and in opposition to plans proposed by President Reagan urging Israel to establish relationships with Jordan to set up an autonomous government for the West Bank. Settlement and permanent occupation of the West Bank by Israel was what the Arabs long feared, what the U.S. suspected, and what even many thoughtful Israelis continue to worry about.

One such dissenting Israeli was Meron Benvenisti, a former deputy mayor of Jerusalem and a specialist of West Bank affairs. He feared that once the West Bank settlements reached 100,000, it would mean that at least five members of the Knesset out of a total of 120 would be from the West Bank area, which would make it virtually impossible for any of the major parties to later change their minds and move the Israelis out of the disputed area.

Despite claims to the contrary, it is obvious that living standards have risen steadily in the West Bank and Gaza Strip since Israeli occupation. Official statistics show that unemployment in the territories is as low as one percent, and real per capita income has risen 11 to 12 percent annually since 1968. In 1981 the West Bank per capita growth was three times the 1968 figure. Some 80,000 West Bank and Gaza Strip Arabs are employed all over Israel. They enjoy equal pay and the same social benefits that the Israel Labor Federation has negotiated for Israeli citizens. Old people, Arabs and Jews, receive retirement pensions. A retail and building boom on the West Bank itself has created a demand for better homes, furnishings, and clothes. The increased income of West Bank workers has resulted in an expansion of local industry.

Many claims were made that Israelis were destroying hundreds of Arab homes on the West Bank and Gaza Strip every year. Careful scrutiny of the facts shows that only homes of these involved in acts of terrorism have actually been destroyed, in accordance with emergency regulations promulgated by the British mandatory and carried over into Israeli law. Both the State Department and the United Nations Relief and Works Agency state that Israel indeed destroyed hundreds of refugee homes, but only after the refugees had moved into new housing in projects developed by the Israeli authorities.

Claims were also made that the Israelis deliberately separated families, violating international guarantees for the reunification of families, and that they sealed off the West Bank from Jordan and the Arab world. The Israelis claim that they permitted 9,000 family reunions in 1967 and 7,000 in 1968, and 50,000 by the year 1981. There are hundreds of thousands of visitors arriving by air or crossing the Damiya and Allenby Bridges each year.

Despite accusations to the contrary, elections held under Israeli administration have been conducted in conformity with Jordanian law with two exceptions. Under Jordanian law women and those who were not landowners could not vote—under the Israelis both of these groups were allowed to vote.

Because the government, then controlled by Begin and the Likud party, backed the settlement program so strongly, providing low-cost land to developers and low-interest mortgages to buyers, the cost of the new houses and apartments was quite reasonable, making a move to the West Bank territory an attractive option. One young couple, Mazal and Moshe Levi, who had been living with relatives, discovered that they could buy a three-bedroom apartment in a settlement near Jerusalem for a down payment of only $8,000.

Much of the ground being set aside for settlement immediately after the 1967 war was public land, known as Sultan's property in the days of the Ottoman Empire. After 1967 Israel simply declared itself the heir of the Turkish sultan and proclaimed itself owner of the land. However, it was not until 1981 that the vigorous campaign began to attract middle-class Israelis to the occupied West Bank. The government planned to build more than 350 homes in the town of Givon between Jerusalem and Ramallah. The villas were to cost about $65,000, made more attractive by special loans from the government. The houses were sold immediately. The experiment convinced the government that putting 100,000 Jewish settlers in the West Bank territory could be realized.

Since then dozens of other such projects have been started. Along with the settlers would come the protection of Israeli law. One problem faced by the Israelis in settling the West Bank is how to assimilate 1.8 million Arabs into the population while still retaining the Jewish character of the country.

The settlement plan circumvented the apparent need for an annexation of the territory. As Prime Minister Begin put it, "You don't annex your own homeland."

Though the new settlements were in what had been Arab territory, there was still an attempt to avoid conflict by keeping somewhat separate from the Arabs. In fact, one newspaper advertisement describing a new settlement boasted a new road being built from the settlement that would enable new dwellers to go to Tel Aviv without going through Arab towns or villages.

Many felt that the movement into the new territory would not result in assimilation of Arabs and Jews, since the Jewish communities would have little in common with the Arab society around them. The schools and shops would be Israeli, the language would be Hebrew, and culture and entertainment would be available in the Israeli cities just beyond the Green Line, which separates Israel from the West Bank territory captured in 1967.

One such new settler is Dov Verkovits, formerly of Skokie, Illinois, a Chicago suburb. He considers himself to be in a historic battle, as important in some ways as the one that took place centuries ago—perhaps the very territory where he lives in his prefabricated house—when the Philistines overran the Israelites and captured the sacred Ark of the Covenant. "What you see," he said, "is the determination of the Israeli government that there will never be two states in Palestine, that the Jews will always live here."

Several miles away, an Arab who wants to be known only as Bob lives in the village of Turmus Ayya. He is a naturalized American citizen who lived in Chicago for many years and returned to his West Bank homeland where he wants to live for the rest of his life. "Everybody wants to kill us, to force us off our land," he says. "We have no friends."

Settlers have taken over thousands of acres of Turmus Ayya land and surrounding villages. Yet, in that same town, the Arab named Bob has returned from America to his own former homeland, but the Israeli government refused to give him more than a three-month tourist visa. "I don't think it makes sense," he says, "that I was born here and cannot come back to retire. But any Jew from Poland or Russia can come here and get land. Meanwhile, I pay U.S. taxes, which helps make the settlements possible." He was speaking of the foreign aid granted Israel each year by the United States.

Arab farmers who had cultivated land near the village of El-Hadr now have to find odd jobs to feed their families, as 500 acres of their land was expropriated for the nearby Israeli settlement of Efrat. Another Arab village was threatened with destruction by Israeli occupation forces, who refused to let the farmers drill a village well into the big underground water supplies below. Yet water was made available for the use of nearby Israeli settlements, for their swimming pools and well-watered grapevines and citrus trees.

Palestinian Arabs have charged that Israel has been pushing the Arabs out of the West Bank by stealing water from them, drying up their farms. Israel has allowed Jews to drill wells but has not allowed Arabs to drill new wells, they claim. Israel counters by saying that it was the kinds of wells being dug by the Arabs that were forbidden. Arab farmers on the West Bank are served by about 100 springs and 300 wells, many of them being overworked. Restrictions on over-exploitation of shallow wells are in effect to prevent seepage of saline water or total depletion. Some deep-bore wells were dug for Jewish villages to tap new, deep aquifers never before used. These water pools as a rule do not draw from the shallower Arab sources. In one location, near Bardalah, however, it was determined that deep-bore wells at the Israeli village of Mehola may have caused deterioration of shallow wells and springs. Today, the Arab residents of the region are provided with water from the new wells.

The original West Bank residents don't know what to make of the influx of settlers, who place new housing developments side by side with ancient Arab dwellings. Landscapes that have looked much the same since Bible times are now plastered with real estate signs, advertising new homes and apartments. Old villages are now rimmed with new housing projects. For example, the village of Beit Zecharia in the Judean hills looks almost the way it did before Christ was born. Now, just a few hundred yards away are the guard towers and barbed-wire fence of a modern kibbutz.

The West Bank Arabs are fully aware of what is happening to them but can do little to halt the move by Israeli settlers to settle in, set up Israeli culture and social structures, and eventually outnumber and outvote the local Arabs.

Bethlehem's mayor, Elias Freij, said, "We are fighting against time. The Israelis want to grab as much land as they can. They want to make it impossible for us to have autonomy, not to mention a state. We have to talk directly with them. We are at five minutes to midnight, and this is our last chance."

52

WHO IS A JEW?

It will probably come as a surprise to some Christian readers to learn that in the State of Israel today there is still considerable debate over who is and who is not to be considered a Jew. It is actually a rather modern debate and got its start with the enactment of the Law of Return, under which every true Jew has the right to immigrate to Israel and receive immediate citizenship. But the law, both in its original formulation and in its subsequent amendments, does not satisfy everyone, specifically in its wording about converts to Judaism. After every election in recent years, the religious parties have held up the "Who is a Jew" issue and its proper solution as a condition for their joining any coalition. In the end, they have always joined, but the problem still has not been settled.

The problem is often centered on the meaning of two Hebrew words: *lefi ha'halacha*, meaning "according to orthodox religious law." Under the (secular) Law of Return, a person is entitled to citizenship if he is a Jew. As it stands, a Jew is a person born of a Jewish mother or converted. The Orthodox want the controversial phrase added: "Converted according to Orthodox religious law." The non-Orthodox wants the legislation to remain as it is.

The definition of a Jew as being one born of a Jewish mother goes back some way in Jewish history. It was adopted for the pragmatic reason that it is much easier to be sure of the maternity of a child than the paternity. Such a definition, however, was not in effect in Bible times. If it had, Ephraim, Manasseh, and the sons of Moses would not have been considered Jews. And, of course, since David's great-grandmother Ruth was not Jewish and went through no formal conversion, David, Solomon, and all the kings of Judah would not be considered Jews. As one rabbi points out, when the Messiah, Son of David, comes, he may have trouble with the Law of Return.

When the legislation was enacted in 1950, it had no provision that gave a definition of a Jew. A committee of three met in 1958 and concluded that a Jew is a person declaring himself to be a Jew. The committee consisted of three cabinet ministers, one a socialist, one a liberal, and one a member of what is now called the National Religious Party (NRP). That party promptly resigned from the cabinet. Its return to office was made possible by an official directive, issued in January 1960, which stated that a Jew was, for purposes of civil law, a person born of a Jewish mother. After this, the matter quieted down. But soon this definition was challenged by Binyamin Shalit. Shalit was a Jew, married to a non-Jewish Englishwoman. They lived in Israel and had two children. Anne Shalit could have become Jewish by conversion but, like her husband, she was an agnostic, so did not convert.

The Israeli identity card registers a person's status in three ways: by nationality, by religion, and by citizenship. Anne became naturalized, so her entry read: nationality British, religion none, citizenship Israeli. Shalit wanted the entry for his children to be: nationality Jewish, religion none. Under the directive of 1960, that was impossible. Religion could be left blank, but nationality could not then be Jewish. The registry officer entered as the Shalit children's nationality: Jewish father and non-Jewish mother. Outraged, the family petitioned the High Court.

They were raising an explosive issue. The word *Jew* had two meanings, which had never before been separated. It described an ethnic or national grouping, and it described a religious belief. Shalit wanted to be a national Jew (as well as being an Israeli) without being a religious Jew. The High Court, a bench of nine judges, accepted his petition, albeit by a narrow majority of five voices to four. The Orthodox were appalled. They demanded instant legislation to abolish the duality. In their view, an ethnic Jew belonged automatically to the Jewish religion, whether he was a believer or not. An amendment was passed to the Law of Return in 1970. A Jew was henceforth (under Israeli law) a person born of Jewish mother, "provided he or she was not a member of another faith," or a convert to Judaism.

This ban on membersip of another faith was itself something new, and derived from the Brother Daniel case. A Jew called Oswald Rufeisen embraced Catholicism and became a monk, carrying the name Brother Daniel. Yet he was a Zionist (with an excellent war record as a Jewish partisan) and wanted to live in Israel as an Israeli. He applied to the High Court, arguing that under Talmudic law, "A Jew, even if he has sinned, remains a Jew."

The Orthodox, insisting on interpretations even stricter than the Talmud, decided that such a deviation could not be allowed. A Jew converted to another religion is no longer a Jew, either by religion or nationality. That edict shocked many, coming as it did on the heels of the Holocaust. Jews had been martyred for being Jews regardless of the religion they professed. Racial anti-Semitism evoked the bitter phrase, "A Jew is a person that other people call a Jew." According to the Nazis, any person who had even one Jewish grandparent was to be considered Jewish, and it made no difference to them if he had converted to another religion.

Since 1970 the statute books of the State of Israel declare that a Jew must either be born Jewish or converted to Judaism; that religion and nationality shall not be separated; that a person is either a Jew in both respects or in neither.

Actually the dispute, rather than being focused on the question of the definition of a Jew, should more properly be centered on the question of who is truly a convert. Attempts have been made in the past to change the law in question. Various prime ministers have committed themselves to trying to amend the law as it stands as if to appease some of the religious parties, but every effort thus far has been defeated in the Knesset. While Knesset members must normally vote the way their party votes, on religious issues they are usually allowed to vote according to their conscience. The attempt in 1984 was a feverish event, but in the end the vote was not all that close, as the amendment was again rejected. And until the law changes, there will continue to be thorny questions about who has a right to unquestioned citizenship in Israel, since that right is contingent on the question of who is a Jew.

53

WOMEN

Though Orthodox Judaism has always held to strong distinctions of men and women, the State of Israel very early in its history passed a very strong and clear equal rights amendment. The law reads: "There will be one law for women and men; every legal action and every juridical provision which discriminates against a woman, as a woman, is void."

Since the establishment of the State, women have had the right to vote and have held the highest elected offices in the country. When Israel attached the West Bank territories of Judea and Samaria formerly held by Jordan, laws were passed even there enabling women to vote and hold office in the municipalities of that area. Since 1948, throughout all the territory held by Israel, polygamy and child marriages, still practiced by some Muslim Arabs, were abolished.

Women play a large role in almost every sphere of Israeli life. Even ten years ago, women constituted 34.5 percent of the total labor force, and there has been a gradual increase since then. Some of the reasons women find it easier to work outside the home, and still find life easier than most women of the world, are the many provisions made for mother and child care. Health clinics have been set up all around the country, even in West Bank and Gaza Strip areas, to provide full prenatal and postnatal care. Child care centers are set up all around the country to allow women to work outside the home. National Health Insurance allows for twelve full weeks of maternity vacation with full pay to mothers, free hospitalization for all births, and up to six days paid leave annually to care for sick children. The government also pays a monthly family allowance for all children under eighteen years of age. Large families receive extra tax exemptions as well.

Though there are equal rights laws granting both privileges and responsibilities, in some ways women still receive special treatment in areas such as military service. Attempts are made to keep military women out of direct combat, and women are exempted from military service who are married, who have children, or who object on religious grounds.

Women serve in the army for two years, while the law requires that men serve three. Though Israeli women are sometimes pressured sexually from male superiors, the government strongly frowns on it. The commander of the Israeli navy was dismissed in 1979 following his acquittal on assault charges. The military court believed the charges against him but could not convict him for technical reasons.